WORLD REVOLUTIONARY
PROPAGANDA

WORLD REVOLUTIONARY PROPAGANDA

A CHICAGO STUDY

Harold D. Lasswell &
Dorothy Blumenstock

BOOKS FOR LIBRARIES PRESS
FREEPORT, NEW YORK

First Published 1939
Reprinted 1970

STANDARD BOOK NUMBER:

8369-5291-X

LIBRARY OF CONGRESS CATALOG CARD NUMBER:

78-114887

PRINTED IN THE UNITED STATES OF AMERICA

PREFACE

THIS BOOK is a " Middletown " — or, rather, a " Bigtown " — of world revolutionary propaganda. It is a case study of revolutionary propaganda in action. The scene is one of the great industrial cities of the world. The time is the Great Depression. The leading character is the propagandist of Communism.

We are interested in the facts. We have taken care to find them. But we are chiefly concerned with the meaning of the facts for the understanding of the future.

Will Communism conquer America? Are we passing from an " individualistic America " to a " Sovietized America "? Is this part of a world trend from " individualism " to " collectivism "?

We deliberately look toward the future. As students of world politics, part of our problem is to be correct about the future.

This is a bold declaration. Yet it does no more than make explicit what is usually implicit. As living, deciding beings we cannot fail to estimate the future. When we act, as we constantly must, we are influenced by our expectation of what the world has in store for us.

Our expectation about the future may include the destiny of our person, our family, our nation, our race. It may include the destiny of man on earth, and of the earth itself.

With regard to political events, we weigh expectations about the future of influence. From this comes our study of Communism. Will those who are emotionally identified with Communist symbols succeed in ruling America and in unifying the world?

Candid preoccupation with the future — with correct orientation in the context of events which includes the future as well as the past — is one characteristic of our method of political analysis. The method was called the "configurative method" in a book published by one of the authors in 1935 (*World Politics and Personal Insecurity*).

We are not prophets, although we are concerned about the shape of things to come. We cannot gather facts about the future because there are no facts about the future.

How, then, do we proceed? The starting-point is a developmental construction. We set up tentative expectations about the course of history. We use some words to refer to future events, and other words to refer to past events. We treat intervening events as approximations of one pattern or the other.

Such constructions may enter into political propaganda and affect the course of history. Thus the propagandists of Communism declare that the world is passing from "class states" to a "classless" society. Whatever approximates the "classless society," or increases the probability of its appearance, is "revolutionary." Whatever repeats the pattern of "class states," or strengthens it, is "counter-revolutionary."

As propaganda, developmental constructions are mythology. But such constructions are not always — or not only — propaganda. If tentatively and critically held, they are means to the end of orientation.

Hence developmental constructions are related both to method and to myth. And method must evaluate their potential effectiveness as myth. This leads to uncertainty, since uncertainty is inseparable from the consideration of the future. We have to do with comparative probabilities and not with inevitabilities. Probability is a category of method; inevitability is a tool of myth.

Developmental constructions are not scientific laws. They are not knowledge. We have knowledge (and laws) only of elapsed events; developmental constructions include selected events of the future as well as the past.

If such constructions are not knowledge, why make them?

They are aids to knowledge. They are selective guides to the study of the past (which leads to knowledge) and to the preparation of the study of the future (which also leads to knowledge).

They are aids to a special kind of knowledge: namely, knowledge that is explicitly relevant to orientation. They assist in selecting events in the past and future that are significant for the estimation of the future.

This investigation was undertaken as a means of evaluating the future prospects of Communism. We devoted our attention to events in Chicago because they were accessible and important. Chicago is a major industrial center in a major power. Chicago recently shared in the collapse of economic life. Case histories of Communist propaganda in such situations were not at hand. We decided that a case study of Chicago would usefully supplement available data for the appraisal of Communism in America and in the world.

Our expectations about the future have been greatly matured by the experience of collecting facts about Communist propaganda in Chicago. The careful exploration of events has given us a surer sense of the direction and the tempo of political movement. (Our conclusions need not detain us; they are abundantly evident in the report.)

While our expectations about the future of Communism are important to us, they are only helpful to others if we communicate them in a way which shows what we actually saw and how we saw it. Hence the body of detail in this book.

Events are not only described in simple chronological order. To some extent they are treated comparatively; that is, they are described as quantitative changes of variables. This pattern of thought — which is often assumed to embrace all of scientific method — leads to the quest of ever more satisfactory indices of variables. (In contrast to the "developmental pattern," this is here called the "equilibrium pattern" of analysis.)

Our attempt to apply an equilibrium pattern of analysis to past politics shockingly revealed the discrepancy between the data which we needed and the data at hand. We grew increasingly critical of what the past had left us. We could not decisively confirm or disconfirm hypothetical propositions about causal interrelationships. Observers had not been sufficiently trained to examine past events. They had not invented adequate methods of making significant and comparable records.

This is a typical result of studying the past. Hence we turn toward the planned observation of the future. This is the sense in which comparative history (social science) is in the future. This is the sense in which we have little to learn from the history which has been described in the past, and nearly all to learn from the history to be described in the future.

The developmental construction which has been set up with reference to world politics has been sketched, rather than elaborated, in this book. Other patterns are eligible for inclusion in the pattern of the epoch. No doubt the tendency to abolish unemployment — at least symbolically — will prove to be as universal as the tendency to moderate income differences.

In conducting this investigation, practical aid has been received, and is hereby appreciatively acknowledged, from the Social Science Research Committee of the University of Chicago. Acknowledgment is also made for the students made available through the National Youth Administration. Voluntary assistance has been forthcoming from many individuals, only a handful of whom can be singled out for our cordial thanks. Access to important sources was facilitated by the helpful co-operation of Mr. Joseph L. Moss, Director, and Mrs. Edward J. Lewis, Assistant Director, of the Cook County Bureau of Public Welfare, and Lieutenant Make Mills, of the Police Department of the City of Chicago. Dr. Gabriel Almond was particularly active in connection with the study of case histories and organizations of the unemployed. George Blumenstock, Jr., gave important statistical aid. At successive stages of revision the manuscript benefited greatly from precise criticism by Dr. N. C. Leites. For many forms of friendly collaboration we are indebted to William V. Morganstern, Lewis E. Gleeck, Garland C. Routt, Leo Shields, and Dr. Leo C. Rosten. For the imperfections of this investigation, the authors have no scapegoats to propose but themselves.

H. D. L.
D. B.

William Alanson White Psychiatric Foundation
  Washington, D. C.

Western Personnel Service
  Pasadena, California

CONTENTS

I. *The Setting of Propaganda*

II. *The Channels of Propaganda*

III. *The Technique of Propaganda*

IV. *The Volume of Propaganda*

v. *The Influence of Propaganda*

ILLUSTRATIONS

PART ONE

THE SETTING OF PROPAGANDA

CHAPTER I

The World Center of Revolutionary
Radical Propaganda

THIS is the Age of Propaganda.

Popular discovery of propaganda was made in the World War of 1914–18. Soldiers and civilians of the warring powers were unceasingly warned against the insidious effects of enemy propaganda. Whoever heard of propaganda learned to think of it as a dangerous and mysterious influence.

When Germany lost the war, the generals tried to shift the blame for the defeat from their own shoulders. They denied that they had been defeated. They declared that the civilians had " collapsed " behind the lines; disaffected elements at home had been easy marks of enemy propaganda. The heroic soldiers of the fatherland had been " stabbed in the back."

The seizure of power by the Bolsheviki in 1917 had already increased the popular prestige of propaganda. It had been hailed as a triumph of mass incitement. From the time of its inception in Moscow in 1919, the Third International was called a world conspiracy against patriotism, a world propaganda against nationalism.[1] The prestige of propaganda was

[1] The immediate background of the Third International is described by Merle Fainsod: *International Socialism and the World War* (Cambridge, Mass., 1935). The general setting is given by Lewis L. Lorwin: *Labor and Internationalism* (New York, 1929).

further advanced in the post-war rise of Fascism in Italy, which was so often attributed in large part to the agitational force and skill of Mussolini. The National Socialist movement in Germany was universally interpreted as another success of modern methods of mass management.

Propaganda consciousness grew among Americans as a result of internal as well as external propaganda. After the end of the World War, many American business groups undertook to throw off the controls over business which had been established during the war, and to withdraw the concessions granted to organized labor. Propaganda campaigns were launched against government and labor, the master theme being the threat of Bolshevism to America.

When the notice of the public was dramatically drawn to the propaganda by business groups, the consciousness of propaganda as a political instrument was made all the keener. Public investigations were made of the extensive propaganda campaigns of the many public utility corporations which acted through the National Electric Light Association.

New fear of Communist propaganda was stimulated when the Great Depression deepened after 1929. In the national emergency the powers of the federal government were greatly extended, especially after the election of President Roosevelt in 1932. Groups which were opposed to the expansion of government promptly rose to their own defense. Propaganda campaigns were begun in order to complain of the use of propaganda by government, and to " pin the red label " on the President and his advisers. Defenders of the " New Deal " promptly replied by seeking to expose the propaganda of these business groups.

National awareness of propaganda was further stimulated by the spectacular success of Senator Huey Long, Father Coughlin, Dr. Townsend, Upton Sinclair, and other heroes of the masses during the depression. After the triumph of National Socialism in Germany in 1933, anti-radical and anti-Semitic organizations multiplied in America. This brought out an answering barrage of protest against foreign propaganda.

As knowledge of propaganda became more general, it was seen that a new skill group had come into existence in modern civilization. The new propagandists operated along distinctive lines. They were not like the old missionaries, who were presumed to be emotionally attached to the cause which they promoted. They were not like the advertisers, who sold copy which was plainly marked and circulated through the several channels of communication. The modern propagandist makes comparatively little use of advertising. He does not necessarily believe what he says or mark what he sells. Clients are served on a business basis. The propagandist may promote a line of radios, a make of automobiles, a hospital, or a demand for national independence at the same time, depending on the fee. The modern propagandist may invent ideas for his clients which gain more public attention than could be bought and paid for. A stock example of this news-making technique is the suggestion that a business corporation add an eminent public figure, like a former president of the United States, to its board of directors. This is itself noteworthy and newsworthy, and the announcement of such an appointment makes headlines across the continent.

A propagandist does not necessarily serve several clients at one time. He may devote himself to one enterprise, serving under names which run all the way from " director of information," " director of publicity," " advertising counsel," " legal counsel," " assistant to the president," to " vice-president in charge of public relations."

The public has not been informed in detail about the extent of specialized propaganda in modern life. A survey of the propagandists in the city of Minneapolis (the best of such surveys) found 82 professional propagandists.[2] A professional

---

[2] Elmo C. Wilson: " Propaganda and Publicity in Minneapolis," M.A. thesis, Department of Journalism, directed by Professor Ralph D. Casey.

propagandist was defined as one who practices the profession of publicity or propaganda expert for hire. Of the 82, 42 were hired by economic groups, ranging from department stores, banks, hotels, theaters, insurance companies, public utilities, milling concerns, to civic (business) associations, employers' organizations, and trade unions; 14 were in the employ of political parties, reform associations, or government agencies; the remainder were scattered among welfare, educational, cultural, and fraternal enterprises. Besides the professional propagandist were some 500 casual and volunteer publicity people, and 570 professional advertisers.

The popular impression that there are more and more propagandists is doubtless correct for democratic countries. Skill in propaganda has become one of the most effective roads to power in modern states. Until recently the most rapidly rising skill group has been the specialist on bargaining (the business man). Released from the surviving restraints of feudal society, the business man came to the peak of his influence in the nineteenth and early twentieth centuries.

The power of the business group was gradually challenged by the specialist on propaganda and on the organization of mass parties. In nations which were demoralized or disappointed by the World War, the propagandists rose to power and curbed the business men. The most spectacular change was in Russia, where the party took supreme control. In Italy and Germany the party limited, though it did not liquidate, business. Lenin, Mussolini, and Hitler, the dominant political figures of recent years, were chiefly propagandists and organizers of mass parties. They set up regimes which were either party bureaucratic states or mixed party bureaucratic states.[3]

[3] See H. D. Lasswell: " Research on the Distribution of Symbol Specialists," *Journalism Quarterly,* XII (1935), 146–56; " Sino-Japanese Crisis: The Garrison State versus the Civilian State," *China Quarterly,* II (1937), 643–9; (with Renzo Sereno) " Governmental and Party Leaders in Fascist Italy," *American Political Science Review,* XXXI (1937), 914–29.

Growing popular consciousness of propaganda was accompanied by more scientific interest in the subject. Some distinguished historians and social scientists had an active hand in American propaganda during the World War.[4] Courses have multiplied in the subject, chiefly in connection with departments of political science, sociology, and social psychology.[5] Research and writing turned more and more actively toward the study of propaganda, especially toward the exploration of propaganda methods in the World War.[6] Contributions to the literature were made by practicing propagandists, journalists, advertising men, revolutionists, psychologists, historians, and social scientists.[7] Scientific periodicals devoted more attention to the field.[8] The idea of measuring the fluctuations of public opinion was materialized in the program of the American Institute of Public Opinion by Dr. George Gallup. The appetite for dependable knowledge about current propaganda led to the creation of a reporting service for subscribers.[9]

[4] Examples: Guy Stanton Ford, University of Minnesota, historian; Charles E. Merriam, University of Chicago, political scientist.

[5] See *Universities — Pathfinders in Public Opinion,* A Survey by Edward L. Bernays, in collaboration with Doris E. Fleischman (New York, 1937).

[6] An example is H. D. Lasswell: *Propaganda Technique in the World War* (London and New York, 1927). Consult Ralph H. Lutz: " Studies of World War Propaganda, 1914–33," *Journal of Modern History,* V (1933), 496–516. Professor Lutz is chairman of the directors of the Hoover War Library at Stanford University, which has a remarkable collection of propaganda material.

[7] A voluminous annotated bibliography was prepared under the auspices of the Social Science Research Council. See H. D. Lasswell, R. D. Casey, and B. L. Smith: *Propaganda and Promotional Activities: An Annotated Bibliography* (Minneapolis, 1935).

[8] The *Public Opinion Quarterly* was launched under the auspices of the School of Public Affairs of Princeton University in December 1936. Editors: DeWitt C. Poole, Harwood L. Childs, Hadley Cantril, H. D. Lasswell, E. Pendleton Herring, O. W. Riegel.

[9] The Institute for Propaganda Analysis. President, Hadley Cantril; Secretary, Clyde R. Miller.

The effect of the war upon political scientists was to stimulate effort in a direction consistent with their steadily growing interest. Students of political institutions had been steadily broadening the scope of their researches. They were interested in discovering why the same legal rules gave very different results in different contexts. They saw that the constitutions of most Latin American states provided for a presidential system of government on the model of the United States, but that the rules worked very differently in practice. For the explanation of these differences they gave increasing consideration to the context in which legal rules are found. They described political parties, and the business, labor, racial, religious, and allied groups which used the parties.

The study of groups led to renewed interest in processes fundamental to all groups, such as control by collective symbols and by leaders. These psychological aspects of political life were described with great penetration, before the war, for English readers by Graham Wallas in his *Human Nature in Politics* (1908). Political science in Great Britain and the United States had reached this stage of development when the World War supplied a new impetus for fresh studies of basic relationships.

For the scientific analysis of politics, it is useful to define the study of politics as the analysis of influence and the influential.[10] By the term " influence " is meant control over values. Representative values are deference, safety, and income. Those who control the most are élite. In the Soviet Union the élite of the government is identical with the élite of the state; but in the United States there are important non-governmental élites of party, business, and church.

Political management is concerned with retaining and extending control over values by the manipulation of the environment. Thus élites manipulate symbols, goods and serv-

[10] See H. D. Lasswell: *World Politics and Personal Insecurity* (New York, 1935); *Politics: Who Gets What, When, How* (New York, 1936).

ices, instruments of violence, and institutional practices; they engage in propaganda, inducement, coercion, and organization.

Political management undertakes to control *attitudes* and *things*. The first is the sphere of *psychiatry* and the second of *technology*. *Public relations* is the management of attitudes external to the enterprise; *personnel management* is concerned with internal attitudes. Among the measures employed to protect democratic governments may be propaganda against dictatorship, the expenditure of large funds for public relief, the strengthening of the armed forces of the state, and the passage of laws prohibiting the use of uniforms by private political organizations.[11]

For purposes of the most general analysis of politics, *propaganda* may be defined as *the control of attitudes by the manipulation of symbols* (symbols are words, and word substitutes like pictures and gestures). Any élite invokes certain symbols to identify itself, to describe its historical mission, and to make demands upon itself and others. In the United States the accepted symbols of the élite include phrases from the Declaration of Independence and the Constitution of the United States. In the Soviet Union the accepted symbols include certain declarations by Marx, Lenin, and Stalin. Élites which are united on basic symbols make use of propaganda to settle differences among themselves on questions of policy and tactics. Élites may be confronted by counter-élites which invoke propaganda for the purpose of destroying belief in the accepted symbols. This is the role of Communist propaganda in a country like the United States.[12]

[11] See E. Pendleton Herring: *Public Administration and the Public Interest* (New York, 1936); G. E. G. Catlin: "Propaganda as a Function of Democratic Government," in *Propaganda and Dictatorship,* edited by Harwood L. Childs (Princeton, 1936); Karl Lowenstein: "Legislative Control of Political Extremism in European Democracies," *Columbia Law Review,* XXXVIII (1938), 591–622, 725–74.

[12] For technical purposes the *basic symbols* of an élite or counter-élite may be called the *political myth.* When the myth is accepted

There are several terms which are closely allied in popular usage with propaganda and from which propaganda may properly be distinguished. It is convenient to distinguish between propaganda and education as follows: *propaganda is the manipulation of symbols to control controversial attitudes; education is the manipulation of symbols (and of other means) to transmit accepted attitudes (and skills).* This means that the advocacy of Communism in America is propaganda, but the inculcation of traditional Americanism is education. In the Soviet Union, on the other hand, Communism is presumably the accepted tradition by this time, and the transmission of Communism is therefore education. The spread of individualism in the Soviet Union would be propaganda.

It will be noticed that propaganda is exclusively concerned with the control of attitude, but that education includes attitude and skill. Propaganda is also limited to the manipulation of symbols, but education may use other means as well (like corporal punishment to stimulate diligence and proper deportment). *Civic education* refers to (1) the transmission of ideology, and (2) the transmission of skills which are believed to be serviceable to the state.[13]

---

within a state by a large fraction of the people, it is *ideology.* When many persons within a state reject the ideology and project an alternative, their symbols are called *utopia.* These definitions imply no judgment of truth or falsity. They have grown up in the literature called into existence by the writings of Karl Marx on " ideology." Reference may be made to the contributions of Sorel in France, Gaetano Mosca and Vilfredo Pareto in Italy, Roberto Michels in Germany and Italy, and Max Weber in Germany. See the volume by Karl Mannheim: *Ideology and Utopia,* translated by Louis Wirth and Edward Shils (Chicago, 1937).

[13] The skills may include skill in the analysis of the conditions and consequences of ideology in general. The most extensive comparison of systems of civic education is the Civic Training Series, edited by Charles E. Merriam. The summary volume by Mr. Merriam is *The Making of Citizens* (Chicago, 1931). The definition given above of

The propaganda which is investigated in this report is an example of world revolutionary radical propaganda. Communist propaganda in Chicago is revolutionary because it demands fundamental changes (rather than reforms) in the institutional practices of America. Communist propaganda is also radical, because it circulates demands for drastic, rather than moderate, methods of achieving political results. Communist propaganda is a propaganda of world revolution because it speaks in the name of a world group, the proletarian class; predicts the completion of a world revolutionary process in which the proletariat will triumph; and demands active support of existing initiatives to complete the world revolution which transformed Russia after 1917.

Communist propaganda is by no means the only world revolutionary propaganda of recent world politics. There were other agencies of world revolutionary radical propaganda when the Communist International was established. The Second International, though badly split by the World War, was

---

propaganda includes the idea of "premeditation" ("manipulation") in propaganda. The unintentional circulation of Communist symbols is not propaganda, but may be a result of propaganda. This rejects the category of "unintentional propaganda" proposed by Leonard W. Doob: *Propaganda, Its Psychology and Technique* (New York, 1935), p. 89. By *news* is meant timely and interesting symbols which are brought to the focus of general attention. *Publicity* is the act of manipulating news in order to extract tangible advantages from the attitudes molded by it. *Advertising* is paid publicity. Publicity may be *informational* or *sensational*. Communists speak of propaganda as the spreading of doctrine, and of *agitation* as the utilizing of incidents to improve the reception of dogma. In practice the two are merged in "agit-prop" work. Propaganda is *dispersed* or *concentrated;* when concentrated upon a few persons, it is *persuasion*. Expressions like "propaganda of the deed" have grown up to refer to acts like assassination which are expected to have an influence upon attitudes which is disproportionately greater than usual for an act of the kind (the killing of an official is thought of as arousing larger responses than the killing of an unknown citizen). Strictly speaking, the assassination is coercion and not propaganda.

still in existence; most of its spokesmen demanded fundamental change, many of them wanted universality, and some
of them called for the use of drastic methods. The anarchists
and the syndicalists were in organized existence in 1919, and
in distinction to the Second International, all of their leaders
unambiguously used radical, revolutionary, and world-inclu-
sive symbols.

During the lifetime of the Third International new agencies
of world revolutionary radical propaganda have emerged. For
a few years of the early post-war period the " Left wing " of
the Second International enjoyed organizational independence
and had the label " Two and a Half " pinned upon it; later on,
the Fourth International, whose primary nucleus was composed of adherents of Trotsky, challenged the claim of the
Third International to champion the true proletarian revolution.

The Third International is distinguished from other inter-
nationals by the intimacy of its association with the rulers of
an established state. Although nominally divorced from the
government of the Soviet Union, and merely receiving " hos-
pitality " in Moscow, the Third International has been dominated by the ruling élite of Russia. It was called into existence
by Moscow, and it survives as an agency of the élite which
seized power at the center of the latest world revolutionary
wave.

For the understanding of world political developments it is
vital to discover whether the acts of propaganda of the Third
International, together with other acts committed in its name,
will probably succeed in unifying the self-assertive, " sove-
reign " states of western European civilization. Can an international propaganda agency which is obviously dominated by
the rulers of one of the great powers revolutionize the other
great powers and add them to the Soviet Union?

This possibility is not to be lightly dismissed without rational
discussion. The technical advances of modern civilization
have brought the world into more intimate contact than ever

before, and the World War of 1914 demonstrated the horrors
of war among major powers armed with the weapons of the
machine age. The war fostered, at least temporarily, demands
for a common reign of law to end international anarchy. The
recurrent ground swells of collective insecurity which are connected with the irregularities of modern economic life furnish
incentives as well as opportunities for mass action under the
guidance of new symbols. In many quarters it has long been
a commonplace that " what the world needs is a new religion,"
since unity that lasts is based on unity of conviction.

Is the Third International the champion of a secular religion
which is capable of inaugurating the new day of peace, union,
and justice?

Communism, conceiving of itself as the spear-head of opposition to the capitalistic order of society, strives to profit from
the discontents which arise, from whatever cause, throughout
the capitalistic world. This is always a potential strategic advantage of the " party in opposition," and Communism bears
the onus of responsibility only within the boundaries of the
Soviet Union. The goal of the Third International is to create such hyper-concentration of striving and faith that the
" dictatorship of the proletriat " will spread among the peoples
not already affiliated with the U.S.S.R.

The struggle between the Third International and its ad-
versaries is world-wide and must be viewed as a whole. Major
conflicts control lesser conflicts, and if we are to deal properly
with the intricate interplay of personal, party, class, race, religious, economic, and national antagonisms, we are bound to
see them in relation to the disjunction between those who are
emotionally identified with the Third International and those
who are identified with its enemies.

A great question mark in world politics, then, is this: Will
the Third International succeed in universalizing the Soviet
Union? Regardless of local failures or concessions, will the
trend of history be toward world union in the name of Communism?

We are not wholly at a loss for objective ways of approaching this question. From one point of view it is a problem of diffusion and restriction, and such processes have been studied by several specialists in the social sciences. The most vigorous discussion of the technical issues involved is found in the literature of students of comparative history and of primitive society. Some of their methods may profitably be applied to the understanding of the political events with which we are concerned.[14]

Russia may be taken as the world center from which a revolutionary pattern is spreading. Beyond the boundaries of the Soviet Union the Third International rises and falls in influence. Its geographical dispersion at any given time is the net result of the factors which affect the total process of diffusion and restriction. Our problem is to discover the relative strength of these factors, and in the light of the total world picture to evaluate the possibility of development toward all-inclusiveness.

World revolutionary waves are not unique in the history of modern civilization. Those who seized control in France at the end of the eighteenth century spoke in the name of all mankind, prophesied the age of reason, and demanded active support for the realization of the rights of man.

The world revolutionary waves of the past have come short of universality. The élite which seized power at the world revolutionary center was restricted by the play of the balance of power.

Our judgment of the world-unifying potentialities of the Communist revolution depends upon the analysis of the relative strength of factors making for diffusion and restriction of world revolutionary initiatives.

Among the possibilities we may distinguish the following:

[14] An important theoretical statement by Edward Sapir is *Time Perspective in Aboriginal American Culture*, Memoir 90 (Canada, Geological Survey, 1916), pp. 30 ff. Useful discussions are found in the publications of Roland Dixon, Leslie Spier, Alfred Kroeber, Paul Radin, Bronislav Malinowski, Ralph Linton, Wilson Wallis.

1. *Total diffusion.* The world beyond the boundaries of the Soviet Union may eventually adhere to the new order, and the new order may retain its revolutionary characteristics.

2. *World unity with restriction from within.* The world adheres to the Soviet Union, but in the meantime the revolutionary characteristics of the center are modified by the reactivation of older social patterns.

3. *Restriction of the scope of the world revolutionary center from without by the reactivation of older social patterns.* One well-established pattern is loyalty to local regions (national territory); and nationalistic sentiment may be utilized to block the spread of control from Russia. This may be called restriction by geographical differentiation. Old feudal practices may be reinstated as a means of emphasizing local distinctiveness.

4. *Restriction by partial incorporation.* The restriction of the élite in control at the center may proceed by incorporating some of the distinctive characteristics of the revolutionary pattern. Some incorporation may be limited to symbols: " Socialist revolution," " soldiers' and workingmen's councils." Some may include practices: the monopolization of legality by a single political party, the governmentalization of organized social life.

5. *Restriction by functional differentiation.* The restriction of the élite at the center may involve the rejection of the claim of the élite to bear the true revolutionary burden, and a call for a new revolutionary initiative.

The understanding of the diffusion-restriction process calls for case studies of communities of different characteristics at varying distances from the center of the world revolutionary wave. This report on Communist propaganda in Chicago is such a case study. Chicago is an urban manufacturing center with a large wage-earning population; hence it may be presumed to offer favorable conditions for the spread of Communism. Chicago is located in a nation which is one of the major powers and which, though it is at some distance from the Soviet Union, is important for the Communists to revolutionize, if the world revolutionary wave is to attain universality.

Communist propaganda in Chicago is studied during a period which was particularly favorable for revolutionary activity — namely, the years of the Great Depression.

The study also coincides with the period in which an isolationist strategy was followed by the Third International. At the Sixth World Congress of 1928, Socialist and liberal parties were stigmatized as Social Fascists. This was a declaration of war on the leaders of liberal and "proletarian" parties and mass organizations in all countries. In the autumn of 1935 this isolationist policy was changed. The Third International called for collaboration with all anti-Fascist elements and made overtures to Socialist and liberal groups. Our study shows how the policy of isolation worked in practice.

By examining communities of different types at different distances from the center of world revolution, we may hope to discover some laws of political change. We may for example consider certain hypotheses about the relation between revolutionary innovation and the incidence of crisis elsewhere in the world. The fact of crisis does not signify that the full pattern will be taken over. Restrictive processes may be more potent than diffusion processes. But the fact of crisis shows where the *potentiality* of incorporation is particularly high.

The appearance of a new center of world revolution is a *deprivational* change in the environment of all who are emotionally attached to established ideologies. The influence of established ideologies is diminished in the world. The élite which seizes control at the new center challenges, by the mere fact of its existence, the self-confidence of all other élites. When the leaders of the Russian revolution spoke in the name of the "proletariat" and indicted the "bourgeois" world, they became positive threats to legally constituted authority beyond the boundaries of the Soviet Union. Within these states rose challenging élites in the name of the triumphant language of the revolution in Russia. The leaders at the world center sought to instigate, guide, and co-ordinate all anti-bourgeois elements by means of a newly formed weapon of revolution, the Third International.

Three factors may be said to determine the intensity of crisis beyond the borders of the world center of revolution: proximity, bipolarity, and level of insecurity.

Proximity refers to distance from the Soviet Union, our expectation being that states which are close to the revolutionary center are more susceptible to crisis than states which are remote.[15]

Bipolarity refers to the intensity of attitudes for and against the revolutionary pattern. Where some features of the revolutionary pattern are fervently supported and fervently opposed previous to the success of the pattern at the world center, we expect crisis to be intense. Where attitudes are overwhelmingly favorable, hostile, or indifferent, the local crisis will probably be less intense.

The level of insecurity refers to dissatisfactions which are not explicitly related to details of the successful pattern of revolution. Attitudes which are expressly organized toward the revolutionary pattern are taken into consideration in determining the degree of bipolarity which prevails in a given state. Previous to 1917 there were attitudes of acceptance and rejection of " world revolution " and the " proletariat," which were leading symbols of those who seized power in 1917. All dissatisfactions, however, were not laid at the door of " capitalism." Discontents were often evidenced by quarrelsomeness in private affairs, by drug addiction, by suicide. Such indices depict the level of insecurity.

When the states of the world are classified according to

[15] Strictly speaking, we are using proximity as an index of intimacy of contact, the most inclusive hypothesis being that states in most intimate contact with the revolutionary center are most susceptible to crisis. As indices of contact one may take such factors as war, trade, travel, symbolic interchange. In the age of the airplane one may presume the existence of increasingly close correlations between such indices and proximity.

proximity, bipolarity, and level of insecurity in relation to the world center of revolution, the United States occupies an intermediate position. For this reason the study of the United States is especially important for the understanding of the factors which condition the diffusion or restriction of world revolution. Unless the Third International can conquer states like the United States, its dream of universal revolutionary unity is a mirage.

Proximity may be measured in terms of state-contiguity to the Soviet Union. One zone of states and near-states is immediately adjacent: Finland, Estonia, Latvia, Poland, Rumania, Turkey, Afghanistan, China, Japan. A second zone is one state removed by land from the boundaries of the Soviet Union (or separated by a common sea or strait). The United States falls in this zone, if we count Alaska, which is across the Bering Strait from the Soviet Union, as the northern boundary of the nation. If we count distance from the main body of territory which comprises the United States, the nation would come in the third and not the second zone. The third zone is removed by two states, or by a state and narrow waters,[16] and includes the strait and Canada as the barriers between the Soviet Union and the United States. The third zone embraces the states of Europe not included in the first and second zone, and certain other states (Great Britain, Irish Free State, Saudi Arabia, Egypt, Canada). A fourth zone includes the remaining states of Africa, and Australia, New Zealand, and the Americas.

Subdivisions may be made within each state. The city of Chicago comes within the north-central zone of the United States, occupying a position which in this respect is roughly comparable with that of Berlin in Germany, Manchester in England, Paris in France, Milan in Italy. If the number of miles from the nearest boundary of the Soviet Union is taken as an index of proximity, Chicago's intermediate position is

[16] Or is situated in contiguous continents and islands, or borders on enclosed seas connected with such areas.

emphasized. The city is the same distance from the Soviet Union as Tulsa, Oklahoma, El Paso, Texas, Ottawa, Canada, and the city of Singapore. The cities of Central and South America, of course, are farther away from the Union than Chicago.

The United States (and Chicago) also occupy an intermediate position with respect to bipolarity of attitudes toward the pre-revolutionary and the post-revolutionary patterns of the Soviet Union. We expect revolutionary crises to be severe in states which in many traits closely resemble the pattern which was superseded at the revolutionary center. Pre-revolutionary Russia was an absolute monarchy and possessed an influential aristocracy and plutocracy. The liquidation of all three institutions would constitute a more serious menace to the ruling élite of a state like Hungary than to the ruling élite of one like the United States, since Hungary possessed a monarchy (though limited), an aristocracy, and a business hierarchy, while the United States had no monarchy or aristocracy.

On the other hand the ruling élite of the United States was more seriously threatened than that of some other states; for the United States had a class of factory workers and a few propagandists of world revolution at the time of the Russian upheaval. The vanguard of the Russian revolution was furnished by workers in the huge factories of Moscow and Petrograd. In states like New Zealand there were fewer points of similarity to the pre-revolutionary pattern of Russia than have been enumerated for the United States.[17]

---

[17] A high degree of pre-revolutionary similarity is *generally* accompanied by a low degree of post-revolutionary similarity (Hungary in relation to Russia). A low degree of pre-revolutionary similarity is *often* accompanied by an equally low degree of post-revolutionary similarity, *as well as* by a high degree of post-revolutionary similarity. The primitive patterns of life in Ethiopia, for example, offered relatively few similarities to pre-revolutionary or to post-revolutionary Russia. Australia offered few points of similarity to pre-revolutionary Russia, and more points of similarity to post-revolutionary Russia. We expect revolutionary crises to be least severe in states which most extensively

If we consider the United States and Chicago from the standpoint of the level of insecurity, as well as proximity and bipolarity, we strengthen the conclusion that they occupy intermediate positions among states and regions. The United States has not been subjected to recent defeat in war (like Germany), or to diplomatic frustration (like Italy at the Peace Conference). But the industrial recession of 1920 was sharp though transitory, and the crisis after 1929 was far more severe than in France, for example.

The present case study of Communist propaganda in Chicago during the Great Depression fits into the study of Communist propaganda in places and times which occupy intermediate positions on a scale of probable sensitivity to world revolutionary radical propaganda emanating from the latest center of world revolution. Whether we think of Chicago (and the entire United States) in terms of proximity to the Soviet Union, or in terms of bipolarity or level of insecurity, we see that Chicago (and the United States) stands between the extremes of "dullness" and "hypersensitivity." Hence our detailed consideration of developments in Chicago is of special interest for the evaluation of the long-run prospects of Communism.

Since the empirical investigation of symbols is a comparatively new field of scientific activity, there is much opportunity for the invention of useful observational and verbal devices. As yet there is no large measure of agreement about the best ways of measuring the volume, describing the technique, appraising the skillfulness, or discovering the influence of propaganda. This study presents several new devices which it is believed will prove serviceable in research and practice.

Case studies of Communist propaganda enable us to improve our understanding of many strategical and tactical aspects of propaganda in general, and of revolutionary propaganda in

---

and sharply diverge from (or coincide with) the pattern which succeeded at the new revolutionary center.

particular. Propaganda is directed toward strengthening attitudes which facilitate the desired goal and toward weakening attitudes which obstruct it. Revolutionary propaganda in a given state has the following main tasks: (1) to direct discontents, however caused, against the symbols and practices of the established order; (2) to organize favorable attitudes toward symbols which can be manipulated by a counter-élite during revolutionary crises; (3) to prevent hyper-concentration of hostile influences until the probability of a successful revolutionary action is attained.

CHAPTER II

The Local Balance of Indulgence
and Deprivation

WHEN the Great Depression hit Chicago, the city had been passing through a long period of mounting prosperity. Wages had steadily improved. New industries had risen to take the place of declining industries. Chicago was a thriving, vigorous citadel of industrial capitalism.[1] The workers of the city, when organized, were devoted to "business unionism" and to the political tactics of "rewarding your friends and punishing your enemies." There were, it is true, reminiscent sparks of a more militant past. The Haymarket riot was a gory milestone in the history of Chicago. There were vestiges of the Socialist movement which had won tangible, though limited, victories before the World War.

More potent, however, were memories of frustration connected with the brief period of militancy in the years just after the war. The Chicago Federation of Labor had raised the flag of revolt against the traditional tactics of the American Federation of Labor. Chicago itself had been the dynamic center of national Communism. But militancy and radicalism had gone down to smashing defeat. The Chicago Federation of Labor lost out in the Illinois Federation and in the American Federation. The old-line leaders of the A. F. of L. had won

[1] For important details consult Appendix.

out all along the battle-front. Chicago unions relapsed into passivity. Chicago also declined as a national center of Communism. Publications were moved to New York. The Chicago party lived a puny existence during the glittering years of the Great Prosperity. Near their end there was some borrowed glory from the herculean efforts of the Soviet Union to execute the Five-Year Plan. But there were no laurels for local achievement.

A small band of the faithful held out during the lean years of prosperity. The Great Depression finally came. Would it bring a great upsurge of mass feeling, revitalize the older revolutionary tradition, and set the proletariat on the road to power with the Communists in the lead? Would the depression vindicate the soundness of the Communist analysis and justify the strategy and tactics of the Third International?

For the proper evaluation of what happened in Chicago after 1929, we must see what the Great Depression meant for the social groups to which the Communists addressed themselves.

It is taken for granted by revolutionary propagandists that protest will thrive among those who get less of what there is to get rather than among those who get relatively much. Therefore revolutionary radical propaganda is primarily directed to the lower layers of the value pyramids and has as one of its immediate aims the spreading of the statement that they are excluded from a fair share in the available values in the community. Communist propaganda concentrates upon the wage-earners, the unemployed, the lesser middle classes, which are the strata of the nation which obtain less deference, income, and safety than the wealthiest groups.

Just how close is the connection between the acceptance of propaganda and changes in the environment? As a means of exploring this relationship in Chicago, we have classified the years and quarters after 1929 according to the predominance of *indulgence* and *deprivation*. Deprivations are changes which impair the position of persons with reference to the distribution of values. Income is a value in western European civilization; hence reductions in income are deprivations. Deference is also a value; hence exclusion from agencies which consult on public policy is a deprivation. Indulgences are improvements in relation to the values. They consist in augmentations of income, safety, deference, and whatever other values are present in the situation.[2]

The principal indices selected for this study are as follows: changes in *employment;* changes in number of *evictions;* changes in total *relief-case count;* changes in the amount of *work relief;* and, finally, changes in *average relief expenditure per case* (excluding work-relief expenditures).

Changes in these factors have been studied by quarters, and, principally on the basis of such figures, quarters have been classified as deprivation or indulgence quarters. Thus, for example, the first quarter of 1932 was a deprivation quarter: these were severe winter months; there was a relief crisis, with general uncertainty as to who would foot the relief bill for the future (federal, state, local, or private sources); the number of evictions rose 182 per cent over that of the previous quarter; employment indices continued to fall. On the other hand, the final quarter of 1932 was an indulgence quarter: these months saw the first upturn in employment figures since the beginning of the depression; the relief case count rose 16 per cent; the number of evictions dropped 43 per cent under that of the previous quarter; and presidential elections allowed release of collective aggression through the defeat of Herbert Hoover, and a wave of general optimism regarding the future.

Not all quarters, however, were found to fall definitely into the classification deprivation or indulgence quarters. Some three-month periods when taken as a whole presented no net change in deprivation or indulgence. Such quarters will be called " activity quarters " if considerable changes are taking

[2] Different values from income, deference, or safety may be taken for purposes of analysis. The important point is not to reach agreement on the categories, but to make clear the categories which are used.

place in them, but if the changes of indulgence character are approximately compensated by changes of a deprivational character. And such quarters will be called "inactivity" quarters if no considerable changes of either an indulgence or deprivational character are occurring in them.[3] Thus, for example, the first quarter of 1933 was an *activity* quarter in which many aspects of the environment were changing and when deprivation and indulgence factors were both prominent: employment dropped 8 per cent, although the previous quarter it had risen slightly for the first time in several years; the bank crisis of February and March paralyzed the resources of many persons who up to that time had been able to carry the burden of unemployment without applying for aid; on the other hand, during this quarter evictions dropped off 29 per cent and the case load and average expenditure for relief rose; great optimism prevailed in March in appreciation of President Roosevelt's inaugural address and of his decisive and outspoken leadership; the January centralization of complaints at one bureau cut off an important channel of protest expression and was bitterly challenged by organizations of the unemployed, but the police firmly enforced this new measure. The single instance of an *inactivity* quarter is found in the third quarter of 1934; evictions rose 14 per cent over the previous quarter; there were slight decreases in work relief and in case load; employment, however, held steady, and the three-month period was free from much turbulent speech or action in connection with the relief issue; in general, there was a continuation of the general indulgence which characterized the preceding quarter, but no change in this direction.

The five-year period, analyzed quarter by quarter in the manner described above, may be summarized as follows:[4]

[3] Since deprivation and indulgence have been measured in terms of *changes* of certain indices, inactive quarters could not be classified in these terms.

[4] The quarterly variations of the indices on the basis of which these classifications are principally made, are found in the Appendix.

1930: First Quarter: *Deprivation*
       Second Quarter: *Deprivation*
       Third Quarter: *Deprivation*
       Fourth Quarter: Indulgence

1931: First Quarter: *Activity*
       Second Quarter: *Deprivation*
       Third Quarter: *Deprivation*
       Fourth Quarter: Indulgence

1932: First Quarter: *Deprivation*
       Second Quarter: *Deprivation*
       Third Quarter: *Activity*
       Fourth Quarter: Indulgence

1933: First Quarter: *Activity*
       Second Quarter: *Deprivation*
       Third Quarter: Indulgence
       Fourth Quarter: *Activity*

1934: First Quarter: *Deprivation*
       Second Quarter: Indulgence
       Third Quarter: *Inactivity*
       Fourth Quarter: Indulgence

In order to understand in more detail the changes in the environment during this five-year period, and the setting which they afforded for revolutionary propaganda, we shall examine more fully the events of these years.

The cyclical decline in unemployment in Chicago began in the early fall of 1929. The high point in unemployment and pay-roll indices came in September of that year.[5] In October began a steady downward trend in employment which continued uninterruptedly for thirty-six months. It was not until after the federal census of 1930, however, that the extent

[5] "Unemployment and Payroll Indices," *Illinois Department of Labor Bulletin* (Springfield, 1927, 1928, 1929).

of the unemployment crisis became apparent. The figures showed that out of a total of 1,558,949 gainfully employable workers in Chicago, 167,934, or 11 per cent, were unemployed.

During the first half of 1930 little was done toward meeting a situation which was generally felt to be but a temporary one. These months were characterized by obliviousness on the part of the press and the public of the fact that the unemployment situation was one which required special measures of any sort. The press treated the industrial situation as a slump which would shortly be replaced by prosperity. And the famous words of President Hoover: "Prosperity is just around the corner," which later provoked so much ridicule, were, during the first months of 1930, expressive of the generally hopeful attitude of the country.

While private relief agencies staggered under the burden of rapidly increasing case loads, the press of Chicago maintained a cheerful optimism regarding the future. Consequently individuals tended to regard their economic difficulty as a purely personal problem. If a man lost his last savings in stocks, it was because of his personal lack of insight; he should have had enough sense to stay out. The fact that others were caught in the same manner was small consolation. Similarly, if a man lost his job, it was because he was not good enough to hold onto it; the man next door had not lost his. Deprivations were highly personalized, and personal adaptations were sought. The only indulgence was the comforting attitude of the press, which offered condolences for the unfortunate present and reassurances for the future.

During the early fall of 1930, the Committee on Unemployment of the Chicago Council of Social Agencies, a committee which had been previously concerned with means of preventing unemployment, turned its attention to the problem of relief for the unemployed. A general Citizens' Committee on Unemployment was formed to deal with this question. At the same time the chairman of the General Advisory Board of the Illinois Free Employment Bureau recommended that Gov-

ernor Emmerson call a special conference to consider the unemployment situation and ways of meeting it. The Governor
appointed a Commission on Unemployment and Relief, which
was consolidated with the General Citizens' Committee into a
single Commission.

With initial steps toward co-ordinated relief came public recognition of the existence of a problem in which each individual had some social responsibility. The barrage of optimism which had filled the press began to thin out. Instead
emphasis was laid on the help which everyone must give in
working through a difficult and trying situation. The Ro-
tary Club founded the " Goodfellow Movement," to spread
" cheer " through the winter months. A headline in the *Chicago Tribune:* " GOOD FELLOWS WILL CHICAGO TO PROSPERITY —
BUILD HAPPINESS IS AIM OF HELPERS," is indicative of the cheerful
magnanimity with which such private organizations assumed
their obligations toward the unemployed.

A figure of $5,000,000 was set by the social agencies as nec-
essary to meet relief needs. This amount was to be raised
through private contributions. Money was collected, however,
not only from private donations of prominent persons in the
business and social world, but also through such social functions as football games, charity balls, and the like. Society
clubs took it upon themselves to feed poor school children.
Mayor Cermak suggested a " tax-yourself " campaign to aid
the jobless. Sally Joy Brown, a private clearing house for job-
seekers and help-wanters, was introduced by the *Chicago Tribune.* Certain restaurants offered a limited number of free
meals for the unemployed daily.

The earliest public and organized efforts to alleviate the
crisis followed these private and individual forms of charitable
activity, but in the late fall of 1930 came the first of a series
of announcements by private industry indicating a new approach. Samuel Insull announced that " one day's pay for six
months will be contributed by the employees and officers of
the Insull group of Public Utilities to the relief of distress

caused by unemployment." [6] By this plan certain employees, fortunate in having jobs, shared *as a body* with those who were unemployed. Such a move was no longer strictly private in character. Contribution ceased to be purely voluntary. This was an intermediate step on the road to full collective and publicly recognized responsibility.

A recanvass of Chicago by the United States Bureau of the Census in January 1931 showed 448,739 unemployed,[7] or 28 per cent of the gainful workers of Chicago. Unemployment had increased 167 per cent from April 1930 to January 1931, and the employment index continued to fall month by month. Evictions in the city reached unprecedented numbers. Public relief rolls by the beginning of 1931 had practically doubled. At this early stage of the depression, however, this fact in itself must be interpreted as deprivation rather than as indulgence. Public responsibility for the unemployed was not accepted at that time and economic distress was regarded as an individual disgrace rather than as a collective status. To be unemployed was shameful enough, but to be forced to ask for charity was many times more humiliating.

Beyond the material assistance offered by the relief agencies of Chicago in the first winter of the depression, there was a decided increase in the amount of helpfulness, good cheer, and good-fellowship of the kind which had been shown in the early fall of 1930. Local newspapers pleaded for the employment of the unemployed. Good-hearted business men cut their advertising budgets and " backed the bread-line," sometimes getting feature stories in the local press. The move to raise private relief funds by cutting the pay of employees was

[6] This type of contribution had originally been suggested by the Campaign Committee of the Governor's Commission on Unemployment and Relief.

[7] The number of unemployed includes those in classes *A* and *B* defined as follows: *A*, persons out of a job, able to work, and looking for a job; *B*, persons having jobs, but on lay-off without pay, excluding those sick or voluntarily idle.

continued, with added pressure from newspaper sources.

In early March 1931 the first of a long series of relief crises developed. The state legislature failed to pass a bill authorizing the Cook County Board to issue $2,000,000 in bonds for poor relief. It was not until the third week of May that this bill received the signature of Governor Emmerson, and in the meantime the relief rolls were cut, despite the fact that the spring had failed to bring the " cyclical rise in employment " which had been prophesied by the press.

In the middle of July 1931 the $5,000,000 which had been raised in the fall of 1930 and which had been judged sufficient to meet the relief needs until October 1931 was exhausted. Although the bill signed by the Governor in May authorized the issuance of $2,000,000 in bonds for relief purposes, it was necessary to dispose of such bonds before the cash could become available. Furthermore, at that time the private agencies were solely responsible for the distribution of funds, a task which they were not administratively equipped to handle. With rising unemployment, evictions reached a new high. During the summer quarter of 1931, 467 families were put out into the streets, an increase of 51 per cent over the previous three months. The effects of the first series of bank closures also made themselves felt during the summer, when thousands of families had to face the problem of everyday living without the family savings which they had counted upon to tide them over until " better times." Economic deprivations had been steadily accumulating for eighteen or twenty months and reached a maximum. Tensions and affects reached a breaking-point. As a result of spontaneous collective action by the unemployed the fact burst upon the public consciousness that unemployment and the ills occasioned by it were *public* rather than *private* responsibilities. The breaking-point was the bloody riot of August 3, in which three Negroes were killed. From this point on, unemployment was never viewed as a purely individual responsibility.

As a result of the August eviction riots, all evictions were temporarily suspended. This concession was reinforced by a sharp rise in relief expenditures. In August 1931 the Governor's Commission on Unemployment and Relief was reorganized in Cook County as the Joint Emergency Relief Fund, which pledged to raise $10,000,000 before the close of the year, which amount, it was estimated, would provide relief expenditures for the following year. Also joint emergency relief stations, the first *public* relief centers, were established during the fall months of 1931. The first two of these opened their doors on the 1st of October, and by December 1 eleven public stations were in operation. It was characteristic of this period of transition from private to public responsibility that although these Joint Emergency Relief stations were administered by a public commission, they were financed entirely by private funds.

During the entire fall of 1931 the enormous relief drive was carried forward and played up prominently in the press. By the middle of December the Joint Emergency Relief Fund Campaign had reached its $10,000,000 relief quota and on the 20th of the month the drive was ended with $434,659 over its quota. Edward L. Ryerson, chairman of the fund, stated that while the fund would meet the " necessities of life for Chicago's poor through the winter," the fund was not sufficient to meet rents and asked the landlords not to expect rent payments from the fund. Quite aside from the importance of the fund-raising campaign as a source of relief, it reassured destitute families with regard to their future and gave individuals who had contributed to the fund a sense of " having done their duty" and of having disposed of the crisis for some time to come.

The winter of 1931-2 definitely destroyed the illusions which had been fostered by the publicity of the relief drive. Employment figures traveled consistently downward, and the number of people on relief rose so rapidly that by January a new relief crisis was imminent and was brought before the state legislature. Another appeal was made to business and professional men to provide funds to " tide over " the relief stations until legislative action by the state would provide the necessary additional money. A special committee, headed by President Robert Maynard Hutchins of the University of Chicago, hurriedly sought to raise money so that the relief stations would not have to close their doors on February 1. It was due perhaps to the fact that private individuals felt that they could no longer carry the burden of relief needs that the pending crisis was so freely discussed in the press and the seriousness of the situation was treated much more openly than it had been previous to this time. An editorial in the *Chicago Tribune* on January 27, 1932, stated:

" The emergency which the directors of the Governor's relief work have brought to the attention of the Illinois Assembly is beyond debate. . . . Private philanthropy has been drawn upon to the limit and is now exhausted. Neither Cook County nor Chicago can raise the required funds for relief. State aid is possible and essential."

The state legislature acted with phenomenal speed. On the 6th of February a bill appropriating $20,000,000 on a " state credit plan " had passed the House and Senate and been duly signed by Governor Emmerson. The Illinois Emergency Relief Commission was created to distribute these initial funds.[8] The amount appropriated by the state legislature for relief purposes, however, was not an outright appropriation of funds, but had to be raised through the sale of tax anticipation notes — once more a straddling of responsibility between private and public groups. It is noteworthy that the bill was referred to as " poor relief " legislation, thus qualifying state responsibility by attaching a certain stigma to the status of relief clients.

Meanwhile there was a sharp relief crisis in Cook County during the early spring. In January a moratorium on payment of rent from relief funds had been declared by the executive

[8] For a record of Illinois state legislation financing emergency relief for this period, cf. Appendix.

committee of the Joint Emergency Relief Fund. This policy was continued by the Illinois Emergency Relief Commission when it came into being in February. The non-payment of rent by relief agencies was a new policy, and since it was adopted during the time of severe economic deprivation, it resulted during subsequent months in a rapid increase in the number of families evicted from their homes. During the first six months of 1932, 1,032 families were turned into the streets and in July, August, and September another thousand were evicted. The number for the summer months was 146 per cent above the spring figures. It was also during the summer of 1932 that the index of employment reached an all-time low.

Practically all the money used for relief and relief administration from February through July 1932 was state money, but on July 15, 1932 the Illinois Emergency Relief Commission issued the statement that state funds for relief in Cook County would be exhausted by the end of the month. Since it was impossible to secure action from the Illinois legislature in time to prevent a relief crisis, the Commission urged that an appeal be made for federal aid.

During the first part of 1932 the Congress of the United States had considered several bills pertaining to federal funds for relief. These included a bill providing for the distribution of the excess wheat crop to unemployed throughout the country. Finally a relief bill introduced in the Senate under Democratic leadership was agreed upon. On July 21, 1932 a bill was signed which enabled the Reconstruction Finance Corporation to lend $300,000,000 to states for relief purposes. Funds could be secured upon application of the governor of the state, if satisfactory evidence was given that local relief funds were insufficient to meet the relief crisis. Illinois was the first state to apply for aid under this bill and obtained a loan of $3,000,-000 on July 27, 1932.

At first the move toward federal relief was protested by various organizations. Among them was the Illinois Chamber of Commerce, which early in February sent an urgent protest against proposed federal relief to the state's senators in Washington. The Chamber called the federal proposals then pending in the United States Congress "an endorsement of the dole system." However, in the face of the July crisis and the pressure which had been brought upon private individuals in disposing of the state tax-warrants during the spring months, the attitude of this and other organizations was considerably modified. It was during the critical spring and summer of 1932 that anti-Hooverism began to take a real foothold.

At the end of August, J. L. Moss, director of the Cook County Bureau of Public Welfare, announced that the number of applicants for state relief in the month of August had increased so greatly that state appropriations had been overdrawn by $350,000. About the same time a new relief campaign was begun to collect funds for the private agencies, but it was made clear that these funds would be used for free hospitalization, free clinics, child care, and other problems apart from unemployment, which was designated as a public problem. The situation was critical. The state legislature met in emergency session to arrange for the levying of a gas tax as the only hope of raising funds for public relief. The bill was not passed and Mayor Cermak left Chicago hurriedly to appeal to Washington for aid, requesting an additional $8,100,000 from the Reconstruction Finance Corporation. "Until the November elections have been decided it is a political impossibility to get the Illinois legislature to adopt an adequate relief program," Chicago spokesmen were reported to have said as they filed the loan. The Reconstruction Finance Corporation granted to the state $5,000,000 with which to meet the emergency.

In general the situation after the September crisis developed indulgently. During the month of October 1932 funds were collected from three sources: private, state, and federal. The urgent call for funds may be looked upon as an indulgence factor in itself. Every type of appeal was used, and there was a throwback to private forms of self-sacrifice where individuals gave publicly to the unfortunate. Thus, on the 1st of November, James Simpson, chairman of the Board of the Commonwealth Edison Company of Northern Illinois and of the People's Light, Coke, and Gas Company, gave his entire six months' salary from those positions to "charity." Private funds were solicited through the Goodfellow Clubs and a fresh campaign was launched to feed Chicago's hungry school children. The number of families receiving relief rose to 168,000. The employment index, which had begun to rise in August, continued to move upward, and although the increases were very small, they held steady till the end of the year. Evictions during October, November, and December dropped 43 per cent from the summer figure.

One of the most important factors which served to ease the situation in the fall of 1932 was the presidential election, which afforded the unemployed an opportunity of expressing their grievances at the polls. The general insecurity level diminished with the November elections, and with the coming of Roosevelt a new wave of optimism swept the country.

In 1933 began a period of social and economic readjustment. In his campaign speeches as well as in his party platform Roosevelt held out the hope of a New Deal for "the forgotten man." His election assured a program of federal action. The relief problem was placed on an entirely new basis, in which economic responsibility was definitely lifted from the shoulders of the private individual and placed instead on the broad back of the federal government. Furthermore, the federal government promised not only alleviation of depression conditions but a decisive program moving toward recovery.

In January 1933 the number of families on relief in Chicago reached an all-time high (including the rest of the depression). The amount of money spent on relief increased to an even greater extent, so that more money was spent on each family. The number of evictions fell off considerably.

With the let-up of the tension of 1932, the relief administra-

tion in Chicago acted to check the direct pressure which had
been brought upon the relief stations during the preceding two
years. Until the end of 1932 demonstrations at relief stations
as a means of securing relief demands had been steadily growing in size and number. In January 1933 this channel of pressure was blocked by administrative order of the relief agencies,
and an office called the Public Relations Bureau was created
to deal with all complaints of organizations regarding relief.
Complaints were to be submitted through a committee. These
restrictive orders were emphatically opposed by the unemployed organizations, but were rigidly put into force by the
police. One immediate result of the consolidation of social responsibility in the New Deal program was that for the first
time relief was planned beyond a month-to-month basis of
operation. At the beginning of 1933 the Illinois Emergency
Relief Commission estimated that at least $92,000,000 would be
required from state or federal funds to furnish relief in Illinois for the ensuing year; $80,000,000 of this would be needed
in Cook County alone.

During the first half of 1933 a series of bills were passed in
the Illinois state legislature appropriating funds for relief purposes. Relief funds were drawn from the motor fuel tax, from
the levying of a general sales tax, and from the retailers' occupation tax.[9] In the early months, additional direct loans were
made to the state by the Reconstruction Finance Corporation.

Although the first months of 1933 were definitely filled with
the optimism of Roosevelt New Dealism, during the early
spring a serious situation developed. Bank failures in Chicago,
as elsewhere throughout the country, deprived hundreds of
thousands of their remaining savings. There was a considerable cut in relief expenditures per family. Evictions once more
assumed distressing proportions. In the midst of this gloom
President Roosevelt was inaugurated. Then followed the first
federal emergency measure, the bank moratorium.

In its relief policy the federal government for the most part

[9] Cf. Appendix.

followed the program outlined by President Roosevelt in his special message of March 21. The Federal Emergency Relief Administration, approved May 12, 1933, provided $5,000,000 which was to be used in direct grants-in-aid to the states. Half of this appropriation could be granted only to those states which would match such grants with twice the sum.

During 1933 the desire to get men back on jobs favored the development of a large-scale public work-relief program. Although, on the one hand, the federal government had made clear its acceptance of responsibility for relief of the unemployed, it was felt that a system of dole was contrary to the principles of American democracy and that in order to retain his self-respect the unemployed person must earn the money paid out by the government. It was also pointed out by the New Deal administration that work relief, besides being productive in itself, would tend to stimulate private employment.

The idea of work relief did not originate with the New Deal. As early as the summer of 1930 the first work-relief fund had been started. One of Chicago's public-spirited citizens had contributed $25,000 with which to put unemployed men to work. The plan for putting able-bodied men, especially heads of families, to work on this fund at $50 a month was worked out by the United Charities in co-operation with the Illinois Free Employment Bureau. The first group of men sent out on this fund went to work in October 1930 for the South Park Commission.[10] A work-relief plan had been part of the program of the Chicago social agencies since that time. The initial work fund of $25,000 was the nucleus of a Special Work Fund, later expanded under the Governor's Commission. The Joint Emergency Relief Fund (set up in August 1931) had continued a work program. In 1930 the amount spent by the Special Work Division of the Family Relief Agencies in Chicago had constituted 6 per cent of the total spent on relief. In 1931 this figure rose to 8 per cent. Actually only several hun-

[10] Linn Brandenburg: *Chicago Relief and Service Statistics, 1928–1931,* p. 8.

dred people received work relief during these early years. By February 1932, owing to lack of funds, the work-relief program in Cook County had become practically non-existent. Almost directly after the formation of the Illinois Emergency Relief Commission, however, the first public funds for work relief were appropriated, and limited allocations for this purpose were continued. The work-relief program had spluttered and floundered along through the series of relief crises.

In 1933, however, work relief was lifted to a new level by the federal government. The formulation of a special federal work-relief program tended to dissociate work relief from the regular relief process. In July 1933, 20,371 persons in Chicago were put to work on work-relief rolls. During that month $665,860.46 was spent in this manner. The adoption of the work form of relief on a large scale came about as a sequel to the assumption of full responsibility for unemployment by the federal government. Putting men on the federal pay-rolls through such programs as the CWA and PWA also tended to dignify the status of those dependent upon the public for a livelihood.

In accordance with expectations, the summer of 1933 brought a definite upswing. The series of emergency acts instituted by the President began to take form. The very existence of a decided policy and of decisive action revived hope for the future. There were a marked increase in employment and for the first time since 1929 a reduction in the number of persons receiving relief in Chicago. Employment figures rose steadily through the spring and summer, reaching a high for the year in September.

But rising prices and increased relief standards partly counteracted the effects of decreasing case loads on the amount of relief expenditures. Notwithstanding this, the total relief expenditures of the major relief agencies in Chicago fell from $4,636,707 in March 1933 to $3,866,103 in December 1933.[11] In November 1933 the state of Illinois issued bonds to the

[11] *Social Service Yearbook,* 1933, p. 14.

amount of $30,000,000 to be used for relief purposes. Funds were also diverted from the retailers' occupational tax for the same purpose. A total of $101,943,301.86 in obligations for unemployment relief and administration was incurred in Illinois in 1934, as against $79,107,936.59 in 1933. Throughout the year 1934 social work in Chicago, as throughout the country, was greatly affected by the policy of the Federal Emergency Relief Administration. Furthermore, the work-relief program of the Civil Works Administration brought with it a marked decrease in the scope of operations of the other agencies. But this program fell off considerably already during the early parts of the year, reaching a minimum figure in April, when only about 24,800 men were put to work on it. This development, in its turn, necessitated a corresponding expansion of the operation of other relief agencies, since no significant change in the employment situation had come about.

The foregoing summary of the local balance of indulgence and deprivation depicts the framework within which, and upon which, the propagandists of Communism were at work. Disregarding some of the minor fluctuations referred to above, one may say that the first half of the Great Depression was a time of deprivation; the second half was a time of indulgence. What was the connection of Communist propaganda with this ever shifting scene?

PART TWO

THE CHANNELS OF PROPAGANDA

CHAPTER III

The Channels of Propaganda:
Demonstrations

THE PRESENT section of this book describes the channels used by the Communist Party and its affiliated organizations in the circulation of Communist propaganda during the first five years of the depression in Chicago. The Communist Party relied so extensively upon demonstrations, publications, and cover organizations that these channels have been singled out for special treatment. In this chapter we consider demonstrations; they involve the concerted activity of persons for protest purposes. Forms of demonstration comprise public gatherings, tag days, strikes and picketing, official investigations, joint resolutions, telephone campaigns, and consumer boycotts.

Mass Demonstrations

Although demonstrations have been lauded by the Communists since the Russian revolution as a supreme method of reaching and activizing the masses, mass demonstrations leaped into prominence only with the deepening of the crisis. A welling flood of demonstrations among the unemployed was " headed " or " assisted " by the party to the best of its ability. The degree to which the Communist Party was responsible for these demonstrations should not be overestimated. So desperate were the unemployed that protest was seething through the disadvantaged neighborhoods of the city. The party did its best to capitalize upon the situation by means of mass demonstrations. But the records of the party show that during this period requests for leadership from protesting groups far exceeded the resources of the party.

Nevertheless, during the first five years of the depression the Communist Party led, organized, or participated in 2,088 mass demonstrations in the city of Chicago.[1] Each of these mass gatherings was called in the name of certain political and economic issues. Most of them were planned and advertised in advance, and every effort was made to secure a maximum attendance.

Over 9 per cent of the 2,088 demonstrations were called in celebration of Communist holidays. Memorial days especially were utilized as occasions for demonstration. The anniversary of the Russian revolution (November 7) and May Day (May 1) are two principal holidays of the Communist calendar. The following list of holiday celebrations will give an impression of the types of occasions which called for demonstration. Many of these were perpetuated from year to year:

Sixth anniversary of the *Daily Worker,* party headquarters, 2021 W. Division Street, January 12, 1930

Lenin memorial, Carmen's Hall, Ashland Avenue and Van Buren Street, January 21, 1930

Lenin-Liebknecht-Luxemburg memorial meeting, People's Auditorium, February 9, 1930

National Unemployment Day demonstration, through the West Side, March 6, 1930

International Women's Day, People's Auditorium, March 8, 1930

Celebrate Paris Commune, People's Auditorium, March 3, 1930

Celebrate tenth anniversary of the Red International of Labor Unions, August 15, 1930

Anniversary of the execution of Sacco and Vanzetti, People's Auditorium, August 22, 1930

[1] This number was in excess of the *regular* public meetings held by the party and its affiliated units.

Commemoration of sixteenth anniversary of the youth movement, People's Auditorium, September 5, 1930

Hundredth anniversary of Nat Turner (Negro leader of insurrection), 729 East Oakwood Boulevard, November 18, 1931

Commemoration of the death of Comrade Charles F. Ruthenberg, People's Auditorium, March 2, 1932

Memorial meeting for Sposob (killed year before by the police in a demonstration), October 6, 1933

Mass demonstrations held during the depression have been classified broadly into four main groups: indoor meetings, outdoor demonstrations, socials, and parades. The relative use of these four forms is expressed in the following table:

	Per cent
Indoor meetings	48.3
Outdoor demonstrations	29.6
" Socials "	15.1
Parades	7.0

Indoor meetings, held in public halls, were the most common as well as the most conventional form of demonstration. Such gatherings were generally publicized in advance by leaflets and, if the occasion was important enough, in the radical press. Indoor meetings of neighborhood or branch units of the organizations were generally open to the public free of charge. City-wide events, however, usually provided a small admittance fee of fifteen to twenty-five cents, which helped to pay for the rental of the hall. The program of such occasions invariably included a panel of speakers, Communist members or sympathizers, who spoke on the issue of the occasion in particular or on issues of the day in general. A collection was taken up from the audience. Announcements of future meetings were made from the platform. And Communist songs, including the *Internationale,* were generally sung by the audience. At the larger meetings other events were frequently included.

Outdoor demonstrations tended to be the most militant channel of mass appeal. Gathered together on street corners, in parks, or in empty lots, the demonstrators stood as they lis- tened to the speakers. The outdoor conditions gave these gath- erings an unconventional tone. The speaker, elevated on an improvised speakers' stand (frequently the proverbial soap- box), raised his voice in order to reach all ears in the scattered crowd. At the same time the audience, clustered in small groups, felt free to discuss the subject among themselves. The sense of freedom made it not inappropriate for members of the audience to shout questions or comments at the speaker or to move about and greet their friends as the speech contin- ued. All together, the lack of four walls gave this type of gath- ering a spontaneity which added fire and color to the usual speaking performances.

" Socials " were generally organized by Communist groups as a source of revenue and as a means of increasing the inten- sity of the attachment of members and sympathizers to the party. They were held either in public halls or in private homes of party members or sympathizers, and admission was charged. At many affairs additional charge was made for re- freshments, and favors were sold as a means of collecting funds. The following random collection of announcements of social gatherings suggests the varied nature of such occasions:

A bunco party, June 20, 1931, at the Workers' Lyceum, 2733 Hirsch Boulevard

Annual bazaar and benefit for the Needle Trades Workers' In- dustrial Union, November 11–13, 1932, same place

Dance and boxing match at the Pythian Temple, 3737 S. State Street, May 14, 1932, auspices of the Workers' Ex-Service League

Circus at People's Auditorium, 2457 West Chicago Avenue, January 20, 1934, Youth Section, IWO

International concert and dance, Workers' Center, 4004 W. Roosevelt Road, Section 3 of the party

Hoover " Prosperity Dance," November 26, 1931, Unemployed Council #13

Dance to raise funds for establishing a Trade Union Center in Chicago " where militant trade unionists can gather," West End

"BONUS MARCH," MAY 31, 1932, SEVENTY-SIXTH STREET
AND DOBSON AVENUE, CHICAGO

DEMONSTRATION, MARCH 26, 1932, IN FRONT OF THE
BOARD OF EDUCATION, CONGRESS AND STATE STREETS,
CHICAGO

Club, 37 S. Ashland Boulevard, December 31, 1930, Trade Union
Educational League

Apple dance on Christmas Monday, People's Auditorium, December 26, 1932, YCL

Anti-war jubilee and dance, People's Auditorium, September
29, 1934, American League Against War and Fascism (Youth
Section)

Hallowe'en party, entertainment and eats, 1142 N. Mozart
Avenue, October 29, 1932, Northwest Branch, FSU

Inter-Racial dance, Alvin Dansant, 51st and Michigan, March
19, 1932, Inter-Racial Committee

Tom Mooney street run, 51st Street and Cottage Grove to
37th and State Street, Youth Committee of the International Labor
Defense

Trial of Mayor Cermak (mock trial), 3337 S. State Street, November 24, 1931, YCL

Entertainment on such occasions was frequently connected
with distinctive Communist symbols. The following is a description of a game played at a " social " in 1930:

" The comrades are seated in a circle. They are furnished (secretly) with names of various countries, one for each comrade. A
comrade stands at the center of the circle and calls for revolutions
in two countries. The comrades with the name of these countries
try to exchange seats, the comrade at the center of the circle attempting to take one of the seats. Sometimes world revolution is
called for and everybody tries to get a new seat. It was explained
at one game that Russia was not given because ' there can be no
revolution in Soviet Russia.' "

Picnics and dances were especially popular types of entertainment. Inter-racial dances were frequently promoted in
connection with the Negro-White Solidarity program, and it
was generally recognized that the possibility of dancing with
members of the other race would prove attractive to many.

Parades, the least frequently utilized form of demonstration, were likewise the most complicated to organize and lead.
Invariably, Communist parades were begun or terminated

with indoor meetings or outdoor demonstrations. They carried Communist adaptation of all which the term " parade " connotes: flags, banners, bands, and colorfully decorated marchers. Many parades tended to become conventional expressions of the historic traditions of the movement and lacked the fire and novelty of the street demonstration. On the other hand, during periods of greatest unrest, parades of poorly clothed, hungry-looking, but defiant unemployed through the streets of Chicago in the so-called " Hunger Marches " against the City Hall were powerful channels. Such marches generally passed through several neighborhoods of the city, instead of centralizing at a single location as in the case of the other forms of demonstration, and consequently brought Communist symbols and slogans to the attention of a wide audience.

Communists showed great ingenuity and originality in the way in which they adapted these four demonstration channels to their propaganda purposes. Despite continual blocking by the police, the mass demonstration persisted as an important channel of Communist propaganda. Because of the outstanding importance of this channel of propaganda, subsequent chapters have been devoted to more thorough examination of the number and extent of such events and the techniques employed in their organization and execution.[2]

Trials

A large number of individuals were arrested and tried in Chicago as a result of participation in Communist activities. Trials of party members or of other persons so arrested were often publicized by the party and utilized as channels of propaganda. In each case leaflets were circulated in advance announcing the date and place of the trial and the courtroom was packed with a sympathetic audience. Communist defendants usually demanded trial by jury, and the occasion frequently afforded a chance for the ILD (International Labor Defense) lawyer to present Communist principles to the judge

[2] Cf. below Chapters IX, X, and XII.

and jury as well as to the courtroom. Another variation in procedure introduced by the ILD was for the worker to plead his own case before the jury.

Because of disturbances in the court which occurred on several occasions in connection with Communist hearings, this channel of propaganda was time and again blocked by the refusal of the court to admit an audience.

The importance of trial demonstrations as a channel of propaganda varied with the number of arrests and with the prominence of the Communist defendants on trial. The trials of Communists arrested during periods of violent clash between police and demonstrators were widely publicized. At such trials the police officers were on hand to testify and the Communists sought to use the courtroom as a means of protesting against police tactics. This channel of expression was frequently blocked by postponing cases to a much later date, by which time public interest had cooled.

Attendance at Communist hearings in Chicago inspired a unique type of demonstration at which the Communist Party retaliated by putting the existing authorities on trial. On such occasions invitations were usually extended to the Mayor, the Commissioner of Police, or other individuals who were to be tried in order that they might appear to defend themselves at these " mass hearings." Needless to say, public officials rarely put in an appearance, although on several occasions ward committeemen met the challenge. In any case, the trial was an imitation of what the Communists saw in the municipal courtrooms. Such trials developed after several occasions on which the Communists were barred from the city courtrooms.

Tag Day

Although no tag days were held by the Communist Party itself, the ILD, the WiR (Workers' International Relief), and similar affiliated groups collected funds for Tom Mooney, for the striking miners in Kentucky, and even for the support of the *Daily Worker* (1932). All together, there were perhaps a

half-dozen tag-day campaigns on a city-wide scale between
1930 and 1934. Tag days required a special permit from the
Commissioner of Police and such permits were not readily
granted since they involved the collection of funds.

An adaptation of the tag day, and one which was much
more common in Communist circles, was the selling of buttons by members of organizations to collect funds for specific
purposes. Such acquaintance-to-acquaintance campaigns required no permit.

Strikes and Picketing

The number of strikes in Chicago during the first five depression years was not great, and the number of Communist-
organized and Communist-led strikes was negligible. According to available information, there were at the most 16 strikes
in 1930, 17 in 1931, and 27 in 1932. During these years the Communist Party was too busy organizing the discontent prevalent
among unemployed groups to devote any large share of its
energies to strike activities. In 1933, when a wave of strikes
arose in Chicago, as elsewhere, in connection with the enforcement of the NRA codes, the party found itself in the position of favoring strikes but of having definitely committed
itself against the Roosevelt codes. Shop papers of this period
reflect this dual attitude by focusing attention not on the issue
but on general slogans.

School Strikes

The systematic use of the school strike originated with the
Communists. For many years the Communist Party in Chicago has concerned itself with conditions in the public schools.
Indeed, one of the earliest issues taken up by the party in
Chicago in the days when the *Daily Worker* was being published in the city concerned fire-trap schools in poor neighborhoods (1924). The first record of an attempted school
strike, however, is in 1934; it developed around the issue of
racial discrimination in the public schools and was organized

and promoted by the YCL (Young Communist League). Although not widely successful, the strike was given much newspaper publicity. In October 1934 another school strike was held which was more successful. It also developed around the issue of racial discrimination in the public schools of Negro neighborhoods and spread to three or four schools. All the students of these schools were not affected by the strike, but the mass absence of students from classes gave grave concern to school authorities.

During the last years of the depression period student strikes against war were organized on Armistice Day. At eleven o'clock students walked out of their classes and demonstrated against war. Such strikes and demonstrations against war were held in Chicago not only in the high schools, but also in colleges and universities throughout the city. The strikes were usually led by radical student organizations, but many nonradical groups participated in them.

Official Investigations

" When in doubt, investigate " is almost a standing order of the Communist Party. Chicago Communists were constantly investigating the conditions of workers in factories or the methods of relief administrators. These investigations were usually made by affiliated organizations particularly concerned with the problem at hand rather than by the party proper. The purpose of each investigation was to bring to light facts which could be used for propaganda purposes. The inquiries were carried on with a blare of publicity before and after. They occurred frequently as part of a general campaign on an issue which circumstances had brought before the public. Less often they were instituted to focus public attention on a new subject.

These investigations were often initiated by party resolutions and afforded many opportunities for this form of appeal as they were carried on.

Protest Resolutions and Petitions

Resolutions and petitions were favorite channels of Communist protest when there were violent clashes between police and demonstrators. These protests were frequently signed by groups of organizations. Resolutions were often mimeographed and signed by many different branches of the unemployed council or the ILD. The following telegram, for example, was sent on January 20, 1933 to Commissioner of Police Allman and was signed by the League of Struggle for Negro Rights, Unemployed Council, and the ILD:

Commissioner of Police Allman
City Hall, Chicago

We the Workers of the 42nd Ward gathered together in mass protest meeting protesting the terror carried on by police and detectives squads questioning and threatening Negro and white workers on the street as commissioner we hold you responsible for these actions — these actions must stop.

League of Struggle for Negro Rights Unemployed Council
ILD

Wm. Wilson as Committeeman

January 20, 1933

Typical of the frequent resolutions on police terror is the following resolution *On Police Brutality and Conditions in the Chicago Bridewell* which was sent to Mayor Cermak and Police Commissioner Allman in September 1932:

To Mayor Cermak, City Hall, Chicago, Ill.
To Police Commissioner Allman, City Hall, Chicago, Ill.

In the past few weeks the efforts of the workers in Chicago to better their conditions, to seek some improvement in the miserable relief furnished them; their struggle to prevent the eviction of destitute working class families and the exercise of their constitutionally guaranteed rights of free speech and assemblage, has met with a police attack accompanied by the most brutal assault on individual workers, both at the time of arrest and while in custody in police stations. The series of unprovoked attacks by the police with the accompanying beating of individual prisoners in police stations, shows the identity of control in the city administration by the big bosses who hope to further increase their profits by terrorizing the workers into accepting ever worse relief conditions.

When our fellow workers are sent to jail in the city prison known as Bridewell, they are compelled to exist under the most indescribable sanitary conditions. The north and south cell wings of this institution are completely lacking in any sanitary facilities. Prisoners go for hours without water, subject to the whims of brutalized guards. The food conditions are so bad, with food served of such very low quality that the prisoners have been compelled to resort to an organized protest in the dining room in the three weeks of August.

We demand the stoppage of police brutality and interference with the rights of free speech, and assemblage in all organizations.

We demand the immediate stoppage of the beating of prisoners in police stations and that the commanding officer of the North Ave. Station and of South Chicago Station be brought to trial because of their personal responsibility of the beatings in the stations, commanded by them.

We demand that the prisoners in Bridewell be given sufficient food, of a sufficient and varied character to make it possible for them to live without impairment of their health. We demand that this diet include milk, butter, sugar and fresh vegetables, to stop the profiteering of these items within this prison.

We demand free smoking for all prisoners within this penal institution. We demand the immediate installation of running water. We demand that prisoners sent to Bridewell for their working class activity should be allowed the right to receive all working class literature books, pamphlets, publications of all kinds.

We pledge our support to the struggle until our aims are accomplished.

Unemployed Council (20 members)
3855 W. Chicago Ave.

Philip Martino
Chairman
September 27, 1932

Another form of protest was petitions on which individuals undersigned demands for relief or general betterment of conditions. Such petitions were usually mimeographed and circulated through the branches of one or more organizations and subsequently presented by a committee to the authority to which they were addressed. Typical of this type of petition is the following, addressed to Mayor Cermak and the City Council with regard to the imprisonment of workers arrested during a demonstration:

Mayor Cermak and the
City Council,
Chicago, Illinois.

Gentlemen:

We the undersigned protest the imprisonment of our fellow workers who are serving from one to three and a half months in the House of Correction. Their only crime was to fight for immediate relief and unemployment insurance for themselves and their fellow workers, all unemployed and unable to secure work.

Today fifteen are serving. They are confined to vermin filled cells, are forced to hard labor and are given filthy and insufficient food. We demand their immediate and unconditional release.

In addition there are one hundred and twenty-six who will go to trial on or before November 16th. They likewise are facing jail directly as a result of their working-class activity. We demand the dismissal of all charges against these workers.

Further we declare that we will defend the workers' right to demonstrate for immediate relief and unemployment insurance. The workers are entitled to the streets and we demand a cessation of the police and judicial terror now being exercised against them.

(Space for signatures)

International Labor Defense
Chicago District
23 S. Lincoln Street

Individually undersigned protest resolutions and petitions were most common during the early part of the depression, in keeping with the individual sense of responsibility current at that time. During the latter part of 1931 and in 1932 protest came to be registered in the name of organizations rather than individuals.

Telephone Campaigns

Besides the communications by telegraph or mail of protest resolutions and petitions, there were telephone campaigns carried on by the Communist Party or its affiliated organizations from time to time. The telephone campaigns were in some ways more effective than written protests since they tied up the wires of government agencies and forced attention on the subject of complaint. Telephone campaigns have high nuisance value.

Canvassing

The Communist Party and its affiliated organizations have from time to time used door-to-door canvassing as a method of organizing interest or raising funds. This form of propaganda is very closely related to the protest forms already discussed.

In the 1930 election campaign and in subsequent elections held in Chicago the Communist Party necessarily resorted to this means of securing signatures in order to put Communist Party names on the ballot. In the local campaign of 1932 the agitprop department of the Communist Party and the YCL issued special directions about soliciting signatures. This one-sheet manual was circulated among party officials and among the officials of some affiliated organizations like the Unemployed Council. The sheet said that the solicitation of signatures was as much an act of propaganda as a means of getting on the ballot.

" While of course we want to get as many signatures as possible, our aim is to carry the message of the party to the masses. This means that we should not work only for signatures but also explain to the workers about the party so that they will vote for

the party as well. Non-English speaking comrades can be utilized
as they can go together with the more experienced Comrades."

Persons soliciting signatures during any of the election campaigns carried an ample supply of literature. The Communists
concentrated their energies upon working-class sections, and
particularly those hard hit by unemployment.

Lists of signatures were used as membership sources for the
party and its affiliated organizations. Canvassers frequently
marked after the signature the organization for which the individual appeared to be a potential member. From the election
petitions special lists were made up on the basis of these notes
and distributed to the appropriate organizations.

Canvassing was used mostly by the party itself during elections. Several other organizations, notably the unemployed
councils, canvassed for members during certain campaigns.

Consumers' Boycotts

The consumers' boycott was used on more than one occasion
in Chicago. The boycott of German goods, which was vigorously supported by left organizations in 1933 and 1934, was
one of the more important campaigns of this kind. The American League Against War and Fascism was most active in the
anti-German boycott and was responsible for much of the publicity against the buying of German goods.

The anti-German boycott was national rather than local
in nature, and was participated in by many non-Communist groups. Certain boycotts local to Chicago developed and
spread in the wake of the consumer co-operative movements.
A consumers' boycott in protest against the high price of meat
took place in New York City; housewives planned menus
without meat on Thursdays. The movement had its counter-
part in Chicago and, although it did not grow to the same
proportions as in New York City, it received general publicity.

A consumers' boycott was also used as a weapon of pressure
in connection with the Communist-led bread strike on the

west side. West-side sympathizers pledged themselves not to buy bread until the strike was settled.[3]

The consumers' boycott is an extremely diffuse type of activity which is very difficult to control or measure. Consisting in "passive resistance" by a large number of individuals widely spread through the community, this channel is as difficult to block as it is to organize effectively. It has not been much used in Chicago, except in very local instances where the boycott was directed against an individual merchant who was known to be intolerant of Communist activity.

[3] Strikes and boycotts go beyond propaganda. Propaganda is the manipulation of symbols, and symbols are parts of the environment which refer to other parts. Strictly speaking, the slogans used in strike and boycott are the only propaganda connected with these events.

CHAPTER IV

The Channels of Propaganda:
Publications

THE PUBLICATIONS issued by the Communist Party included magazines and newspapers which were official or semi-official organs of the party and its affiliated groups; books published by the several publishing houses which specialized in the printing of Communist literature; pamphlets published by Communist organizations; leaflets issued by the hundreds of thousands throughout the Great Depression; and posters, placards, and banners.

Magazines and Newspapers

The chief periodical of the Communist Party in America is its official organ, "*The Daily Worker* — America's only Class Daily Newspaper." The *Daily Worker* began publication in Chicago in 1924, but in 1927 it was transferred to New York, where it remained. The idea of a Communist daily in English received the approval of Lenin himself several years before the founding of the paper, according to Robert Minor, who wrote in the tenth anniversary edition:

"We decided to ask Lenin to help us with advice. Comrade Lenin was the busiest man in the Congress. . . . He told us wistfully that the only free hour he had was after midnight on a certain day! So, at one minute after midnight we Americans, I think there were six, filed into a dingy little office to meet Lenin.

"Yes, he said, by all means — he believed the American comrades are right who say they must immediately set the whole party to work to establish a great daily newspaper to reach the native American masses. . . . He insisted upon the role of the paper as a popular mass organ for leadership and organizing of the day-to-day struggles of the working class — a popular revolutionary paper reaching out far beyond the narrow circles of the workers, and into the depths of the native working class steeped in the traditions and ways of the country.

"Yes, the Party already had a press, several daily newspapers in foreign languages. Ah, yes, he knew that a large proportion of the workers in the basic industries were foreign-born. But it was nevertheless out of the question to think that the American Communist Party could become the leading force in the American masses and give consistent every-day guidance in their struggles in all political questions. Yes, it would be tremendously hard to establish and maintain such a big enterprise. But couldn't we see that the very demand upon the masses for their support of such a paper would be itself a political matter of importance?"

After 1927 there was no party newspaper of any substantial size published in Chicago. But the *Daily Worker* continued to circulate in the city, and the Chicago circulation was the largest outside New York. In 1931 the *Daily Worker* began to devote a page a week to news of the Chicago district. News for this page was prepared in the Chicago office and forwarded to New York. The separate page was initiated in connection with the election campaign, but proved sufficiently popular to remain as a permanent feature of the paper. In 1933 it was believed that this district was strong enough to support its own newspaper, and on June 25 the *Workers' Voice,* a weekly newspaper selling at three cents per copy, appeared in Chicago. On August 4 the *Voice,* a four-page sheet, made its bow, but before the end of the year it had become a semi-monthly and during the following year passed out of existence.

Although Chicago failed to support its own newspaper, the

circulation of the *Daily Worker* in Chicago rose through the depression. There was sufficient local interest to support several small papers which were distributed in some of the more radical communities. Section 4, for example, launched a penny organ in 1934 on the west side of Chicago. The *West Side News* was circulated free by the Young Communist League in 1933. Such ventures, however, usually vanished after a brief existence and copies of such publications survive by chance.

The Communist Party published shop papers for the purpose of stimulating political activism among employed workers. The first shop paper of which there is a certain record is the *Harvester Worker*, which was issued by the McCormick Works unit in 1926. After 1930 shop papers became more numerous; there is a record of 22 such publications in District 8 between 1930 and 1934 (18 were distributed within the city limits of Chicago). Such periodicals were usually put out every month, but in only three cases did they appear regularly over several years. The form did not differ appreciably from shop to shop. Most of the papers were mimeographed, although from time to time a few were printed. Some sold for one or two cents; others were distributed free. The shop unit was usually responsible for gathering the material, and a special shop-paper committee was usually formed in the unit. Copy was supposed to be checked with the section or district before publication as a means of hewing sharply to the party line.

The party recommended that the distribution of shop papers should take place inside the plant several days before any outside distribution was made. Inside distribution had to be carried out with the utmost secrecy, since exposure usually meant the loss of a job. When it was not practicable to pass out the shop papers inside the place of work, they were distributed near the factory gates, often by workers from other concerns or by the unemployed.

Until 1929 most of the Communist publications in Chicago

SHOP PAPERS (USUALLY MIMEOGRAPHED) CIRCU-
LATED BY THE COMMUNISTS, THE MOST DISTINCTIVE
CHANNEL OF PROPAGANDA

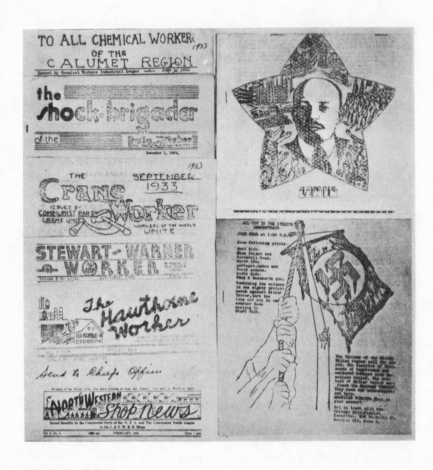

SHOP PAPERS

were printed for a national audience. Until 1926 there was no organ issued in the city which was designed for local circulation only. As national organs were shifted to New York, the need for local papers made itself felt. Thus, as shown in Table I, the number of Communist periodicals having purely local circulation rose from 1 in 1926 to 24 in 1933, the year when they constituted 80 per cent of the total number appearing.

It is possible to arrive at an estimate of the degree of control which was exercised by Communists over "radical" publications by comparing the number of Communist organs with the number issued by the two main rival protest organizations, the Industrial Workers of the World and the Socialist Party. Before the splits of 1919 began, there were 28 radical magazines and newspapers published in Chicago. Of these over half (54 per cent) were issued by the Industrial Workers of the World, and the rest by the Socialists. By 1924 the total number of "radical" publications of these three major groups was apportioned as follows: Industrial Workers of the World, 9 per cent; Socialist Party, 32 per cent; and Communist Party, 59 per cent.

As headquarters for national publications were gradually moved to New York, the Communist share of the "radical" press of Chicago dwindled slightly. When local Communist publications began to spring up at the onset of the depression, the Communist share increased steadily until, in 1933, 79 per cent of the total was Communist. In 1934 the last Industrial Workers of the World publication disappeared, leaving the Socialist Party as the only outstanding competitor of the Communist Party in the field of radical publications. (Cf. Table II.)

During the period 1919–34 the Communist Party published more periodicals in English than in foreign languages. Of the 77 different Communist newspapers or magazines appearing in Chicago during the sixteen-year period 84 per cent were in English. In that period 1930–4, 90 per cent (44 of 49) of the

TABLE I

Communist Periodicals Published in Chicago Showing Number and Percentages Having Local, and Local and National, Circulation, 1919–34

	Local Circulation		Local and National Circulation		Total	
	Number	*Per Cent*	*Number*	*Per Cent*	*Number*	*Per Cent*
1919						
1920			3	100	3	100
1921			5	100	5	100
1922			8	100	8	100
1923			21	100	21	100
1924			26	100	26	100
1925			16	100	16	100
1926	1	9	10	91	11	100
1927	1	9	10	91	11	100
1928	3	30	7	70	10	100
1929	6	50	6	50	12	100
1930	10	62	6	37	16	100
1931	13	76	4	24	17	100
1932	15	75	5	25	20	100
1933	24	80	6	20	30	100
1934	13	72	5	28	18	100
Unduplicated count of publications	44	57	33	43	77	100

Communist periodicals appeared in English. On the other hand between 1919 and 1934, 59 per cent of the Socialist Party and 75 per cent of the Industrial Workers of the World periodicals were published in languages other than English. (Cf. Table III.)

Books

The elaborate intellectual structure of Marxism has produced an extensive library of books on dialectical materialism and upon the details of mass movements throughout the world. Chicagoans have contributed nothing to the theoretical structure of Marxism, and in recent years Chicago has served only to a very limited extent as a publishing center for new contributions. Most of the books published by the Communists were reprints of the works of Marx, Engels, Lenin, and Stalin.

The book-publishing center has been New York, and Chicago's role has been that of a consumer. Books, however, have never reached far beyond the student group. The pamphlet has been better suited to the pocketbooks and the inclinations of the ordinary Communist.

Chicago has to some extent contributed to the " proletarian novel." During the depression James T. Farrell rose to national eminence for his novels of life among the Irish youth in the " back of the yards " district of Chicago's south side. " Studs " Lonigan, whose life was so intimately depicted by Farrell, became a permanent figure in the gallery of American social types. The creator of " Studs," following in the footsteps of many artists reared in Chicago, moved to New York City and figured in " Leftist " circles there.

There is no example of a sustained application of Marxist categories to American data which can be attributed to a Chicago Communist. The intellectuals who were spokesmen of " liberalism " or " Leftism " during the depression were not connected with the Communist Party; indeed, they were usually in sharp opposition to it. Frederick L. Schuman, then a member of the Political Science Department at the University of Chicago, published a vigorous study of *The Nazi Dictatorship* (New York: Alfred A. Knopf) early in 1935 which attracted wide attention. This was undoubtedly the most substantial book written by a Chicago intellectual on

TABLE II

*The Number of Periodicals Published in Chicago by the
Communist Party, the Socialist Party and the Industrial
Workers of the World and the Percentage Each Rep-
resents of the Yearly Totals, 1919–34*

	Communist Party		Socialist Party		Industrial Workers of the World		Total	
	Num-ber	Per Cent	Num-ber	Per Cent	Num-ber	Per Cent	Num-ber	Per Cent
1919			12		15		27	100
1920	3		12		17		32	100
1921	5		12		13		30	100
1922	8		11		8		27	100
1923	21		13		5		39	100
1924	26		14		4		44	100
1925	16		12		4		32	100
1926	11		9		4		24	100
1927	11		9		3		23	100
1928	10		8		4		22	100
1929	12		9		4		25	100
1930	16		8		4		28	100
1931	17		7		4		28	100
1932	20		6		3		29	100
1933	30		7		1		38	100
1934	18		8				26	100
Unduplicated count of pub-lications	77		27		24		128	100

a hotly controversial subject during our period. Dr. Schuman
was without political connections, and especially without
Communist connections. Paul Douglas, economist, of the
University of Chicago, called for the formation of a third

TABLE III

Number and Percentages of English and Foreign-Language Periodicals Published by the Communist Party, the Socialist Party, and the Industrial Workers of the World, 1919–34

	Foreign Publications		English Publications		Total	
	Number	Per Cent	Number	Per Cent	Number	Per Cent
Communist Party	12	16	65	84	77	100
Socialist Party	16	59	11	41	27	100
Industrial Workers of the World	18	75	6	25	24	100
Total for all organizations	46	36	82	64	128	100

party in the United States; his sympathies were definitely " liberal " and " Socialist " and explicitly anti-Communist.

The Communist Party published books for different audiences, including children. One of the most popular books in Communist homes continued to be the *Fairy Tales for Workers' Children,* which was translated from the German of Herminia zur Mühlen and first issued by the Daily Worker Publishing Company in Chicago (May 1925). Class consciousness comes to the child from the Rose-bush, the Gardener, the Sparrow, the Little Grey Dog, and a Dryad. The evil characters are rich. A wealthy factory-owner orders that a Rose-bush with withered branches and flowers be dug up and thrown away. The illustrations give point to the significant events of the story. The Rose-bush is shown scratching the ugly, fat, rich lady. A street scene depicts the extremes of work and idleness. There are beggars and workers, and the workers carry heavy bundles. A military man struts with sword and medals. A carriage with two coachmen is passing by. In another illustration a group of slaves toil under the glare of an overseer with a whip. Later a slave is shown lying beaten; the overseer with the whip is walking off. One illustration shows a child standing in front of a haughty Catholic sister.

The tale begins with the Rose-bush becoming indignant because her owner is a woman who owns a big factory where the workers drudge. As the woman bent down to pick the flowers, " the Rose-bush hit her in the face with a twig, stretching out all her thorns like a cat stretching out its claws, and scratched up the woman's face." Resolving that she would "no longer bloom for idlers," the Rose-bush shriveled up. The factory-owner then ordered a worker to remove the bush. With her last remaining strength, the Rose-bush besought the worker to take her home. When she was transplanted there, she bloomed and bloomed and was even able to restore the health of the worker's wife. The moral of the tale comes from the Rose-bush to the children: " Little children, when you are grown up, you will no longer stand sadly before the gate. The whole world will belong to those who work, the whole world! "

Another tale concerned the Sparrow. The young Sparrow was a student in Professor Swallow's school of architecture and artistic nest-building. But discontent welled within him. He resented building houses for aristocratic birds to live in. He proposed to migrate to warm climates, just like the rich birds. Mother Sparrow was shocked, and Father Sparrow was indignant: " Be silent, you lost soul, you whipper-snapper. You talk like a Bolshevik. My son must not rebel against law and order." The old Blackbird minister, black-frocked and solemn, sermonized to the impatient young Sparrow, saying that God himself had decreed that Sparrows must spend their winters in the north. But the bold young Sparrow flew away to Egypt where he was encouraged by the Sphinx.

Pamphlets

The pamphlet has been a flourishing channel during depression years. Between 1920 and 1927, the Communists published 50 pamphlets in Chicago. In 1927 the center of publication was shifted to New York, and the following year only six pamphlets are on record as published in Chicago. This was a low point for pamphlet publication there. In 1929 there were 14; in 1930, 23; in 1931, 30; in 1932, 56. Apart from this, Chicago has been a steady consumer of the New York output.

Pamphlets have been popularized in the sense that they have been shortened and cheapened. During the '20's the pamphlets were rather comprehensive treatments of their subjects, which sold for twenty or twenty-five cents. Especially after the beginning of the depression, pamphlets became smaller, cheaper, and more numerous and circulated more widely. Sometimes they sold for as little as one cent a copy.

As the pamphlet was popularized in form, it was more devoted to the issues of the day than to involved discussions of party principles. Pamphlets appeared discussing relief, unemployment insurance, and other current problems. In the election campaign of 1932, pamphlets explained the platform of the Communist Party to the masses; there were also other pamphlets which sold for from one to five cents each discussing the platforms of the Republican and Democratic Parties. The Communist Party proper has been responsible for only a share of the pamphlets published. Communist affiliated organizations used the pamphlet channel regularly. The Trade Union Educational League put out 27 pamphlets in 1926 and 1927. The Friends of the Soviet Union published 24 pamphlets in the years 1931–4. Among the other organizations the International Labor Defense has been active (since 1926) with a pamphlet program. The Red International of Trade Unions put out pamphlets from time to time (14 in 1927).

The authorship of Communist pamphlets appearing between 1919 and 1934 has been distributed among many individuals. Of the 272 authors represented, 197 wrote but a single pamphlet, 41 wrote 2 pamphlets, 12 wrote 3. Only 5 individuals contributed more than 10 pamphlets for the entire sixteen-year period. Earl Browder was responsible for the largest number of pamphlets published by any American. His contributions were more numerous than those of William Z. Foster or Scott Nearing, the only other Americans who figured conspicuously in the list. The leading Europeans were Bucharin, Engels, Lenin, Marx, Molotov, Piatnitsky, and Stalin.

As the pamphlets became popularized they became increasingly attractive (when sold for more than a few pennies). The covers were illustrated by photographs, and special cartoons and designs were frequent aids to vividness.

Leaflets

The leaflet channel of propaganda is particularly well adapted to the Communist task of galvanizing the masses into action. A leaflet can be prepared quickly and run off in large numbers. Variable in form and size, it can be adapted to many occasions. It can be terse and telling, and it can be distributed widely; but, most important, a leaflet is cheap and can be distributed free.

Years when the masses are in motion are years when the leaflet is most frequently found as an auxiliary of demonstrations. During the depression, 1932 and 1934 were the high points of leaflet activity for the Communist Party (and the Young Communist League) and for the auxiliary and co-operating organizations. The number of leaflets distributed varied from year to year as follows:

1930	1931	1932	1933	1934
162	161	312	278	335

The year 1934 is somewhat over-represented in this tabulation. Leaflets are among the most fugitive of all fugitive materials, and our leaflet file thus tends to be weighted toward the most

LEAFLETS AND ANNOUNCEMENT CARDS

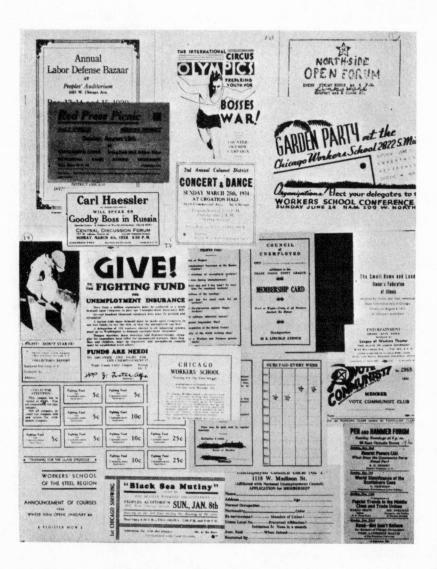

LEAFLETS AND ANNOUNCEMENT CARDS

recent months. The year 1932 was undoubtedly the year of greatest increase in leaflet activity, and it is probable that it marked the high point as well.

The form of the leaflet also changed considerably during the depression. At first leaflets were printed on a fairly good grade of paper and were obviously edited with considerable care. As the amount of activity increased, however, during 1931 and 1932, and as the use of leaflets became more prevalent not only by the central organization but by the many affiliated organizations, the leaflet clearly became popularized: it was usually mimeographed rather than printed, the paper used was of a cheaper grade, and the printed matter itself was obviously written in some haste and none too well edited.

On important party occasions such as May Day or special revolutionary holidays a carefully prepared leaflet was circulated in great numbers throughout the city. Varicolored paper sometimes added greatly to the attractiveness of the leaflet. During 1933 and 1934 it was increasingly common to use drawings on party leaflets.

There were many variations in the form of Communist leaflets. On some important occasions a rather heavy, durable grade of paper stock was used. One popular variation was the sticker, a small leaflet with a glued back surface, which could " plaster up the city."

The circulation of leaflets always caused some anxiety since persons discovered passing them out were subject to arrest by the police, especially during crises. Communists who were arrested were generally booked on charges of disorderly conduct.

Records of the party show that leaflets were distributed very widely all during the depression. Ten to a hundred thousand copies of a single leaflet might be printed. These were passed to the party locals and to the branch offices of affiliated organizations. Sometimes each sponsoring organization printed separate announcements, and four or five different leaflets would appear concerning the issues of the demonstration.

The following leaflet attracted favorable comment from the national directors of "agitprop" work for the party:

WORKERS
of the
CHICAGO SCREW CO.

A Grievance Committee has been formed in the shop to protest against

OIL DRIPPING
THROUGH THE FLOORS

ALL DAY LONG
DOWN OUR NECKS
ON OUR HEAD
INTO OUR EYES

Drops of OIL — OIL — OIL
Seeping thru the Floors on us

This condition can be prevented by the company and we DEMAND that the dripping of oil STOP at once!

Workers, join in this demand!

GRIEVANCE COMMITTEE
Chicago Screw Co.

Posters, Placards, Banners

Chicago police persistently refused to allow Communist posters to be put up in the streets, and consequently posters have been limited to use inside halls, auditoriums, offices, and homes. Persons apprehended in the act of sticking up a poster were liable to arrest on a disorderly-conduct charge, and the possibility of evasion is not great; the same prohibition against the distribution of leaflets has proved much less enforceable. When mass meetings were held inside buildings, the hall was always decorated with posters and banners carrying the slogans of the day. For outside demonstration purposes these posters were converted into placards carried by a single marcher, or by two or more individuals who spanned the marching columns. Placards were also used in picketing strikes, although police restrictions were constantly to be reckoned with.

The most noticeable change in poster technique has been the pictorial poster. At first slogans and emblems were solely relied upon, but gradually the range of illustrations has been greatly expanded. The frequency of the use of posters is most directly connected with the number of mass meetings held, and no doubt the high point of increase was 1932. Communists and Communist sympathizers decorate their offices and homes with pictures of Marx, Stalin, Lenin, and with pictorial and cartoon posters (or with photographs of them).

CHAPTER V

The Channels of Propaganda:

Organizations

ALTHOUGH there were some organizations which were closely related to the Communist Party before 1930, there was comparatively little effort made to draw clear lines of effective demarcation of personnel and activity between the party and special purpose associations. Before the depression the personnel of all affiliated organizations was largely Communist, and in practice there was little separation from the general party line. For many years there had been discussions in world, national, and district congresses of the potential significance of " front " or " cover " organizations. It was universally recognized that " front " organizations might be an effective means of bringing the active membership of the party into direct contact with persons who, if properly cultivated, might be drawn into the central corps of the party. Even if the auxiliary associations yielded few members, they could broaden the scope of the party and contribute to the radicalization of the masses.

The potentialities of the " front " organizations were thus well understood. Yet for various reasons which will develop in the course of this report, there was an immense gap between theory and practice. The party was actually not the center of a spider-web of associations which stood in all degrees of proximity to the seasoned nucleus of the party. The most prominent subsidiary organization previous to 1930 was the Trade Union Educational League (Trade Union Unity League after 1929), which had been organized by William Z. Foster in 1920 and worked closely with the Communists after 1921. This organization had a meteoric career until its efforts to " bore from within " aroused effective counter-measures on the part of the established leadership of the American Federation of Labor. The only associations which have been continually active throughout the life of the Communist Party in Chicago were the foreign-language federations. These, indeed, antedated the party. They seceded from the Socialist Party in 1919. The *foreign-language* federations found active during the period 1930–4 were:

Bulgarian Workers' Education Club
Czechoslovak Educational Association
Freiheit Gesang Verein (Jewish singing society)
Greek Workers' Educational Club
Greek Workers' Club
Hungarian Workers' Home
Irish Workers' Club
Italian Workers' Club
Jewish Workers' Club
Lithuanian Alliance of America
Polish Chamber of Labor
Polish National Alliance Lodge
Polish Workers' Club
Scandinavian Workers' Club
Slovak Workers' Home
Ukrainian Women Toilers

The largest " cover " organization of the depression period was the Unemployed Councils, which had at least 80 locals. This figure includes only those which gave some substantial evidence of having been effectively established. On the fringe was a flotsam and jetsam of councils, semi-councils, and wholly dubious councils which shade off to the vanishing-point. Sometimes the " council " was a single energetic person who tried to buttress his individual demands on the relief agencies by dignifying himself with a more inclusive name. Sometimes a committee came into being, lodged a series of protests, and vanished into the void. In the milling confusion of the depression years, " crystals " were in all degrees of differentiation. The Socialist-controlled organization of the unemployed was the Workers' Committees, which accounted for perhaps 70 local branches. The Communist-controlled Councils attracted by far the most attention from the authorities in charge of relief, from the police, and from the community at large.

It should not be assumed that the Unemployed Councils invariably behaved to the satisfaction of the party. During 1930 and 1931 the demonstrations of the unemployed threatened to get out of hand, and the party was constantly instructed about the proper method of handling such mass organizations through the technique of " fractional control." The District Bureau of the party, for example, had occasion to complain that a demonstration on February 25, 1931, " International Day of Struggle Against Unemployment," had undesirable features:

". . . 'left' opportunism has been developing in Chicago which registered itself in the slogan ' CITY HALL OR BUST '; issuing stickers with the slogan ' DEMONSTRATE AGAINST BREAD LINES '; not raising to forefront in leaflets, the struggle for the Social Insurance Bill; issuing instructions and making other proposals of a ' leftist ' nature." (Resolutions of the District Bureau, March 4, 1931)

Besides the foreign-language federations, which remained quite stable, and the Unemployed Councils, which were numerically preponderant during the depression, there was a variety of associations which were rather closely connected with Communist activities. In most cases they were affiliated, but in a few instances they merely co-operated in a number of special operations. Table I gives a picture of the number of organizations of certain kinds which were to be found in Chicago from year to year. They are divided into " unions," " cultural," " defense," " Negro," " farm," and " others." In 1930 there were 22, and by 1934 there were 60. The annual rate of growth was from a third to a fourth of the total for the preceding year. All told, 79 "front" or " co-operating " organizations are accounted for.

TABLE I

Communist Affiliated and Co-operating Organizations Existing in Chicago, 1929–34

(*exclusive of foreign-language federations and Unemployed Councils*)

	1930	1931	1932	1933	1934	Total (no duplication)
Unions	10	10	11	12	20	24
Cultural	2	6	9	11	12	15
Defense	2	3	3	3	4	5
Negro	2	1	1	2	1	3
Farm				3	2	3
Others	6	10	16	20	21	29
	22	30	38	49	60	79

Too much importance need not be attached to the numbers, but there is little doubt that the trend is accurately shown. Many tiny neighborhood groups which came and went during the depression are not included in the table. Also excluded are the many short-lived committees which were constantly being formed by larger organizations to promote specific issues. The table is limited to organizations having city-wide influence and with some degree of permanence and functional independence.

In the category of "unions" are included the unions of the Trade Union Unity League, which continued to function during the early part of the period. Perhaps the strongest was the Packing House Workers' Industrial Union, which launched many special campaigns in the Chicago stockyards. It protested wage-cuts, led hunger marches against the packing plants, and participated in the strike of 1934. But a serious failure was that it did not manage to lead this strike.

Another extremely active union was the Needle Trade Workers' Industrial Union. This, like the packing-house union, was one of the early labor groups. It supported the Needle Trade Workers' Educational Club and the Needle Trade Workers' Youth Club, both of which have been included among the union organizations. The Steel and Metal Workers' Industrial Union, although organized as a metal workers' union previous to the depression, was reorganized and began to function with some effectiveness in 1933, when a strike was threatened in the Chicago steel district.

During the latter part of the depression the Communists sought to create unions among the government and " white-collar " groups. The Civil and Public Workers' Union was formed for individuals on PWA and other government projects. The Association of Professional and Technical Workers was formed, together with the Office Workers' Union.

Other labor unions or councils affiliated with the Communist Party were: Building and Construction Workers' Industrial League, Food Workers' Industrial Union, Hotel and Restaurant Workers' Industrial Union, Machine Workers' Industrial Union, National Railroad Industrial Union, Red Industrial Labor Union, Stock Yard Labor Council, Fur Workers' Industrial Union.

It will be noticed that the Communist Unions were industrial unions, and in this sense were forerunners of the CIO type of organization.

In the group of " cultural " organizations are groups organized for cultural, social or recreational purposes. Among the more serious clubs were the Palm Club, the local organization for " proletarian arts, letters, and music," and the Workers' Cultural League, the Workers' Theater League, and the

Midwestern Workers' Cultural Federation. The most important group of this kind was the John Reed Club, a national organization represented in Chicago. In its membership were the more prominent artists and writers of Communist and near-Communist movements. Social and recreational groups include local units like the Big Time Social Club, the Labor Sports Union, the Workers' Sports League, the Workers' Film and Photo League, and the Workers' Camera Club.

The proletarian theme was uppermost in the life of these associations. The Workers' Camera Club was specially interested in pictures with social and economic implications, and the Palm Club qualified its objectives, " arts, letters, and music," by the term " proletarian." The athletic clubs sought to break down racial barriers by encouraging the participation of Negro youth in their activities.

" Defense " organizations were busy during the depression. The International Labor Defense, the Labor Defense Council, and the Committee for the Protection of the Foreign Born were intimately bound up with the party. The United Front Scottsboro Committee is included in our list of defense organizations as an exception to the rule excluding committees devoted to special issues. The Scottsboro campaign figured so prominently in Communist tactics that the Committee received wide public notice. The Chicago Civil Liberties Committee was not a Communist affiliate, but it comes within our definition of a " co-operating " organization because of the frequency with which it rendered aid to members of the Communist Party. The liberals and Socialists who controlled the Committee during the depression were at great pains to emphasize their individual disapproval of the Communist Party. They were constantly attacked as " red " by many persons in the city who did not discriminate between outright Communist affiliates and organizations which pursued some objectives which, in particular cases, were parallel to the goals sought by the Communists. The Communists had a separate agency, the ILD (International Labor Defense), which was very close to the party, even though it, too, included many liberals and " non-political " trade unionists.

The ILD not only maintained its own branches throughout the city, but served as an affiliating body for many radical groups. A party report for November 1931 shows that at that time the ILD maintained 49 branches, having a membership of 1,905 in Chicago and its suburbs. In addition there were 64 organizations affiliated to the ILD, including four A. F. of L. locals. At that time there was a city committee of the ILD consisting of nine members, of which four were Communists and five non-party members. The district bureau of the ILD, however, consisted of eight party members and one non-party member.

The ILD and the Chicago Civil Liberties Committee were both active throughout the depression in raising bail for persons arrested for radical activities and in pleading cases in court. The Communist Party urged its members to accept the assistance of ILD lawyers when in trouble.

The " Negro " groups active in Chicago during the depression were the following: the American Negro Labor Congress, League of Struggle for Negro Rights, Negro Tenants' Protective Association, Universal Negro Improvement Association. Of these the most active has been the League of Struggle for Negro Rights. This organization affiliated with the ILD during its earlier history and carried the burden of the propaganda regarding the Scottsboro case in Chicago.

The " farm " organizations, of course, were not active in Chicago except as fund-raisers. Farm groups met in Chicago from time to time, however, particularly during the latter part of the depression, when more attention was devoted to farm issues.

The farm organizations which were active in Chicago to some extent during the first five years of the depression were: Farm Labor Political Federation, the Farmers' National Committee for Action, the United Farmers' League.

Among the remaining groups which have been lumped

together are three of the most vigorous organizations of all. The American League Against War and Fascism and the Chicago Committee to Aid the Victims of German Fascism were extremely active in connection with the advent of the Hitler régime in Germany in 1933. In addition, such groups as the Friends of the Soviet Union, although disclaiming intimate association with the Communist Party, were in fact largely under its control. The FSU was much more loosely controlled than the ILD.[1]

It is worth reiterating the point that " front " and " co-operating " organizations were not necessarily puppets to be manipulated at will by the officials of the Communist Party. The degree of party control varied from organization to organization, and within each organization from time to time and place to place. Communist Party members were sometimes the active influence on the central committee of the affiliated association, but frequently the Communist leadership was nullified or partly discredited. Party control depended upon the caliber of the leadership furnished by Communist members.[2]

The theory of the Communist Party in relation to affiliated organizations was summed up in the principle of " fractional control." By this was meant that party members should devote time to the organization of special groups, seeking to assume leadership and guide policy along Communist lines, while preserving a certain amount of distinctiveness in the symbols and practices of the organization. In practice, how-

[1] One group of organizations not included in Table I are the special press organizations. Included might have been the " Boosters Club " to support the *Daily Worker,* and news agencies like the Federated Press, the personnel of which was largely Communist, and the Midwest Bureau, which was entirely so.

[2] Some of the organizations included above were founded independently of the party and are included only because they had enough specific goals in common to join with the party in mass demonstrations and similar events. On the other hand, some of the organizations listed here were little more than letterhead organizations improvised by the party.

ever, as we shall see, and as the Communists recognized from time to time, this procedure often led to one of two extremes: the leading fraction of an organization (that is, the group at the center rather than the groups in the branches) was the only nucleus which effectively sought control of the organization; or fractions in control assimilated the symbols and practices of the affiliated organization completely to those of the party.

It is regrettably difficult to arrive at satisfactory estimates of the membership even of organizations of permanence and prominence. Party officials have often been poorly informed about the facts. A 1931 party report for District 8 supplies the following meager details:

Organization	Branches	Membership
ILD	33	1,670
Organizations affiliated with ILD	64	not given
IWO	35	1,444
FSU	none	198
TUUL (9 organizations)	17	835

So sporadic and speculative are membership figures for most of the auxiliary and co-operating organizations that a sounder picture of their role is obtained by studying the meetings which were sponsored in their name than in piecing together the isolated details of membership.

The record of sponsorship has the additional advantage of indicating the extent to which the party receded behind the " front " organizations during the depression years. Table II shows that in 1930 the party was solely responsible for over two-fifths of the total number of meetings held during the year which were sponsored by the party and/or by its affiliated and co-operating organizations. In 1933, the low point of sole party sponsorship, only a little more than an eighth of the total were accounted for by the party.

TABLE II

Number of Meetings Sponsored by the Communist Party and/or by Communist Affiliated and Co-operating Organizations

	1930	1931	1932	1933	1934
Party	63	96	88	28	51
	42.28%	37.94%	24.65%	13.59%	21.07%
Affiliated	86	157	269	178	191
	57.72%	62.06%	75.35%	86.41%	78.93%
Total	149	253	357	206	242
	100.00	100.00	100.00	100.00	100.00

CHAPTER VI

Channels of Propaganda: Supplementary Media

COMMUNIST propaganda was too versatile to rely exclusively upon the demonstrations, publications, and cover organizations which have been described in the preceding chapters. Nearly every means of communication was drawn into the network of channels in which the propagandists of Communism placed the symbols which they chose to circulate.

The Party School

An important medium of propaganda, and one which the Communists have not neglected, has been the party school. For many years the Communist Party has sponsored workers' schools in Chicago, in the hope of educating leaders for the working-class movement.

The activity of the Chicago Communist Workers' School between 1930 and 1934 is indicated by the number of courses offered during these years. An analysis of the school announcements, which began to be published in 1931, shows that the number of courses increased from 12 in 1931 to 35 in 1934, and that the total teaching time increased from 1,220 hours in 1931 to 3,150 in 1934. This is an increase of almost 300 per cent in the number of courses given, and of about 435 per cent in the number of teaching hours. The number of different courses offered during each of these years is as follows:

1930	1931	1932	1933	1934
no figures	12	28	33	35

Although previous to 1930 the Workers' School in Chicago had been used mainly as a training school for Communist propagandists, during this year its function was shifted to a greater emphasis on immediate propaganda rather than on the preparation of persons for future propaganda. A bulletin issued by the Central Committee of the Communist Party in 1930 pointed out that Communist education must be interpreted in the broadest sense.[1] This shift in the function of the school resulted in immediate and continuing expansion. In keeping with the broader educational policy, it was reorganized under a director with an advisory committee. The school opened new headquarters at 2822 South Michigan Avenue and began operating as a separate organization. It held fall, winter, and spring sessions, and non-Communist educators of liberal views were invited to offer courses.

The new propaganda function of the Workers' School was reflected in its curriculum. The curriculum supplied more courses of general interest and fewer courses directly related to Communist theory and practice. In this way the school sought to attract workers who were not already committed to Communist doctrines. Courses making this general appeal included those in public speaking and journalism, English, and especially subjects which would be of interest to foreign-born working groups. The courses devoted to cultural subjects also grew in number.

In 1933 the Chicago Hearst press " discovered " the existence

---

[1] This policy with regard to the functions of the Workers' School was paralleled by the development of study groups or study circles in the Communist units. These groups were organized on an informal basis and sought to educate new members by immediately drawing them into a study of Marxism.

of this " Left " educational center and as a result of pressure from this and other sources, the Workers' School abandoned its Michigan Avenue headquarters and retreated to 550 South State Street. Party determination to make good use of the school was evidenced by its continuation under these adverse conditions and by the organization in 1934 of a branch school in the steel mills district of Chicago's south side.

The Chicago Workers' School during depression years was open to the public; a charge was made for tuition to help meet running expenses. Tuition was nominal, however, and never exceeded two dollars a course. Party functionaries were allowed special rates and were sometimes offered scholarships. Tuition fees continually failed to meet running costs, and additional funds were raised from sympathetic individuals or organizations in order to maintain the school. A financial statement for the last half of 1934 indicates that operating expenses for the year 1934 were approximately $2,000. Income from tuition during this same year was about $1,000, or half of the total operating expenditures. The total income of the school for 1934, including tuition fees and solicited funds, was approximately $2,500.

In addition to the regular classes which met daily, the school was a meeting-place for all kinds of informal social gatherings of Left organizations.

Camps

Another channel of propaganda closely associated in function with the school was the summer camps. The party itself in Chicago at no time directly maintained any institutions of this sort, but the Young Pioneers, who were responsible for educating the children of the movement, did hold short summer camps during this period.

Several other associated organizations also ran camps during several successive summers. The camps were close to the city and afforded a meeting-ground for the sons and daughters of those interested in Communist Party activity.

While classes were not generally held, some Communist customs, such as certain distinctive holidays, were observed, and in their casual contacts with the adults who organized and ran the camp centers the children were taught to identify themselves with the Communist cause.

Bookstores

The principal function of the bookstores was to distribute the leaflets, pamphlets, books, and periodicals which carried the message of the party to the public. But they were also important as informal meeting-places for groups of individuals.

In 1930 the main bookshop in Chicago was located at 2019 West Division Street. With the beginning of the depression, however, several new shops sprang up in poor sections of the city. Some of these were established and operated by party members. Others were run by individuals who were sympathetic to the movement and included a representative collection of Communist literature in their stock.

Persons affiliated with the Communist movement frequently gathered at the bookstores for informal discussion of current political and social events. Such personal contact aided in the consolidation of the party. Possibly this means of group identification was most helpful during times of comparative inactivity. The bookstores were havens of reassurance during moments of psychological depression.

The Theater

The Communist organization which originally sponsored a Left-wing theater group in Chicago was the John Reed Club. At the beginning of the depression this organization arranged short dramatic performances which were staged at Communist demonstrations throughout the city. As the depression deepened, those interested in the development of a Left theater movement originated a theater center where the productions of the group were given. The unemployed were admitted free, their Unemployed Council membership cards serving as identification.

This idea of a workers' theater, organized mainly for the entertainment and education of the unemployed through the presentation of plays with a radical theme, met with opposition among certain leaders of the theater movement. One group wished to use the theater as a medium for artistic expression rather than as a propaganda channel. These two opposing schools of thought formed separate groups and pursued different lines of development. Ultimately the Works Progress Administration in Chicago absorbed many members of both groups in its theater projects.

The proletarian drama which was played informally before workers' groups was an important channel of propaganda during a period of several years. It played strictly to working-class audiences and staged performances mainly in working-class neighborhoods. It afforded an opportunity for attending theatrical performances to groups which would otherwise have found it difficult during the depression to do so. However, this movement was neither large enough nor sufficiently well organized to be of far-reaching significance in a city as large as Chicago. During 1934, nevertheless, the year in which this group was most active, it added color and interest to many occasions sponsored by the Communist Party and its affiliated organizations.

Motion Pictures

In its use of the motion picture as a channel of propaganda the Communists depended largely upon Soviet films. Early in the depression the Punch and Judy Theatre in Chicago began showing foreign films, a great many of which were of Soviet origin. Showings were advertised by Communist organizations and they were supported chiefly by Chicago radicals.

After weathering some depression years, however, the Punch and Judy Theatre was playing to empty houses and closed its doors. It was reopened after some months as the Sonotone Theatre and continued to show foreign films.

The party itself has on numerous occasions sponsored the showing of Soviet films at meetings or social occasions. The general opinion is that Soviet motion pictures have been excellent channels of propaganda. The vitality and conviction of Soviet pictures was extremely stimulating to Chicago audiences sympathetic to the " Left " cause.

The Communists were unable to take full advantage of this excellent channel. If the party had been able during the low point of the depression in Chicago to show Soviet pictures in working-class neighborhoods and to allow the movie-starved population free admittance to these performances, the motion picture might have had far-reaching effects. But the use of the motion pictures was neither widespread nor persistent. For 1933, the banner year, there is a record of only 17 sponsored performances.

During 1933 and 1934 a small group of amateur photographers in Chicago became interested in the idea of using motion pictures as a means of bringing local conditions to the focus of attention. Pictures were taken of areas in which depression conditions were particularly deplorable and these were shown with a running commentary regarding the social and economic implications of such conditions.

Such films, however, had a comparatively limited value. The American public have long used the motion picture as an escape from pressing or unpleasant realities. Particularly during the depression, motion pictures increasingly played such a role in American life. Simple documentary pictures of the misery and desolation of depression-struck communities were scarcely acceptable to a public which saw too much of this in its day-to-day existence. No dramatic talent appeared on the scene equal to the task of fusing these details into vehicles of mass incitement.

Radio

Even in depression years the radio came to be accepted not as a luxury but as a necessity. Yet this important channel of propaganda was not used by the Communists during depression years. It was not open to them. On several occasions when the Communist Party attempted to go on the air, they were not granted the time even though they were willing to pay for it.[2]

The importance of the radio as a channel for political propaganda even in time of political peace was most fully realized by President Roosevelt when he began his series of fireside talks to the American people in 1933. The fact that this important medium of propaganda was closed to the Communist Party during the depression low point of 1932 doubtless accounted in part for its failure to capitalize more fully upon the serious economic situation.

Painting and Sculpture

The John Reed Club has been the special organization to which Communist members and sympathizers interested in the arts have belonged and through which they have shared and developed their talents.

Throughout the depression John Reed Club members created posters and placards for demonstrations and painted stage sets for Communist productions. During 1933 and 1934 they were drawn more closely into the production of leaflets, shop papers, and other written forms of propaganda by supplying more and more illustrations for such local publications.

Many young artists in Chicago's " Latin Quarter," the near north side, were attracted by the proletarian theme and through their work became associated with the movement.

[2] This was nullified later by a federal ruling which declared that stations could not discriminate in granting radio time to political parties. Communist speakers were heard over national networks several times during the 1936 political campaign.

The John Reed Club during depression years gave exhibits of the work of its members. Outstanding Chicago artists of the Left movement during this period were Peter Topschevsky and John Groth. Robert Minor, associated with the early Communist movement in Chicago, returned to the city and contributed as painter and cartoonist to the output of the Chicago group.

The development of work projects for the white-collar groups, and especially the art projects, stimulated the productivity of this group.

Music and Ballet

Artists of the proletarian movement in Chicago experimented with music and the ballet as a means of arousing class consciousness. These movements, however, were not as prominent in Chicago as in centers like New York and Detroit. From time to time Eastern groups gave performances in Chicago which were enthusiastically received.

Songs

The Communist Party has been fairly successful in its use of song as a medium of propaganda. The *Internationale,* which was sung throughout the depression on all occasions of importance, was the official party hymn and battle-cry. Audiences always rose to their feet as the first strains were heard, and began the chorus with upraised fists. Its singing was upon many occassions a dramatic and stirring performance:

THE INTERNATIONALE

Arise, ye prisoners of starvation!
  Arise, ye wretched of the earth,
For justice thunders condemnation,
  A better world's in birth.
No more tradition's chains shall bind us,
  Arise, ye slaves, no more in thrall!
The earth shall rise on new foundations,
  We have been naught, we shall be all.

(*Chorus*)

'Tis the final conflict,
  Let each stand in his place,
The International Soviet,
  Shall be the human race.

(*Repeat*)

Next to the *Internationale*, *The Scarlet Banner* was one of the most popular. This was a particular favorite with the Young Communist League.

THE SCARLET BANNER

Arise, ye workers,
Fling to the breezes
The scarlet banner,
The scarlet banner!
Arise, ye workers,
Fling to the breezes
The scarlet banner triumphantly!

(*Chorus*)

Wave, scarlet banner, triumphantly!
Wave, scarlet banner, triumphantly!
Wave, scarlet banner, triumphantly!
FOR COMMUNISM AND FOR LIBERTY!

Another favorite of depression days was *Solidarity Forever*:

SOLIDARITY FOREVER

When the Union's inspiration through the workers' blood shall
    run,
There can be no power greater anywhere beneath the sun.
Yet what force on earth is weaker than the feeble strength of
    one?
But the Union makes us strong.

(*Chorus*)

Solidarity forever!
Solidarity forever!
Solidarity forever!
For the Union makes us strong!

The party also taught the public many less serious songs. Some of these were taken from the collection of IWW tunes, as was the extremely popular *You'll Get Pie in the Sky When You Die,* which is sung to the tune of the *Sweet Bye and Bye.* The song was adapted to current situations by the addition of appropriate stanzas.

Numerous original songs were written with special reference to the Chicago scene. One of these voiced a dual protest against the insurance racketeers of Chicago's south side and the social workers who demanded that applicants for relief terminate their insurance payments:

LIFE INSURANCE RACKET SONG

(To be sung to the tune of *Fighting on the Picket Line*)

Oh, there was an old man
On Sixty-third Street,
He slaved for forty-eight years.
The insurance company
Took all his dough
While he slaved for forty-eight years.

On the line!
We're fighting fakers on the line!
They'd rob the old man
Of his burial right
So we're fighting on the picket line.

Oh, the Charity Fakers at Forty-seventh Street
Said: " Sign on the dotted line!
Give up your life insurance,
Or we'll give you no bread,
Sucker, sign on the dotted line."

On the line!
On the line!
We're fighting on the picket line.
They'd rob the old man
Of his burial right
So we're fighting on the picket line.

The *Depression Blues* is another example of the songs of this character:

THE DEPRESSION BLUES

Listen to my plea, dear, I can't wait any longer:
My stomach is crying, my heart is growing weaker.
Please hurry, Miss Case Worker, I am starving
And the rent is due. I am sick and dying.

(*Chorus*)

Please hurry, can't you see I'm starving?
How long must I wait: till I'm dying?
Feet aching, children crying for eats,
No gas, electric, and house without heat!
Miss Case Worker, how long can this go on?

Still other songs were improvised to be carried by popular tunes current at the time:

HE FALLS DOWN AND GOES—BOOM

(Parody on the song *I Faw Down and Go Boom*)
— George G. Allen

Where's the big man of success,
Of success, of success?
His stake is getting less and less,
He falls down and goes — Boom!
When he's broke and on the bum,
On the bum, on the bum,
Out the window he will come!
He'll fall down and go Boom!
Who cries? Who cries and says it's not fair?
Who'll starve and die while " big shots " never know or care?

Humpty-dumpty on the wall,
On the wall, on the wall,
Down comes Humpty, wall and all —
He'll fall down and go — Boom!

2

Lots of room up at the top,
At the top, at the top —
And a nice long way to drop
He'll fall down and go — Boom!
He climbs the ladder, one — two — three,
One — two — three, one — two — three,
Going up is hard, but gee!
He'll fall down and go — Boom!
    Who'll cry, who'll cry for the poor millionaire?
    Just try, just try to eat like he does anywhere.
When he stays at Hoover House,
Hoover House, Hoover House,
With the bedbug and the louse —
He'll hit the bottom and — Boom!

Another type of song sprang up in Negro neighborhoods. A
favorite among the Negroes was *That New Communist Spirit:*

THAT NEW COMMUNIST SPIRIT

(To be sung to the tune of *Gimme That Old-Time Religion*)

Gimme that new Communist spirit,
Gimme that new Communist spirit,
Gimme that new Communist spirit,
It's good enough for me.

It was good for Comrade Lenin,
It was good for Comrade Lenin,
It was good for Comrade Lenin,
And it's good enough for me.

Dozens of verses were improvised to fit this simple but effective song.

The words of songs to be sung at large meetings were mimeographed and distributed among the audience. At special demonstrations in large halls like the Coliseum, groups of Young Pioneers or Young Communist League members frequently sang the Communist songs in chorus from the stage. The party also published a collection of songs in the *Red Song Book,* which was on sale at all large meetings.

Many of the Communist tunes were written in march time and were sung as marching tunes during Communist parades. The youth sections in the parades generally had a song leader who led the section. It was the custom in passing the City Hall to sing the *Internationale;* and so many parades passed the City Hall during depression years that many City Hall employees unwittingly learned this Communist hymn.

Cheers and Chants

At many of the demonstrations held in large meeting-halls, cheers were given for working-class heroes. During 1933 and 1934 the Young Communist League organized cheering sections which added much to the enthusiasm of the meetings. During intermissions, between speakers, or while the crowd was still gathering, a cheer leader would lead his sections in the enthusiastic shouts typical of American sporting contests. The " Yay-rah-rah-YCL " given in unison and with proper enthusiasm was an explosive adaptation of American football spirit.

Cheers were also common during parades. Often they were started spontaneously by a small group of marchers and taken up by the crowd. During the May Day march of 1932, as the parade passed through Chicago's Loop, someone started to cry: "We want Hoover — with a rope around his neck." This cheer was enthusiastically taken up by the crowd and was passed along the whole parade. Slogans of the day were frequently given as cheers during the parades (with or without benefit of a cheer leader).

The cheer, like the song, was designed not only to heighten the spirit of the participants, but to impress the spectators. The thousands of people who stood along the lines of march of the depression parades were often visibly impressed by the defiant slogans shouted in unison by the marchers. The cheering thousands put across the idea that the Communist movement was strong and articulate.

Jokes

Perhaps because so many other channels were available for Communist propaganda, political jokes were not extensively used during the depression. Occasional jokes appeared about the capitalist and his simple idea that the workers would submit indefinitely to exploitation. Probably the most effective and popular form of humor was the parody. The following parody of the twenty-third Psalm, written by a seventeen-year-old party member, is representative of the depression output:

THE HOBO'S PRAYER

Hoover is my Shepherd, and I am in want
He maketh me to lie down on the park benches,
He leadeth me beside the free soup houses.
He leadeth me in the path of destruction for the Parties' sake.
Yea, though I walk through the Valley of Starvation, I die for evil,
    for thou art against me.
Thy Republican Party are the profiteers, they do frighten me.
Thou preparest a reduction in my wages before me in the presence
    of mine enemies.
Thou annointed my income with taxes.
Mine expenses overrunneth my income, surely poverty and unemployment will follow me all the days of his normalcy administration.
I will dwell in a rented house forever.

Flags

Early in its history the Communist Party in the United States adopted the red flag with the white hammer and sickle symbol as its official banner. It was the appearance of this Soviet flag in party demonstrations that intensified the characterization of the Communist Party movement in America as something definitely Russian, foreign, and anti-American.

In 1930 the scarlet banner still appeared at important cele-brations. It was given a place of honor on the platform in meeting-halls and was carried proudly in the front ranks of parades. Following military custom, the Soviet banner draped the coffins of several persons who were killed during the vio-lent clashes between police and demonstrators during this pe-riod.

The importance of the flag as a symbol is suggested by the fact that in 1933, although demonstrators were permitted to march through Chicago's Loop, it was specifically ruled by the Commissioner of Police that no red flags would be allowed. The May Day parade of 1933 marched flagless through Chicago streets. As the parade reached the corner of Jackson and Michigan Boulevard and filed into Grant Park to demon-strate, a young party member was hoisted on the shoulders of the crowd and triumphantly fastened the Communist banner to a street lamp. The flag was quickly hauled down by police.

The story was also told of an occasion in 1934 when the Communist banner was found one morning flying gaily from the Michigan Avenue building which housed the German Consulate.

As the new " United Front " policy developed (which was made official at the Congress of the Third International in 1935), the Communists began to make more frequent use of the American flag on the Communist platform and in Com-munist parades.

Insignia and Uniforms

The Communist Party in Chicago did not develop insignia and uniforms as significant channels of propaganda. No doubt this is to be attributed in part to the poverty of the workers and to the comparative absence of a " uniform " tradition in America.

BUTTONS AND BADGES

BUTTONS AND BADGES

Red arm-bands were occasionally used to great effect in parades or demonstrations, but this was not standard practice. The Young Pioneers would sometimes parade in red and blue uniforms.

Another factor which helps to account for the underdevelopment of this channel of propaganda was the uncertain legal status of the Communist Party in the United States. All through the depression there was a tendency on the part of members and officials to conceal the identity of party members. This secretiveness prompted the use of numerous aliases by party members and leaders.

In Chicago, as elsewhere in the United States during the depression years, potential members were partly identified by poor clothes. A well-dressed individual was looked upon with suspicion at Communist gatherings; middle-class intellectuals connected with the movement donned their old clothes to attend Communist functions. As the new " United Front " and " People's Front " policy of the Communist Party developed, attention was focused less upon the unemployed and more upon the employed worker. The better-dressed individual became less of an object of suspicion as the party reached out for skilled workers and white-collar groups.

PART THREE

THE TECHNIQUE OF PROPAGANDA

CHAPTER VII

The Technique of Slogans

SINCE propaganda is the circulation of symbols to influence attitudes on controversial matters, the analysis of the meanings of the symbols is central to the study of any propaganda. While the selection of channels for the symbols is important, greater opportunities are offered for flashes of creative imagination in the act of inventing and adapting symbols.

The scientific analysis of the symbols which lie strewn in the wake of practicing propagandists may appear stale and dull in comparison with the zest and sparkle of the original campaign. Periods of wild inventiveness, hours of provocative argument, moments of lucky accident are rarely duplicated in the methodical calm of scientific autopsy. When the symbols of yesterday lie stiff and cold on the slab of the dissecting scientist, the bystander may turn away in disgust or indifference.

However, the distance between post-mortem and ante-vitam is closer than it might seem, for all is not superheated fantasy in the creation of propaganda symbols. Wholly apart from the tedious and highly repetitive details of lay-out and channel, there is often little elbow room for the flights of genius. The highest acumen is often displayed in cases in which the propagandist deliberately prefers the trite and sure to the new and doubtful. Ways of presenting a given set of symbols are quickly molded so that the elaboration of basic ideas tends to follow well-beveled grooves. On the other hand the scientist's concern with the general features of a problem occasionally stimulates the manipulator into a furor of exciting and profitable discovery.

The present chapter is more concerned with the technique of the autopsy than with the technique of propaganda. Existing ways of describing and comparing propaganda campaigns leave so much to be desired that something may be done to direct attention to the abundant possibilities which lie unexplored. These early studies may contribute little of direct value to our knowledge of propaganda, but the patient application and expansion of the procedures devised may ultimately vindicate themselves to practitioner and theorist alike.

What we need to know about propaganda symbols in general and revolutionary symbols in particular is clear. We want to find out under what conditions some symbols win out over some other symbols. The symbols which are circulated by the propagandists are part of the environment of all whom he hopes to influence. If the predispositions of the community are known, which symbol patterns will be accepted?

One of our initial tasks is to invent ways of describing symbols which enable us to compare changes in the symbol pattern of particular propagandas from one time to another. In reference to Communist propaganda in Chicago, this task has been partially accomplished and the results are presented here. In the long run we must make sure that our categories enable us to compare any given propaganda with each of its rivals, whether revolutionary or not. To some extent we have made use of our categories with reference to propagandas which were rivaling Communist propaganda in Chicago. But this task was only partially completed. Hence we cannot be sure that these categories can meet every relevant problem of comparison. But there is little doubt that many of these categories will win acceptance among specialists.

It was necessary to devise new ways of describing propaganda symbols because the existing procedures were unstandardized and in many respects unsatisfactory. The existing literature, however, abounds in stimulating suggestions.[1]

How may symbols be classified for descriptive and comparative purposes? Our categories have been adapted from those previously proposed by one of the authors.[2] Symbols are classified (for many basic comparisons) into symbols of " demand," " identification," and " fact." [3]

Symbols of demand are symbols of preference or determination for certain events to take place. Revolutionary propaganda symbol patterns are distinguished from non-revolutionary patterns according to the presence or absence of demands for fundamental change. That is, revolutionary symbol patterns by definition include demands for fundamental substitutions in prevailing symbols and practices. Communist propaganda during the depression years always included demands for such fundamental changes.[4]

Radical revolutionary symbol patterns are distinguished from moderate revolutionary patterns according to certain demand symbols. Radical patterns demand drastic methods of making fundamental change; moderate patterns do not. Communist propaganda during the depression years was more drastic than its revolutionary competitors in the Chicago

---

[1] A guide to the existing literature is H. D. Lasswell, R. D. Casey, and B. L. Smith: *Propaganda and Promotional Activities: An Annotated Bibliography* (Minneapolis, 1935). Current literature may be followed in the *Public Opinion Quarterly*.

[2] H. D. Lasswell: *World Politics and Personal Insecurity* (New York, 1935). Chapters II–VI discuss symbols.

[3] Symbols of fact include among other sub-categories "the symbols of expectation" of the book just cited. The latter may be defined as symbols of fact which refer to the future.

[4] The strictest procedure would require us to specify the minimum frequency with which such demands must appear before the pattern is called revolutionary. We might say, for example, that unless the demand for fundamental change is made in at least one per cent of the demands circulated during a given period, the propaganda will not be classified as revolutionary.

situation. Communists championed many more incitements to extreme modes of action than Socialists.[5]

Revolutionary (as well as other) symbol patterns may be distinguished from one another according to identifications rather than demands. Demands may be made in the name of many different groups: some revolutions have been in the name of classes (like the proletariat); others in the name of nations. Communist propaganda invokes the "world proletariat." In this respect it differs quantitatively and not qualitatively from Socialist propaganda, which also speaks in the name of the world proletariat. During the depression Communist propaganda more often demanded world-wide revolutionary action by drastic methods, and more often invoked the world proletariat than Socialist propaganda. Hence Communist propaganda was more "world," "radical," and "revolutionary" than its immediate rivals.[6]

Still another way to draw useful distinctions among revolutionary (as well as other) propagandas is according to the symbols of fact, rather than demand or identification. Symbols of fact are terms referring to objects other than persons or groups, or sentences which assert something about events without affirming preference, and without being symbols of identification. For the purposes here in question symbols of fact may be classified not according to their "truth value," but

[5] The strictest procedure would call for the specification of the minimum frequency with which drastic demands must be made in a propaganda in order to enable us to call it a revolutionary one. The term "drastic" is to be understood with reference to prevailing community standards of preference before the depression. Acts regarded as justifiable — if ever justifiable — only under conditions of great emergency are "drastic."

[6] The strictest procedure would require, as before, the choice of a minimum frequency with which certain identifications (names) have to be invoked before the propaganda pattern in which they appear shall be said to proceed, as a whole, in these names. Identifications include all names of persons or groups; some are "self" references, some are "other" references.

according to their meanings. The words "the coming world revolution" are fact references because they expressly allude to events which may occur in the future. They are not a demand symbol because they do not explicitly affirm approval or disapproval of the events in question. Persons may agree that a new world revolution is probable; but one man may deplore what another man acclaims. Communist propaganda was radical world revolutionary propaganda in the factual as well as in the demand and identification sense; it circulated symbols which affirmed and demanded the completion of world revolution in the name of a group symbolically associated with this process.[7]

The categories of demand, identification, and fact have thus far been helpful in making basic distinctions among revolutionary propagandas. Such categories indicate how it will be possible to improve our instruments for the description of propaganda.[8]

By means of the categories of demand, identification, and fact we can assemble more relevant data than heretofore about potentially significant features of the symbols circulated by propagandists.

The hypothesis has been stated that skillful revolutionary propaganda depends upon provoking crises of conscience as means of emancipating persons from the compulsions of the

[7] Strict procedure would call for the choice of a minimum frequency with which certain facts would have to be invoked before propaganda would be classified according to them. Sentences in which certain probabilities are assigned to events lying in the future of the speaker, or terms referring exclusively to such events ("the coming world revolution") will be called "symbols of expectation."

[8] A pioneer contribution to the orderly investigation of symbols is George Carslake Thompson: *Public Opinion and Lord Beaconsfield* (2 vols. London, 1886). A recent use of "counting" which yielded fruitful results is by Svend Ranulf: *Moral Indignation and Middle Class Psychology* (Copenhagen, 1938). Pamphlets and other publications of the English Puritans are described with great exactness. See pages 59–95.

"old" conscience.[9] The contents of the individual conscience determine what the "mores" of the community are. Unless patterns of conduct are incorporated within the consciences of the overwhelming proportion of the community, they should not be called "mores." Since the attainment of revolutionary objectives depends upon the dissolution of certain of the mores, it is essential to stimulate "counter-mores" attitudes. So peremptory are the exigencies of conscience that appeals in this direction which are not in their turn presented as legitimized by other elements of the mores are apt to fail of their purpose. That is to say, a simple incitement to perform a counter-mores act ("Smash the Constitution") may arouse rejection rather than acceptance. We may therefore expect that a skillful device of revolutionary propaganda is to divide consciences against themselves; that is, to use symbols which appeal to conscience (mores) on behalf of symbols which violate the conscience (mores). We may therefore describe revolutionary propaganda according to the proportion and the interconnections of conscience and counter-conscience symbols (mores and counter-mores symbols).[10]

Closely connected with the foregoing discussion are the hypotheses concerning the precise proportion between "positive" and "negative" expressions of preference. Since one plain purpose of revolutionary propaganda is to arouse hostile attitudes toward the symbols and practices of the established order, symbols of hostile (negative) preference must play a prominent part. But another purpose of revolutionary propaganda is to organize love and esteem with reference to certain substitute symbols (some of which refer to practices not yet established) and practices (for example, those of the revolutionary movement), and this calls for the circulation of

[9] Consult H. D. Lasswell: "The Strategy of Revolutionary and War Propaganda," in *Public Opinion and World-Politics,* Lectures on the Harris Foundation, Quincy Wright, editor (Chicago, 1933).

[10] Hypotheses about skillful magnitudes of these proportions are not proposed for lack of data in sufficiently precise form.

positive preferences. Is there a proportion of maximum skill-fulness between positive and negative preferences in revolutionary propaganda? Our description of the Chicago data will probably modify some existing impressions about the answer to this question.

Propagandists must keep certain symbols constant as a means of stabilizing attitudes. At the same time they must vary symbols as a means of reinforcing the key symbols, of adapting themselves to the shifting composition of the focus of attention, and of enlarging the attention group. What is the skillful proportion of " repetition " and " innovation " in revolutionary propaganda? What is the obsolescence rate of symbols in revolutionary propaganda?

Another basic propaganda problem concerns the " comprehensiveness " of symbols. We may examine the proportion of " definite " to " indefinite " symbols. We may describe the " inclusiveness " of the symbol pattern with reference to the demands of specific groups.

Since it is often (not always) one of the plain purposes of revolutionary propaganda to incite the masses to rather immediate action, the " dynamic " quality of the symbols is worthy of investigation.

The problems which have been posed in this study by no means exhaust the possibilities of symbol analysis. They are representative of the questions which appear, at this stage of research, to be particularly important.

The material which is described in the present chapter comes from the slogans which were printed on the leaflets circulated by the Communist Party in Chicago during the Great Depression.

For the study of revolutionary propaganda in its application to the masses the " slogan " is peculiarly important. Revolutionary propaganda is mass-orientated propaganda, and symbols for the masses must be terse, clear, and strong. Slogans are synoptic words, phrases, or sentences directed to the masses for their guidance. By Communists the world over, the slogan is the recognized unit of propaganda. Every policy is deliberately and almost universally reduced to slogans. So deeply embedded is this in Communist practice that the veteran party member, speaking of past history, automatically begins: " Our slogan of that time was . . ."

For the study of revolutionary symbols the slogans found on leaflets furnish a highly valuable body of material. The leaflet speaks the slogan language to the masses. The leaflet, like the poster, is primarily a channel of mass appeal.

The ephemeral character of the leaflet renders it peculiarly difficult of access for comparative analysis. Libraries are not accustomed to handle such fugitive material, and there is no agency devoted to the task of assembling these transitory clues to the experience of the masses. The leaflet collection of the present study, built up over several years, can be relied upon to give an entirely dependable picture since 1931. Although the leaflets remaining from 1930 are few in number, they exhibit distributive characteristics so similar to those of their successors that they may be treated with confidence. Several hundred leaflets of Communist auxiliary, co-operating, and rival organizations have been assembled, many of which are analyzed in the course of this report.

For immediate purposes, attention will be strictly confined to the leaflets which were directly sponsored by the Communist Party and its youth organizations, the Young Communist League and the Young Pioneers. The 315 leaflets which fit this description were distributed as follows:

1930	1931	1932	1933	1934
20	99	93	44	59

These 315 leaflets yielded 1,659 slogans:

62	455	591	261	340

The average number of slogans per leaflet varied from 3 to 6:

3	5	6	6	5

Slogans are patterns of words or word-sequences. Some slogans contain no demands:

REFORESTATION CAMPS ARE NO AID TO THE UNEMPLOYED
(May 1, 1933)

Such slogans affirm facts. The following make demands:

VOTE FOR THE COMMUNIST PARTY
(November 4, 1934)

AGAINST FASCISM!
(May 1, 1934)

"Vote" is a demand symbol which indicates "method." Method demand symbols are usually verbs which call for an act from the persons addressed. "Goal" demands show an end to be attained by the act which is explicitly or implicitly prescribed. The words "for the Communist Party" describe the object to benefit from the "vote." The words "Against Fascism" depict goal without stating method. From this point of view slogans may be classified as "method-goal," "method," or "goal" slogans.[11]

Even a casual glance at any collection of Communist demand slogans will reveal the emphatic quality of the words used: FIGHT! SMASH! RESIST! DEMAND! PROTEST! DEMONSTRATE! ORGANIZE! STRIKE! JOIN! VOTE! SUPPORT! COME! ATTEND! DRIVE OUT! MOBILIZE!

Method symbols can be readily classified into forms which are serviceable in tracing the dynamic characteristics of Communist propaganda slogans between 1930 and 1934.

Form 1. Imperative form of the verb, with the object of

[11] Note that there may be many goals in a slogan, some of which bear an instrumental relation to the others. Often there is more than one method symbol in a slogan. Examples: ORGANIZE AND FIGHT! (October 17, 1931); ORGANIZE! FIGHT! STRIKE! DEMONSTRATE! (March 8, 1932). Actual count showed that the Communist slogans which contained any method symbols averaged two per slogan.

address either stated or understood (most commonly the latter).

DEMONSTRATE AGAINST WAR!
(*August 1, 1932*)

Form 2. Fuller imperative form of the verb in which the object of address is always stated.

THE WORKERS MUST FIGHT FOR THE UNEMPLOYMENT INSURANCE
BILL!
(*1930*)

Form 3. Subjunctive of wish.

LET US ORGANIZE TO POSTPONE WAR!
(*August 1, 1934*)

Form 4. Action phrase: an elliptical phrase with action meaning.

OUT ON THE STREETS ON MARCH 6TH!
(*March 6, 1930*)

The first form, the simple imperative, is obviously more forceful than the second and third forms. The fourth form, like the first, is more emphatic than the second and third.

The simple imperative form of method demand was by far the most frequent in Communist propaganda during the period studied. Out of a total of 732 demands for action, 91 per cent, or 670, were phrased in this way. The action phrase (Form 4 above) accounted for 6 per cent, or 41, of the total number. The distribution between the four forms was as follows:

Per cent

Form 1 91
Form 2 1
Form 3 2
Form 4 6

The simple imperative form accounted for 95 per cent of the action demands invoked in 1930 and 1932. It was used least frequently in 1933, during which year only 79 per cent of the method demands appeared in the simple imperative. During this latter year the mild subjunctive form appeared in over 8 per cent of the cases, the high year for use of this form. In 1934 the simple imperative was again less strikingly frequent than in its two banner years; this time the benefiting supplementary form was not the subjunctive of wish, but the action phrase. There is no hesitation in saying that 1933 was the year with the least dynamic styles of demand symbol.

In the study of revolutionary propaganda we are interested in the "comprehensiveness" of symbols. Both method and goal symbols may be classified as "definite" (that is, specific and particular in reference) or as "indefinite" (that is, general and universal in reference). The terms "specific" and "general" refer to the nature of the methods or goals represented by the symbols; the terms "particular" and "universal" refer to the position of these acts or goals in time and space as explicitly formulated or understood.

Thus definite (specific and particular) method demands refer to rather unambiguously indicated and specialized acts to be performed at particular times and places; indefinite (general and universal) method demands refer to events which are more ambiguously defined and less localized in time and place. Hence method words like "vote" and "attend" are definite and specific, whereas terms like "protest" and "prepare" are indefinite and general.

The number of different method symbols appearing in Communist Party slogans was comparatively small, and there were few uncertainties of meaning. Sometimes, however, the symbol was definite and specific in one context and indefinite and general in another. The symbol "demonstrate" in a slogan like DEMONSTRATE AT UNION PARK ON MAY DAY is definite as well as specific, while the same word in another slogan, DEMONSTRATE YOUR STRENGTH, alludes to a wide range of ambiguously defined possibilities. The same differences in meaning are shown by the term "join" in two slogans, JOIN THE

YOUNG PIONEERS OF AMERICA and JOIN THE FIGHT AGAINST WAR.

A goal symbol is definite (specific and particular) if it refers to an unambiguously defined objective of specialized character which is to be realized in a circumscribed time and place; a goal symbol is indefinite (general and universal) if the nature of the objective is subject to alternative interpretations and if the time-space range for which the change is postulated is inclusive. Thus a demand for RECOGNITION OF THE SOVIET UNION is definite and specific; a demand to STOP THE MISTREATMENT OF THE NEGRO PEOPLE is indefinite and general.

The space characteristics of goal demands are convenient indicators of the geographical comprehensiveness of propaganda. For this reason a special study was made of the " space " reference of goal demands. They were for this purpose classified as " local," " regional," and " world " (and " spaceless "). A goal symbol is " local " if it refers to an objective wholly within Chicago; a goal symbol is " regional " if the objective is anywhere outside Chicago or in an area which includes Chicago but is less inclusive than the world; a goal symbol is " world " (or " spaceless ") if the objective refers to the world as a whole or if no space reference is stated.

For the sake of convenience the following abbreviations may be applied to the terms of classification given above:

Definite (i.e., specific and particular) goal or method symbols   A

Indefinite (i.e., general and universal) goal or method symbols   B

In addition:

Local goal symbols (i.e., Chicago)   1

Regional goal symbols (i.e., outside Chicago, or inclusive of Chicago but less inclusive than world)   2

World or spaceless goal symbols (world or no place reference)   3

Using these abbreviations the various types of goal demands are illustrated below. In each instance the symbols are given in the slogan context.

Examples of A1 (specific, local goal symbols)

EXTENSION OF STREET CAR SERVICE AT 47TH, 59TH, CICERO AND
CRAWFORD AVE. NO DOUBLE FARES WITHIN CITY LIMIT. FIVE
CENT CARFARES.
(January 31, 1933)

THE REPLACEMENT OF THE OVERCROWDED SCHOOLS, LIKE THE
BRYANT AND THE MASON, WITH SANITARY BUILDING, JUST AS
IN THE WARDS INHABITED BY THE WEALTHY PEOPLE
(February 4, 1931)

B1 (general, local goal symbols)

LONG LIVE THE UNITED FRONT OF THE WORKING CLASS OF CHICAGO!
(February 17, 1934)

ONE SOLID UNITED CHICAGO WORKING CLASS AGAINST THE
BOSSES AND THEIR LACKEYS!
(July 1934)

A2 (specific, regional goal symbols)

FOSTER FOR PRESIDENT
(November 1932)

AGAINST THE DIES DEPORTATION BILL
(August 1, 1932)

B2 (general, regional goal symbols)

FOR A WORKERS AND FARMERS GOVERNMENT IN THE U.S.A.
(November 7, 1933)

FOR DEFENSE OF THE SOVIET UNION
(March 14, 1931)

A3 (specific, world or spaceless goal symbols)

6 HOUR DAY, 5 DAY WEEK
(May 1934)

FREE FOOD FOR UNEMPLOYED
(March 8, 1932)

B3 (general, world or spaceless goal symbols)

FOR THE INTERNATIONAL SOLIDARITY OF THE WORKING CLASS!
(March 10, 1934)

AGAINST IMPERIALIST WAR
(July 15, 1932)

We may now summarize the results of the study of method and goal symbols. In the case of method demands it appears that general symbols predominated. In no single year did general demands constitute less than 55 per cent of the total, and 58 per cent was the average for the five years. Specific method demands were most frequently used in 1932 and least frequently in 1933. The percentages of specific method symbols were as follows:

1930	*1931*	*1932*	*1933*	*1934*
39%	41%	45%	36%	44%

The most specific goal symbols were almost always local, and thus classified as " A1 specific, local goal symbols ". in the scheme outlined above. It will be remembered that symbols were sorted according to their explicit content; hence only those symbols which expressly mentioned local objects were included in this category. The result of this strict treatment was to hold down the entries in this division (4 per cent of the total number of symbols classified). Persons exposed to a slogan like FOR PROMPT RELIEF would often take it for granted that the demand applied only to Chicago. But this demand would fall into the A1 class only when formulated in ways such as FOR PROMPT LOCAL RELIEF or FOR CHICAGO RELIEF. Specific, local goal demands, the most limited in reference to time, place, and act, varied in relation to the total number of goal demands as follows:

1930	*1931*	*1932*	*1933*	*1934*
5%	6%	1%	0%	2%

The category at the opposite extreme is B3 (general, world or spaceless goal symbols). The year 1931, which according to the previous tabulation ranked highest for specific local symbols is shown to rank lowest for " general, world and spaceless ":

1930	1931	1932	1933	1934
58%	38%	52%	47%	54%

Another means of studying comprehensiveness is to consider inclusiveness. An index of this is the number of groups whose special demands are incorporated in the slogans issued. Sometimes the special demands of local groups were directly linked with general, universal and spaceless goal symbols:

EX-SERVICE MEN! WORKING-CLASS FATHERS AND MOTHERS! FROM COLEMAN BRONZE, SEARS ROEBUCK, DRYDEN RUBBER, CHICAGO SCREW! COME TO THIS DEMONSTRATION OF INTERNATIONAL WORKING-CLASS SOLIDARITY — INTERNATIONAL YOUTH DAY.
(*August 31, 1934*)

Groups which were addressed by Communist propaganda, and whose specific demands were incorporated, are shown in the tableaux of slogans which are published at the end of this chapter. Groups have been classified as follows: class; skill; family status, age, and sex; race and nationality; locality. A glance at the slogans conveys something of the hectic atmosphere of the disturbed days when Communist propaganda was especially active.

Under the general term " comprehensiveness " we have described certain symbols as specific, particular, or inclusive. In respect of definiteness (specificity and particularity) certain years have been found with distinguishing characteristics. Thus the data are in a form which admits of the careful consideration of interrelationships. (This task, however, is beyond the scope of the present chapter.)

The description of the slogan symbols will be continued with reference to certain other significant differences. The

Communist movement is a world-wide movement which plans to preserve its consciousness of identity in many countries through many years. Aside from organizational bonds, the most important factor working in this direction is the common body of symbols which enter into the experience of Communists everywhere. In Canton or Chicago, no less than Moscow and New York, incorporation of common symbols implies that uniformity of experience which fosters concerted action. No matter how many subgroup appeals may be taken up, there remains the vital necessity of preserving symbolic uniformity in space and through time by means of the repetition of a nuclear collection of representations.

A major symbol, of course, is " Communist," which was found on the leaflets in such contexts as the following:

LONG LIVE THE COMMUNIST INTERNATIONAL!
(*November 24, 1934*)

VOTE FOR THE ONLY PARTY OF THE WORKING CLASS — THE COMMUNIST PARTY
(*November 4, 1930*)

FIGHT WITH THE COMMUNIST PARTY AGAINST LYNCHING AND TERROR!
(*November 4, 1930*)

JOIN THE COMMUNIST PARTY, THE PARTY OF LENIN, THE PARTY OF STRUGGLE, THE PARTY OF THE MARCHING VICTORIOUS PROLETARIAT OF THE WORLD!
(*November 7, 1931*)

This symbol of identification was intended to arouse favorable responses among prospective members and followers of the party, and is hence a symbol of positive identification. The term figured a comparatively small number of times in the slogans which were featured on the Chicago leaflets. The absolute numbers give a more vivid impression than percentages, although both are given below in order to show both actual and relative usage:

1930	1931	1932	1933	1934	Total
40	17	6	21	29	113
65%	4%	1%	8%	9%	7%

"Soviet" referred not only to the Soviet Union but to the form of organization to be used in and after the coming revolution:

FORWARD TO SOVIET AMERICA!
(*November 24, 1934*)

DEFEND THE SOVIET UNION!
(*March 18, 1932*)

DEFEND THE SOVIET UNION, THE CHINESE AND CUBAN PEOPLE!
(*November 7, 1933*)

DEFEND THE SOVIET UNION — THE FATHERLAND OF THE WORKERS OF THE WORLD!
(*May 1, 1932*)

DEFEND AND FIGHT FOR YOUR FATHERLAND — THE UNION OF SOCIALIST SOVIET REPUBLICS!
(*October 1930*)

The term "soviet" was used 125 times during the five years. The relative usage is shown by the following percentages:

1930	1931	1932	1933	1934	Total
8%	10%	9%	7%	2%	8%

Other symbols of positive identification which are closely connected with one another are intended to refer to the social group in whose names the party operates: "workers," "working class," "toilers," "masses," "proletariat," "oppressed." Representative slogans:

LONG LIVE THE SOLIDARITY OF THE INTERNATIONAL WORKING CLASS
(*February 26, 1934*)

WORKING CLASS AGAINST CAPITALIST CLASS
(*January 1, 1931*)

FOR WORKING-CLASS UNITY AGAINST HUNGER AND WAR!
(*August 1, 1934*)

WORKERS OF THE WORLD, UNITE!
(*September 14, 1930*)

TOILERS OF THE UNITED STATES! UNITE WITH THE OPPRESSED
OF ALL COUNTRIES!
(*January 1933*)

WORKERS OF EUROPE ARE HOLDING HIGH THE BANNER OF
PROLETARIAN EVOLUTION!
(*February 26, 1934*)

WORKERS! COMRADES! HELP THE PARTY OF YOUR CLASS
(*November 1934*)

The term " workers " was the most frequent one, being used 383 times in slogans of the five-year period. The relative usage is shown in the following percentages:

1930	*1931*	*1932*	*1933*	*1934*	*Total*
3%	30%	8%	31%	28%	23%

The expression " working class " was used 83 times between 1930 and 1934 as follows:

1930	*1931*	*1932*	*1933*	*1934*	*Total*
11%	4%	1%	7%	9%	5%

The other symbols were quite sporadically employed.

The term " class " appears in negative as well as positive combinations, when expressions like the " capitalist class " or " class enemy " (as against the " working class ") were used. An instance of negative meaning:

FIGHT AGAINST OUR CLASS ENEMY — THE RICH OPPRESSORS!
(March 8, 1931)

Another key symbol which often had opposite " signs " was
" Socialist." In certain cases the symbol was positive:

HAIL — VICTORIOUS — SOCIALIST CONSTRUCTION
(November 4, 1934)

(This alluded to the Second Five-Year Plan in the Soviet
Union.) In other cases the term was unequivocally negative:

DOWN WITH THE A. F. OF L. AND SOCIALIST TOOLS OF THE BOSSES!
(August 1, 1931)

In many cases an effort was made to keep the symbol positive
and eliminate any negative effects of its appearance in a negative combination by imputing that the symbol was falsely used
by those of whom the party disapproved:

THE COMMUNIST PARTY FIGHTS AGAINST: A. F. OF L. AND " SO-
CIALIST " FAKERS!
(April 3, 1931)

The great negative symbols, " capitalists " and " capitalism," [12] appeared in such slogans as:

DOWN WITH CAPITALISM
(March 14, 1931)

DOWN WITH BLOODY CAPITALISM WHICH BREEDS WARS,
HUNGER, STARVATION AND UNEMPLOYMENT!
(August 1, 1933)

CAST YOUR VOTE ON NOVEMBER 4TH AS A BLOW AGAINST
CAPITALISM — AGAINST POLICE TERROR, WAGE-CUTS, SPEED-UP,
MASS UNEMPLOYMENT, PART-TIME EMPLOYMENT, AND THE
COMING IMPERIALIST WORLD-WAR
(November 4, 1930)

---

[12] By special rule " capitalism " is taken to refer to " those who accept capitalism." It is an identification symbol as previously defined.

The symbols " capitalism " and " capitalist " were invoked 38 times during the five years. Their significantly infrequent usage in each year is suggested by the following percentages:

1930	1931	1932	1933	1934	Total
0%	4%	3%	2%	1%	2%

The term " bourgeoisie " was almost entirely absent. " Middle Class " was also ignored.

The principal demand symbol which unifies a revolutionary propaganda is the demand for " revolution " itself. There were very few explicit goal demands for " revolution " or method demands for " civil war " during the period. Among the occasional slogans:

FOR THE REVOLUTIONARY WAY OUT OF THE CRISIS
(*April 10, 1934*)

LET US BUILD OUR UNITED POWER TO TURN WAR INTO CIVIL WAR FOR THE VICTORY OF THE WORKERS AND TOILING MASSES AGAINST THE CAPITALIST CLASS!
(*August 1, 1934*)

WE CALL FOR THE UNITY OF ALL WORKERS IN ONE REVOLUTIONARY STRUGGLE FOR IMMEDIATE RELIEF AND FOR THE FINAL OVERTHROW OF CAPITALISM
(*March 14, 1931*)

The total number of different symbols of identification used in the Communist Party leaflets was tabulated for the period 1930-4. This included all of the symbols referring to persons, associations, unorganized groups, and communities. The total was 549. These symbols were used 3,009 times. The nuclear terms just referred to account for from 20 to 30 per cent of the total use. The proportions of usage per year:

1930	1931	1932	1933	1934
54	240	126	141	161
32%	30%	19%	20%	25%

Turning now to the analysis of symbols from the standpoint of the deeper psychological requirements of revolutionary action, we broach the interesting question of the relative emphasis upon negative and upon positive symbols. By the nature of the case revolutionary propaganda seeks to turn hostility toward symbols and practices which have been revered, and from which loyalty is now detached, and to attach loyalty to new symbols and practices which may previously have been abhorred. Plainly the bringing about of these adjustments in the sentiment life of the masses requires emphasis upon targets of affection as well as upon targets of destructive self-assertion.

In the Communist slogans from 1930 through 1934 a little over 70 per cent of the net number of identification terms were positive. Even larger is the relative frequency with which positive as against negative symbols of identification were utilized:

	1930	1931	1932	1933	1934
Pro	85%	78%	71%	81%	76%
Anti	15%	22%	29%	19%	24%

These figures contradict the usual belief that negative symbols (hostile affects) universally predominate in revolutionary propaganda. On the contrary, positive symbols (positive affects) appear to receive far greater emphasis.

The subordinate role of symbols of identification of specific persons is clearly brought out. Only 10 per cent of the 549 terms which were used during the five years were names of individuals. References to these persons constituted only 5 per cent of the total number of uses of symbols of identification during the period. The year-by-year record (percentage of use of personal symbols among symbols of identification):

1930	1931	1932	1933	1934
	1%	10%	5%	8%

Thus, slogans like the following were comparatively infrequent:

ORGANIZE AND STRUGGLE AGAINST THE FORD-HOOVER-CERMAK
GOVERNMENT OF STARVATION, TERROR, AND WAR!
(March 18, 1932)

ANSWER THE HEARST FASCIST ATTACK!
(December 28, 1934)

DOWN WITH HITLER!
(June 24, 1933)

AGAINST ROOSEVELT'S STRIKE-BREAKING, UNION SMASHING
NRA!

(August 1, 1934)

One of the objectives of revolutionary propaganda is to break
through the code of restraint which protects constituted authority; that is, revolutionary propaganda does battle with
some of the mores standards (the sanctioned patterns of de-
cency and right). The masses must be emancipated from the
sense of duty to abide by the established forms of government
and of property; for a political order is running smoothly only
as long as the fundamental practices of the community are
sustained by the consciences of the overwhelming proportion
of the population.

Since all men are born babies, they begin life as free of conventional rules of conduct as they are of clothes. The activities
of the infant and the growing child are gradually chastened
into the forms of expression which are held permissible in the
situation in which they are reared. At first the code is imposed
by the environment by means of rewards and punishments,
but gradually the child exacts from himself conformity to the
commands and restraints of the environment. Instead of bow-
ing to the external commander, he submits to the internal
commander which he has slowly formed.

For technical purposes it is convenient to use special names
for the different channels which make up the structure of the
personality. The primitive channels of impulse (following
psychoanalytic terminology) may be called the " id " channels.

The final paths through which acts of impulse are completed may be named the " ego " channels, whose complexity increases with experience. The basic patterns of self-constraint may be called the " superego," a term which is thus loosely equivalent to " conscience."

Hence it is the typical superego structure of a given group at a given time which must be broken down in part by revolutionary propaganda directed toward persons who are loyal to the constituted authorities of a community. Superego channels protect themselves from antagonistic impulses of the id by turning some of the energies of the personality into the act of blocking the energies of such id tendencies. The intensive study of the personality has shown that any sudden and considerable emancipation from the superego evokes acute anxiety, and that the personality utilizes many means for eliminating anxiety. Resulting compromises may or may not be restricted to lesser modifications of mood or minor peculiarities of behavior.

The strategy of destroying the strength of certain elements of the superego is to divide the superego against itself. Most persons are at most times proof against ·symbolically unsupported incitement to break the codes of law, morals, and manners to which they have given habitual allegiance. They are little tempted by such words as: " Break this law," " Violate this moral duty," " Commit this breach of good manners." But if the words are: " For justice, do so and so "; " For the right, do this and that "; " For the good, do this," the probability that the breach may occur is much enhanced. The task of revolutionary propaganda is to issue demands for revolutionary acts without full and plain disclosure of their countermores character or even with assertion of their mores character when such disclosure would interfere with, or when such assertion would foster, the occurrence of the acts. The conscience is quoted against the conscience in order to minimize the initially unacceptable character of the response solicited.

The task of Communist propaganda consists in weakening

the superego without destroying it; or, to put the matter more exactly, to weaken the superego in certain respects as a stage in the transition to a superego with partially different contents. It is, of course, not the total destruction of self-control, not the lawless life of pillage, but the life of revolutionary discipline that is the goal of revolutionary propaganda. Hence the hostilities which are to be directed against symbols of authority are not to be generalized against all of their functions nor against all symbols of authority, since that would include the authority symbols of the Communist movement itself. Restraints on violence or killing are not to be abolished altogether, but only during the concerted seizure of power, and even then only with reference to certain persons.

Revolutionary propaganda, then, seeks its ends by the redefinition, not the extinction, of conscience. For the discipline of service to established authority is to be substituted the discipline of the present pretender to its succession.

To what extent has Communist propaganda invoked counter-mores symbols, demanding counter-mores acts, thus tending to arouse indignant defensive responses from those bound by conscience to the mores patterns? In this category would come terse demands for revolution in general, and for revolutionary action in America in particular. Thus:

FOR A WORKERS' AND FARMERS' GOVERNMENT OF THE U.S.
(*January 15, 1932*)

FOR A SOVIET AMERICA — THE ONLY WAY OUT
(*August 1, 1934*)

One of the most flagrant violations of established loyalties is the symbolically unsupported demand that law-enforcement officers shall violate their legal duties and that members of the armed forces shall break discipline.

FOLLOW THE EXAMPLE OF THE CALIFORNIA GUARDSMEN WHO
REFUSED TO DO STRIKE DUTY!
(*August 31, 1934*)

(addressed to national guardsmen)

Another counter-mores procedure is to devalue symbols which are highly charged with favorable sentiment. Thus, the designation of a foreign state as the true fatherland of the American worker is one of the deepest conceivable thrusts at the patriotic sentiment organized around " America " and " American."

DEFEND THE SOVIET UNION, THE FATHERLAND OF THE WORK-
ERS OF THE WHOLE WORLD
(April 6, 1932)

DEFEND THE SOVIET UNION, THE WORKERS FATHERLAND
(November 7, 1933)

The emphasis upon the orientation of conduct upon " class " lines is a glancing blow at the symbols connected with " national solidarity " and " individualism." Such a term as " American " was occasionally associated with negative terms of identification, like:

DOWN WITH AMERICAN IMPERIALISM!
(October 20, 1934)

A BLOW AT GERMAN FASCISM IS A BLOW AT THE INTERNA-
TIONAL BANKERS AND ROBBERS, IT IS A BLOW AGAINST AMERI-
CAN IMPERIALISM ALSO
(October 20, 1934)

DOWN WITH AMERICAN & JAPANESE IMPERIALISM!
(January 28, 1933)

This, too, was but a glancing blow at " America," and not a complete rejection of the symbol; not " America " as such was attacked, but " imperialism," against which many adverse sentiments were already current in the community.

Communist propaganda slogans often contained symbols which were firmly implanted in the traditional vocabulary of the nation. Some of these words were positive symbols, designed to make more palatable the specifically Communist symbols which were used with them.

FOR FREE PRESS FREE SPEECH
(April 10, 1934)

PROTECT YOUR CONSTITUTIONAL RIGHTS BY VOTING COMMU-
NIST ON NOVEMBER 6TH
(November 4, 1934)

FOR JUSTICE! FOR HUMAN RIGHTS!
(April 30, 1933)

DEMONSTRATE FOR THE RIGHT TO LIVE AS HUMAN BEINGS
(May 1, 1933)

FOR THE RIGHT TO LIVE
(November 1934)

WORKERS, LETS ORGANIZE AND FIGHT, ONE FOR ALL, AND ALL
FOR ONE
(April 12, 1931)

Closely associated with the connection of the movement with the positively sentimentalized vocabulary of the community is its connection with common hostilities:

FIGHT TO WIPE OUT OPPRESSION!
(November 4, 1930)

VOTE AGAINST HUNGER AND WAR
(February 26, 1933)

AGAINST IMPERIALIST WAR
(July 15, 1932)

FIGHT AGAINST WAR AND FASCISM
(August 31, 1934)

The use by a political movement of symbols connected with foreign countries is no direct violation of the mores of the nation, yet it increases the vulnerability of the movement to counter-attack in the name of the distinguishing symbols of the region in question. It is not a question here of the open counter-mores avowal of a higher patriotism which binds the party to a foreign state, but the question of the more subtle sense of "foreignness" which is conveyed when a movement uses symbols which are connected with other countries. One may distinguish in this context two sorts of such connections. Terms of identification, like "Soviet Union," may be used, which refer to individuals, associations, unorganized groups, or communities outside of the U.S.A. (In this case we speak of "symbols of foreign reference.") Or terms may be used which do not have the characteristics just described, and which "psychologically" are closely associated with identification terms of foreign reference (as the term "Soviet" in the sense of a "Council" calls up "Soviet Union" in the minds of those who hear it). In this case we speak of "symbols of foreign association." A "foreign symbol" is a symbol of either foreign reference or foreign association.

Foreign reference symbols were not infrequently contained in Communist slogans. Representative examples:

AGAINST IMPERIALIST WAR; FOR THE DEFENSE OF THE CHINESE
PEOPLE AND OF THE SOVIET UNION
(May 28, 1932)

DEMONSTRATE AGAINST THE BLOODY JAPANESE IMPERIALIST
BANDITS AND IN SUPPORT OF THE HEROIC JAPANESE REVOLU-
TIONARY WORKERS!
(January 1933)

ATTEND THE COMBINED KIROV MEMORIAL AND ELECTION RALLY!
(December 21, 1934)

The absolute and relative numbers and frequencies of use of identification symbols of foreign reference were counted. About 5 per cent of the 549 symbols of identification were of exclusively foreign reference. This group of symbols accounted for about 11 per cent of the total volume of usage:

1930	1931	1932	1933	1934
10	55	95	140	72
6%	7%	15%	20%	11%

If the symbols previously characterized as the distinctive symbols of world Communism ("foreign association symbols" in the sense defined above) are added to the foregoing, the proportion of "foreign symbols" could be put close to 40 per cent:

1930	1931	1932	1933	1934
38%	37%	34%	40%	36%

A means of reducing the impression of foreignness is the de-emphasizing of certain symbols which are flagrantly recognized as "alien" in favor of more parochial vocabulary. We have already had occasion to remark that the terms "proletariat" and "bourgeoisie" were seldom invoked. On the positive side it is possible to detect the use of certain colloquial expressions. The most prominent example is the word "boss, bosses," as an alternative to "capitalist." The former terms appeared 86 times during the five years and relative frequency of usage is indicated by the following percentages:

1930	1931	1932	1933	1934	Total
10%	6%	6%	3%	3%	5%

Communist propaganda has the delicate task of instigating disrespect for constituted law and order without inciting acts of individual law-breaking. Acts of individual law-breaking are in principle decried by the party, which emphasizes the need for disciplined party action in crises of mass discontent when a seizure of power is possible, and as a corollary asserts the harmfulness of individual outbreaks when the situation is not adjudged to be "ripe." "Guerrilla warfare" is vigorously stigmatized; the battle is to be fought by the army of the proletariat under united leadership, and not by private persons or small groups giving vent to isolated explosions of anger and resentment. Such "romanticism" and "infantilism" are treated with emphatic contempt. Yet some members of the marching masses are bound to step over the line in the turbulence of crises long before the "final" crisis. Hungry and angry workers may occasionally storm the grocery stores in the neighborhood, or hurl brickbats at officers of the law. All of these incidents are officially viewed as regrettable by the spokesmen of the Communist Party; but at the same time they are regarded as inevitable stages in the long process by which the raw masses move toward more complex and disciplined forms of concerted effort. In order to keep in close contact with the more militant sections of the workers, some measure of sympathy must be extended also to such deplorable forms of "subjectively" revolutionary conduct.

The Communist slogans reflect both extremes between which a compromise is struck in this attitude of disrespect-respect for law and order. In general, the Communist slogans refrain from inciting to riot, but they condone in some degree those who have engaged in direct lawlessness. This usually takes the form of implying either that the lawless acts were performed by men and women who were goaded to desperation, or that a greater load of guilt rests upon the officers of the law (and their backers), who indulged in measures of unjustifiable brutality.

Often this takes the form of unmitigated denunciation of the police, and the treatment of those injured by the police as "martyrs." Thus:

WORKERS! PREPARE TO PARTICIPATE EN MASSE, AT THE FUNERAL OF OUR MURDERED FELLOW WORKERS

(August 3, 1931)

DEATH PENALTY FOR THE POLICE WHO MURDERED THE WORKERS!

(August 3, 1931)

DEATH TO THE MURDERERS!
(*August 1, 1931*)

Such occasions are seized as opportunities to " unveil " the
class nature of justice and government:

FIGHT FOR THE RELEASE OF THE IMPRISONED KENTUCKY MIN-
ERS, THE SCOTTSBORO BOYS, MOONEY, AND ALL CLASS WAR
PRISONERS!

(*March 2, 1932*)

RESIST THE FASCIST ATTACKS OF THE BOSSES AND THEIR GOV-
ERNMENT

(*May 1, 1931*)

In some cases there was direct incitement to the organization
of violence, expressed, however, in language of " defense ";
thus, quoting conscience against conscience so that the full
counter-mores implications of the suggestion remained beneath the surface:

BUILD YOUR DEFENSE CORPS!
(*July 1930*)

Instances of the kind mentioned are too infrequent to be reported in quantitative form.

The present chapter has described the symbol pattern of
Communist propaganda in Chicago by the use of comparatively novel categories and procedures. Fluctuations in features of Communist propaganda from year to year were disclosed in a quantitative form which makes it possible to search
more carefully for factors which explain the change or for
factors which were affected by the change.

Note on Groups Specifically Addressed
by Communist Propaganda

A. CLASS GROUPS

Workers (Unskilled, Semi-skilled, Skilled)

WORKERS OF THE 46TH WARD! PROTEST!
(*February 3, 1933*)

WORKERS OF THE WEST SIDE: LET US ORGANIZE FOR RESIST-
ANCE AGAINST THE POLICE ATTACKS IN DOUGLAS PARK
(July 22, 1932)

CHICAGO WORKERS STAND BY YOUR BROTHERS!
(June 1, 1934)

WORKERS IN THE STEWART & WARNER LET US JOIN WITH ALL
OTHER WORKERS THRUOUT THE WORLD IN DEFENSE OF THE
SOVIET UNION
(November 7, 1931)

$13 MINIMUM FOR A 30 HOUR WEEK FOR UNSKILLED
$18 FOR 30 HOUR WEEK FOR SEMI-SKILLED
$22.50 FOR 30 HOUR WEEK FOR SKILLED WORKERS
$30 FOR 30 HOUR WEEK FOR HIGHLY SKILLED
(September 24, 1934)

$1.00 PER HOUR MINIMUM WAGE FOR COMMON LABOR,
OTHER TRADES TO BE INCREASED IN PROPORTION
(May 1934)

(For) LIMITING THE NUMBER OF MACHINES EACH WORKER
MUST TEND
(September 24, 1934)

FOUR WEEKS VACATION WITH PAY EACH YEAR!
(August 1, 1931)

HAIL YOUR VICTORY — VICTORY OF SOPKIN STRIKERS!
(July 1933)

FORCE SYMPATHY STRIKES IN YOUR TRADES AND UNION IN
SUPPORT OF THE BUS DRIVERS!
(July 1934)

FIGHT FOR THE RIGHT TO ORGANIZE, STRIKE, AND PICKET!
(1931)

Unemployed ("Proletarianized" skill groups and Unskilled workers)

HONOR THE MEMORY OF THE THREE MARTYRS OF THE UNEM-
PLOYED!

(August 1931)

FREE GAS, ELECTRICITY AND WATER FOR ALL UNEMPLOYED AND
PART-TIME WORKERS

(February 3, 1933)

NO EVICTIONS OF THE UNEMPLOYED!

(August 3, 1931)

FREE RENT AND NO EVICTION OF UNEMPLOYED

(February 2, 1931)

UNEMPLOYED WORKERS SHALL HAVE FREE USE OF GAS, ELEC-
TRICITY, WATER AND STREET CARS

(March 25, 1931)

FOR SOCIAL INSURANCE TO THE AMOUNT OF $15.00 PER WEEK
FOR THE UNEMPLOYED

(August 3, 1931)

Relief Clients and Workers ("Proletarianized" skill groups
and Unskilled workers)

LEARN HOW TO FIGHT AGAINST THE PAUPERS AFFIDAVITS!

(May 28, 1933)

JOBS AT UNION WAGES OR CASH RELIEF FOR ALL UNEMPLOYED
WORKERS!

(May 1, 1934)

FOR RECOGNITION OF RELIEF COMMITTEES AT THE RELIEF STATIONS

(November 24, 1934)

MEN TO BE PROTECTED AGAINST ACCIDENT AND INJURY AS
PROVIDED BY ILLINOIS WORKMEN'S COMPENSATION ACTS

(December 26, 1933)

FULL PAY FOR TIME LOST DUE TO SICKNESS AND BAD WEATHER
(December 26, 1933)

IMMEDIATE AND REGULAR WEEKLY PAY DAYS
(December 26, 1933)

SHELTER AND FIRE TO BE PROVIDED FOR ALL JOBS IN THE OPEN
(December 26, 1933)

UNION WAGES ON ALL JOBS WITH A MINIMUM OF 83 CENTS
AN HOUR
(December 26, 1933)

RELIEF TO BE ISSUED IN CASE OF PART-TIME WORK AND IM-
MEDIATELY AT END OF JOB
(December 26, 1933)

NO DISCRIMINATION AND MISTREATMENT IN THE FLOPHOUSES
(March 8, 1932)

Small Taxpayers (Lesser-Income Groups)

AGAINST THE SALES TAX, FOR REDUCTION OF TAXES OF SMALL
TAXPAYERS AND INCREASE OF TAXES FOR THE RICH
(February 28, 1933)

Small Depositors (Lesser-Income Groups)

STATE TO REFUND LOSSES OF SMALL BANK DEPOSITORS IN FULL
(November 3, 1932)

FOR STATE RESPONSIBILITY FOR DEPOSITS IN FAILED BANKS!
(August 9, 1932)

NO PAYMENT OF CITY DEBTS TO BANKERS, UNTIL ALL WORK-
ING-CLASS DEPOSITORS ARE PAID IN FULL
(February 28, 1933)

Small Property-owners (Lesser-Income Groups)

MORATORIUM ON ALL DEBTS OF SMALL PROPERTY OWNERS.
NO FORCED SALES
(January 31, 1933)

Small Home-owners (Lesser-Income Groups)

NO TAXATION OR MORTGAGE FORECLOSURES OF SMALL HOME
OWNERS
(November 3, 1932)

LOWER TAXES FOR THE WORKERS WHO HAVE HOMES
(February 24, 1931)

UNEMPLOYED WORKERS OWNING THEIR HOUSES TO BE EX-
EMPT FROM PAYING TAXES!
(August 1931)

FOR MORATORIUM ON ALL TAXES AND MORTGAGES OF SMALL
HOME OWNERS FOR UNEMPLOYED AND PART-TIME WORKERS
(February 28, 1933)

Farmers (Lesser-Income Groups)

EMERGENCY RELIEF FOR THE IMPOVERISHED FARMERS WITH-
OUT RESTRICTIONS BY THE GOVERNMENT AND BANKS; EXEMP-
TION OF IMPOVERISHED FARMERS FROM TAXES, AND NO
FORCED COLLECTION OF RENTS OR DEBTS
(June 1932)

SUPPORT THE FARMERS STRIKE
(September 10, 1932)

B. SKILL GROUPS

Teachers and School-Board Employees (chiefly symbol specialists)

DEMAND THE IMMEDIATE CASH PAYMENT OF ALL SALARIES
AND WAGES DUE TO TEACHERS AND SCHOOL BOARD EMPLOY-
EES
(January 1, 1932)

WE DEMAND PAY FOR OUR TEACHERS
(May 1, 1933)

(For) TEACHERS PAY IN CASH NOT PROMISES
(May 30, 1934)

TO ALL PUBLIC SCHOOL TEACHERS OF CHICAGO! ORGANIZE AND FIGHT!
(January 21, 1932)

Ex-Servicemen (Former Specialists on Violence)

FOR FULL PAYMENT OF THE BONUS TO THE EX-SERVICEMEN!
(November 8, 1932)

MAKE THE RICH BANKERS PAY THE BACK WAGES (BONUS) TO THE EX-SERVICEMEN!
(August 1, 1932)

National Guardsmen and R.O.T.C. (Violence)

DEMAND THE COMPLETE WITHDRAWAL OF RIOT TRAINING AND GAS DRILL FROM THE TRAINING SCHEDULE
(August 31, 1934)

NATIONAL GUARDSMEN! MARCH FOR JOBS OR CASH RELIEF!
(November 24, 1934)

Athletes (Body Manipulation)

UNITY OF ALL WORKER ATHLETES!
(July 31, 1932)

MASS PARTICIPATION IN ATHLETICS, AND AGAINST THE SYSTEM OF STARRING ONLY A FEW!
(July 28, 1932)

THE WORKERS' SPORTSMAN IN THE RANKS OF THE WORKING CLASS!
(July 28, 1932)

C. FAMILY STATUS, AGE, AND SEX GROUPS[13]
Families

SOCIAL INSURANCE FOR THE UNEMPLOYED IN THE AMOUNT OF $15.00 PER WEEK AND $3.00 ADDITIONAL FOR EVERY MEMBER

[13] The groups which follow would be treated among *attitude* groups in a classification of politically interesting groups according to *skill, class, personality,* and *attitude.*

OF THE FAMILY, AT THE EXPENSE OF THE BOSSES AND THE GOVERNMENT
(August 8, 1931)

FOR CASH RELIEF OF $7 PER WEEK FOR EVERY MARRIED COUPLE WITH $2 ADDITIONAL FOR EACH DEPENDENT
(February 3, 1933)

Single Persons

$6 PER WEEK FOR ALL SINGLE WORKERS
(February 3, 1933)

RELIEF TO BE NOT LESS THAN $7 PER WEEK FOR ALL SINGLE WORKERS
(May 1, 1934)

Children, Pupils, Parents

CARE FOR BABIES — MILK AND FRUIT
(March 8, 1932)

FREE LUNCHES FOR THE UNEMPLOYED WORKERS CHILDREN!
(February 21, 1931)

FREE LUNCHES AND CLOTHING FOR THEIR (UNEMPLOYED) CHILDREN
(February 4, 1931)

FREE HOT LUNCHES AND SCHOOL SUPPLIES FOR SCHOOL KIDS
(March 8, 1932)

(For) SCHOOLS NOT BATTLESHIPS
(May 30, 1934)

WE DEMAND THE GOVERNMENT GIVE US FREE HOT LUNCHES, CAR-FARE AND CLOTHING IF OUR PARENTS ARE OUT OF WORK AND CANNOT AFFORD IT
(September 8, 1931)

WE DEMAND FREE SHOES AND CLOTHING
(May 1, 1933)

WE DEMAND FREE DOCTOR'S EXAMINATION AND CARE
(*March 26, 1932*)

DEMAND SMALLER CLASSES AND A SEAT FOR EVERY CHILD
(*January 21, 1932*)

PARENTS! SUPPORT YOUR CHILDREN'S STRIKE FOR BETTER ED-
UCATIONAL OPPORTUNITIES! GO WITH THEM ON THE PICKET
LINE!
(*December 1933*)

Youth and Students

FELLOWS AND GIRLS! JOIN THE PARADE AGAINST BOSSES' WAR
AND FASCISM
(*August 31, 1934*)

THE IMMEDIATE GIVING OF A $5 MEAL TICKET WEEKLY TO
UNEMPLOYED YOUTH BY THE UNITED CHARITIES
(*October 13, 1931*)

$5 WEEKLY MEAL TICKET FOR YOUNG WORKERS, TO BE GIVEN
BY RELIEF STATION AND FINANCED BY THE BOSSES
(*October 30, 1931*)

NO FORCED LABORCAMPS, I DAYS WORK PER WEEK, $5.00 CASH
WAGE FOR ALL UNEMPLOYED YOUTH
(*May 1, 1933*)

FOR THE REPLACEMENT OF ROOSEVELT'S CCC AND TRANSIENT
CAMPS BY THE SYSTEM OF UNEMPLOYMENT AND SOCIAL IN-
SURANCE FOR ALL UNEMPLOYED WORKERS
(*July 16, 1934*)

NO YOUNG WORKERS UNDER 21 TO BE EMPLOYED IN NIGHT WORK
(*August 1, 1931*)

EQUAL PAY FOR EQUAL WORK FOR YOUNG AND ADULT WORKERS!
(*August 1, 1931*)

A 6-HOUR DAY, A 5-DAY WEEK FOR ALL YOUNG WORKERS UN-
DER 18 YEARS OF AGE
(*October 30, 1931*)

AGAINST ALL DISCRIMINATION OF YOUNG WORKERS IN NRA CODES
(*July 16, 1934*)

YOUNG WORKERS IN CONTINENTAL CAN: FIGHT AGAINST WAGE
CUTS
(*April 17, 1932*)

THE SECURING OF HOMES, EMPTY ROOMS, ROOMS IN THE
Y.M.C.A. BY THE UNITED CHARITIES FOR HOMELESS YOUTH
(*October 13, 1931*)

IMMEDIATE SUBSTANTIAL REDUCTION IN RENT FOR YOUNG
WORKERS IN " Y'S "
(*September 8, 1931*)

FULL FREEDOM OF DISCUSSION OF ALL POLITICAL QUESTIONS
IN THE " Y "
(*September 8, 1931*)

NOMINATION AND ELECTION OF ALL MANAGERS AND OFFI-
CIALS BY THE MEMBERSHIP (IN Y.M.C.A.)
(*September 8, 1931*)

STUDENTS, TEACHERS, PARENTS, YOUNG WORKERS, NEGRO AND
WHITE! SUPPORT THE DEMANDS OF THE STUDENTS STRIKE!
(*December 1933*)

Women

WOMEN! JOIN THE COMMUNIST PARTY
(*March 8, 1932*)

EQUAL PAY FOR EQUAL WORK
(*March 8, 1932*)

NO NIGHT WORK FOR WOMEN
(*March 8, 1932*)

D. RACE AND NATIONALITY GROUPS

Negroes

NEGRO AND WHITE WORKERS, LET'S UNITE OUR FORCES
AGAINST THE BOSS POLITICIANS AND THEIR PRIMARIES!
(April 11, 1932)

FOR SELF DETERMINATION IN THE BLACK BELT
(November 4, 1934)

RAISE YOUR VOICE HIGH AGAINST THE ONSLAUGHT ON THE
NEGRO PEOPLE!
(April 14, 1933)

SELF DETERMINATION FOR NEGROES!
(September 10, 1930)

AGAINST LYNCHING OF NEGRO AND WHITE WORKERS
(1931)

FIGHT FOR THE RELEASE OF THE SCOTTSBORO BOYS!
(November 7, 1932)

PROTEST THE PLANNED LYNCHING OF THE SCOTTSBORO BOYS
(December 8, 1933)

FOR FULL ECONOMIC, POLITICAL AND SOCIAL EQUALITY FOR
NEGRO WORKERS
(1931)

NEGRO AND WHITE WORKERS! STOP THE KILLING OF THE NE-
GRO PEOPLE!
(July 8, 1934)

DEMAND THE RIGHT OF NEGROES TO SWIM ON ALL BEACHES
(June 14, 1933)

WORKERS OF CHICAGO! NEGRO AND WHITE! COME TO THE
HUGE MASS MEETING TO HEAR EMIL NYGART FIRST COMMU-
NIST MAYOR IN THE U.S.
(February 26, 1933)

NEGRO WORKERS: BEWARE OF THE LANDLORDS, POLITICIANS
AND OTHERS WHO WILL TRY TO MISLEAD YOU AND TURN YOU
AGAINST THE WHITE WORKERS
(August 3, 1931)

MEXICAN, NEGRO, AND WHITE WORKERS COME AND BRING
YOUR FRIENDS
(October 13, 1933)

AGAINST HIGH RENTS IN NEGRO NEIGHBORHOODS
(February 2, 1933)

DOWN WITH THE DOUBLE RENT FOR NEGROES
(August 8, 1931)

JOBS FOR THE NEGRO YOUTH SO WE DON'T HAVE TO GO TO CAMP
(May 1, 1933)

NO JIM-CROWISM OF NEGRO STUDENTS
(September 1934)

DEMAND RECOGNITION OF NEGRO SPORTSMAN!

Jews

NO ANTI-SEMITISM
(August 1934)

Foreign-Born

FOR THE PROTECTION OF THE FOREIGN BORN WORKERS, FOR
THE UNITY OF THE TOILING MASSES!
(December 1932)

AGAINST THE PERSECUTION, REGISTRATION AND DEPORTATION
OF THE FOREIGN BORN WORKERS!
(August 1931)

AGAINST THE DEPORTATION OF MILITANT FOREIGN BORN WORKERS!
(August 9, 1932)

E. LOCALITY GROUPS

Neighborhoods

FOR IMMEDIATE BEGINNING OF A PROGRAM OF PUBLIC WORKS
IN THIS WARD — THAT IS TO INCLUDE PLAYGROUNDS FOR
EACH SCHOOL; ALSO, MODERN BUILDINGS WITH A ROOM FOR
EACH UNEMPLOYED SINGLE WORKER

(February 28, 1933)

COME AND BRING YOUR NEIGHBORS. SHOW YOU STAND ON
YOUR RIGHTS.

(January 23, 1933)

CHAPTER VIII

The Elaboration of Symbols

THE EXTREME brevity of the slogan forbids exhaustive elaboration and reinforcement of the central symbols. These processes may be studied to better advantage in shop papers and speeches. The shop paper, which is one of the chief means of reaching the worker on the job, was an important channel of Communist propaganda. The speeches delivered at mass meetings show the symbol at the point of maximum exposure to those who are expected to be affected by it. Shop papers and speeches, like leaflets, show Communist propaganda in action where action matters most.

The fundamental task of revolutionary propaganda has been stated to be the splitting of the conscience (the superego) against itself. Shop papers and speeches may be utilized to study in some detail the relationship of symbols to assertiveness, weakness, guilt, and love.

Assertiveness may be aroused and redirected by presenting the established order as menacing or obstructive to the actual or desired position of the person or group in the pyramid of values. Reality is thus depicted as deprivational rather than indulgent, and deprivation is attributed to some other agent than the self. The key symbol is: " You lost your job because of the capitalistic system " rather than " You lost your job because of your own inefficiency." Symbols are elaborated to show that the phenomena in question are " Anti-Self by Other," not " Anti-Self by Self."

Human beings reply to hostile acts of the environment by initiating hostile acts of retaliation; but these acts may never be completed. If the external threat is instant and overwhelming, acquiescence commonly results. But even when changes in the environment are less serious, acute and paralyzing fear may result. Such disproportionate anxieties have been investigated by Freud, who showed that these exaggerations depended on the presence and strength of certain impulses of the personality itself. Rejected tendencies of the self were projected upon the outside world (by treating part of it as peculiarly ominous and destructive; this in turn might be followed by directing assertive impulses against the world thus defined).[1]

When kept within limits, the projection of inner hostility upon the outer world aids in mobilizing revolutionary action. But care must be taken to ensure that this does not go so far that the "system" appears as a Frankenstein monster against which all resistance is in vain. In approaching yet unrevolutionized groups it is expedient to choose, as objects of symbols of demand, minor grievances which seem to be capable of immediate remedy, and only gradually to lead up to drastic and fundamental demands, whose acceptance presupposes the belief in the instability of the central symbols and practices of one's environment.

By cultivating the "illusion of victory" one counteracts the tendencies to create a paralyzing picture of the overwhelming strength of the "system."[2] At the same time this enables the person to dispose of his own sense of weakness by projecting it upon the environment, treating the environment as weak.

The ascendancy of the conscience (the superego) is sustained by the sense of guilt which arises because of the existence of

[1] Consult Sigmund Freud: *New Introductory Lectures on Psycho-Analysis* (New York, 1933), Chapter 4, and notice the reformulation proposed by Karen Horney: *The Neurotic Personality of Our Time* (New York, 1937), Chapter 3.

[2] Revolutionary propaganda may be compared with war propaganda on this and similar points. See H. D. Lasswell: *Propaganda Technique in the World War* (London and New York, 1927).

inner impulses toward acts which defy conscience. If this sense of guilt is projected upon the environment, destructive tendencies may then be released against it. It is therefore wise for revolutionary propaganda to represent the established order as immoral and improper, and potential revolutionists as moral and proper.

When human beings are anxious and insecure, the craving for assuaging love is peculiarly intense. Hence it is important for revolutionary movements to furnish targets of love and admiration for the masses, since the superego defiance which is implicit in revolutionary activity heightens the insecurity level of persons engaged in it.

In such ways, then, the turning of the superego against itself can be facilitated by the proper handling of assertiveness, weakness, guilt, and love.

The shop papers were full of anecdotes which appealed to assertiveness by depicting the foreman or the employer as hostile or indifferent to the welfare of the worker.[3] The *Harvester Worker* began publication in 1926; the following typical article was published in the June–July number, 1927:

PROTEST AGAINST BRUTAL FOREMAN IN DEPARTMENT 38

By a Department 38 Tractor Worker

The foreman of department 38 is a mixture of a slave-driver, spy, and ignoramus. He treats his workers contemptibly, like Judge Thayer treated Nicola Sacco and Bartolomeo Vanzetti.

The unfortunate worker who happens to work for this fellow, never heard a decent word from him. Besides he speeds the men to the limit. The men get a miserable $19.00 a week. Anyone who dares to protest is discharged immediately.

---

[3] Such references are *Anti-Self by Other*. When the Other is represented as the violator of some code of morals or taste, the reference is also *Anti-Other*. If the Other is depicted as damaged by the speaker, the reference is *Anti-Other* (caused) *by Self*. Concerning symbol categories, see H. D. Lasswell: " A Provisional Classification of Symbol Data," *Psychiatry*, I (1938), 197–204.

All the workers of department 38 know him to be a s . . . o . . . b. . . . A few months ago this foreman, by his own volition, tried to produce more work with less men.

During that intense period, a worker smashed a finger with a hammer, for paying attention to this brutal foreman, only to be discharged after his finger got well.

In another case, a worker cut off his thumb on a circular saw. This champion foreman made the victim come to the place of work on time every day, for a few dollars a week, until he was well enough to resume his work. (This sort of stuff is carried on by all the foremen all thru the McCormick works. In order not to discredit themselves because of so many accidents, they keep their victims at work.)

Fellow workers! The foreman of department 38 has not the intelligence to be a foreman. He acquired his place by being a ruffian and a slave driver.

If we were in a Workers' Union, we would not be humiliated by such brutal foremen. In a Workers' Union, sick and injured workers would not come to work until they were well and able to do so; they would not have to slave for a pitiful wage of $19.00 a week, under insufferable conditions, with long hours and straight time for overtime work.

Workers of McCormick's: Let us aim to build a real and strong WORKERS' UNION.

The following supplement to the *Armory News* of July–August 1934 was intended to arouse the wage-earners within the National Guard against the enemy among the officers of the Guard:

" Col. H. — executive, Los Angeles First National Bank and Trust Co., commanding 160th Infantry, California National Guard; now on strike duty.

" Col. W. — commanding 107th Cavalry, Ohio National Guard, stockholder Auto-Lite factory where National Guard was used.

" Col. M. — director, Sacramento Water Co., who shut off the water of starving unemployed, leads a regiment against the workers.

" These men, and countless others in your own outfit, are high officers and also capitalists who carried out the orders of the big capitalists and use the National Guard to crush workers. Pres. Roosevelt, our Commander in Chief, and representative of the big capitalists, is directly responsible for training us, preparing us, and calling us out on strike duty."

Conservative trade-union leaders were constantly depicted as enemies of the workers, and their terroristic methods were emphasized. Two successive issues of the *Milkman* contained boxed notices of interest in this connection. In May 1933 the notice read:

" This and future issues will not have a Union Label printed on it.

" Threats have been made by the union gangsters against the shops printing our paper.

" To avoid getting the workers in trouble a new shop has been chosen and the label will be kept off."

In June 1933 this appeared:

" Due to the terrorization and threats of the office force at the address of the milkmen, by gangsters, officials and police bullies we are forced to move to a new address in order to protect the workers in the office, the new address will not be given due to the above reasons.

" Organize in barn groups, more solidly, back your paper ' The Milkman ' more thoroughly; we will be able to devise some method of reaching you, getting your contributions and financial help."

In the March 1933 number similar charges were also made against conservative union officials. The paper exposed the ruthlessness and insolence of the enemy and tried to immunize followers against epithets which might arouse feelings of weakness and guilt.

" When a driver gets up at a union meeting and proposes something constructive for the benefit of the organization and the welfare of the membership, our union officials force him down or refuse to let him finish, and when this driver fights for his rights, the officials call him a RED and try to ridicule him in the eyes of the members.

" When a driver tries to expose the role of our Fakers and the bosses, he is called Rooshian (Russian) and told to sit down.

" When a driver tries to fight for his rights and for justice he is called a com-unist (Communist) and is not allowed to continue."

The Socialist Party figures as an ally of the enemy in such articles as the following, which comes from the *C & N W Worker* (April 1931):

" ' Why is it ' asks a worker in a letter to us ' that the company causes the arrest of Communists when they distribute the shop paper at the gates and never bothers a Socialist Party leader who works in the shops? I am referring to J . . . C . . . who ran for mayor on the Socialist Party ticket.'

" Space does not permit publication of the worker's letter in its entirety. The important question he raises, however, deserves an immediate answer.

" It is because the Socialist Party is the third party of Capitalism. Long before the Chicago mayoralty election, the Socialists had erased every mention of the Class Struggle from their platform. The Socialist Party became a political organization of petty shop-keepers, long-haired intellectuals and wealthy morons. It includes in its membership a number of millionaires, so-called liberals.

" When unemployed workers appeared in the council chambers in New York to demand bread for thousands starving to death, Rev. Norman Thomas, Socialist Party leader, sat in the first row of seats. Upon signal from Tammany's grafting mayor, Jimmy Walker, the police began a murderous assault upon the unemployed, clubbing, beating, and kicking them. Norman smiled at the cops in appreciation of their work on behalf of the capitalist bosses and gave out a lying statement to the press later saying that the unemployed had provoked the riot.

" Unemployed workers demonstrating in the Socialist-controlled cities of Reading, Pa., and Milwaukee, Wisc. have frequently been attacked and clubbed by police and gangsters."

The foregoing extracts have represented part of the workers' environment as menacing and obstructive, insolent and indifferent. This, it is to be expected, will arouse assertive counter-impulses. To guide and strengthen these impulses, specific grievances and demands connected with them are given space in the shop papers. The Communist Party attached much importance to the handling of specific grievances. Beginning in 1931, the party center gave concrete guidance to shop papers by means of the *National Shop Paper Editor;* and much attention was given to the same channel by the *Party Organizer.* Looking back over the year 1931, this latter publication found several unsatisfactory features yet prevalent (January 1932; Vol. 5, No. 1):

" Too often . . . a small item on a lay-off in the shop is printed in a small paragraph somewhere without a comment, and then a long heavy article on our unemployment program somewhere else in the paper, without any shop material whatever.

" More and more the comrades are beginning to suggest action on the basis of some grievance in the shop through the shop paper . . . some of them still confine themselves to saying ' we must do something about this,' when describing a shop grievance."

The reviews of shop papers hammered home the standards of sound practice. The *Party Organizer* for November–December 1932 reviewed a group of shop papers from District 8. Here are some comments about the October copy of the *Illinois Steel Worker:*

" One of the best features of the *Illinois Steel Worker* is the concrete manner in which the conditions and issues of the various departments are dealt with as well as the demands flowing from them. This section deals with such small grievances of the workers as working before official starting time, not getting paid for extra time put in, the need for drinking fountains, etc. The concrete demands formulated on the basis of these department grievances are excellent. However, the comrades fail to formulate the demand around a very important issue in the factory, namely, the struggle against the indirect cutting of wages through the introduction of the six hour day . . . we must demand the same pay the workers received when working eight hours.

"While correctly placing emphasis on the building of the united front organs of struggle — the grievance committees — the paper practically does not deal with building the Steel and Metal Workers Industrial Union.

"The articles on the 15th anniversary of the Russian Revolution and those on the Election Campaign are not linked up with the actual conditions of the steel workers in the plant and fail to contrast these conditions with those gained by the steel workers of the Soviet Union. For instance, the construction of the steel giants, the increase in the wages, no unemployment among steel workers in the Soviet Union, etc., should have been touched upon in relation to the conditions of the workers in the plant."

The November 1932 issue of the *Harvester Worker,* put out by the International Harvester Unit of the Communist Party of District 8, was criticized thus:

"The paper fails to follow up this excellent exposure of conditions (the speed-up, etc.) with a thorough explanation of just how the workers should organize in the plant. We must guard against the habit of merely repeating 'build department committees' — 'build shop committees.' We should explain, in relation to the issues that arise, just how we must organize, just how such attacks can be defeated, utilizing experiences from other sections of the country."

Concerning the *Crane Worker* for October 1932:

"The *Crane Worker* has taken up a struggle against the stool-pigeons concretely exposing them by name. In our task to isolate the stool-pigeons and discredit them before the workers, it is necessary to arouse the indignation of the workers, to create hatred for these rats. On the basis of this, organize this sentiment of the workers to develop a struggle not only to isolate the stool-pigeons from the rest of the workers but to oust them from the shop. This latter task the *Crane Worker* does not bring sharply forward.

"The article on the Hunger March to the City Hall . . . does not sufficiently deal with the relations of the Crane workers to the struggle for unemployment insurance, the insecurity of their jobs, the struggle against part-time work."

About the *Armour Worker* (November 1932):

" The shop paper deals with a problem which embraces all the workers in the plant — the share-the-work system. It formulates the demand, but nothing on how the workers should fight for this demand, and defeat the program of the bosses.

" Similarly, the united front organs of struggle, the building of the grievance committees and department committees, are not raised in this light. Particularly, because this is the second issue of the paper it is essential that these questions be dealt with thoroughly, at the same time bringing out the relation of the Party to these united front organs of struggle and to the revolutionary unions. Furthermore, although the A. F. of L. plays some role in the stockyards, not a single word on the A. F. of L. convention was written to prepare the workers for the decisions and actions at the present A. F. of L. Convention."

With reference to the *Stewart-Warner Worker:*

" While in appearance these issues are attractive, in content, not a single word can be found . . . on the conditions in the plant.

" Something should be done about this by the Chicago District Committee."

Definite instructions for forming a grievance committee are found in the *Illinois Steel Worker* for July 1932:

" Get as many workers as possible together in your departments. Discuss the bad conditions and what your demands will be to change them. Elect a committee who will present these demands to the boss. Before you present these demands to the boss make sure that the committee has the support of the majority of the men in the department.

" You don't need to be a member of the Steel Workers Industrial Union to belong to a grievance committee. But the S. & M. W. I. U. will help you to form and support a grievance committee. For further information write to union at 23 So. Lincoln Street."

The shop bulletins frequently resorted to special devices to enlist the active participation of rank and file workers. Letters were solicited and published; and the " Question Box " was inaugurated in the *Armour Young Worker* (December–January 1934–5):

" We wish to announce that we are reserving this space for a new feature, — THE QUESTION BOX — we will print all questions and answers.

" Everyone is welcome to ask or answer questions about the shop, foremen, conditions, wages or anything else that is bothering them.

DO NOT HESITATE SEND YOUR QUESTIONS AND ANSWERS TO THE

QUESTION BOX — % ARMOUR YOUNG WORKER —

101 S. WELLS ST., RM. 707, CHICAGO, ILLINOIS

" Here are some questions that have been asked so far. See how many YOU can answer.

" 1. Why was the Morris Canning Dept. closed?

" 2. Why did the Beef Boners get a 20% wage cut when there was an 8% raise given to all packing workers in Armours? "

The crossword puzzle was adapted to the task of eliciting more active response. Such sentences as the following were used: "When workers strike, they are thrown into —— " (a four-letter word).

Successes intended to foster the "illusion of victory" are constantly played up.[4] Emphasis upon the triumphs of the Soviet Union, instances of which have already been cited, falls into this category. Such material was supposed to show what workers are capable of doing when capitalists are out of the way. In a more humble and direct form items like the following display " our " strength through organized action, and hence the weakness of the employers when we really unite and fight:

---

[4] Thus fostering the projection of weakness. References to our strength are *Pro-Self,* and they may be asserted *by Self* or *by Other.* The weakness of the other is *Anti-Other* asserted *by Self* or *by Other.*

(Illinois Steel Worker, May 1934):

"The other day a number of the chippers here were laid off for no reason at all. So they got together and refused to go home. The boss got scared, and told them to go to Department #62 to get work.

"They spent half a day there trying to get something to do. Then they went to the main office and protested. The big guys got scared too, and passed out a lot of nice words, and put the chippers to work in dep't 62. This shows what can be done if we get together. What could we do if the whole mill was organized?"

The following brief item serves a plurality of functions. In this case the "scab" is represented as coming to a bad end in a way which emphasizes the ruthlessness and the ingratitude of the employers, while the death itself implies that our enemies perish.

(Gary Steel Worker, February 1933):

"A foreman in the Rail Mill was recently burned to death because Sup't G . . . laid off the regular salamander man and this inexperienced foreman poured gasoline on red coals. This fellow, who was a good servant of the bosses and tried to break the Great Strike of 1919 by working, was killed by the bosses because of their greed for profits."

Extracts like the foregoing show how invidious language of an abstract as well as concrete nature is used to depict the immorality and impropriety (guilt) of certain enemies. Additional extracts of a similar character follow. Chiseling was frequently referred to. Witness the *Illinois Steel Worker* (January 1934):

"In Dep't. #43 the part time work gives Axel and Slim a chance to get some extra change, free drinks and cigars, etc.

"Axel picks mostly on the Mexican workers and Slim mainly on the Polish workers. The method used is to make them bring cigars, take the boss to a saloon and buy drinks or even to make him pay a dollar now and then to get some extra days.

"Workers of Dep't. #43! Let's not stand for this any longer.

Let us get together, and send a committee to the main office and demand a stop to this stuff."

Nepotism was affirmed in a letter published in the *Rock Island Headlight* (July 1, 1934):

" Contrary to instructions of the heads of the Rock Island that men will be put to work in the order of their seniority and that no new men will be hired while there are unemployed on the list, Supt. J. has placed his son as an extra tower man on the Chicago terminal div'n . . . also W., rip track foreman and a great company union man has placed his son on the pay-roll ahead of a number of unemployed."

An attack on an A. F. of L. organizer (*Armour Young Worker,* December 1934–January 1935):

" W. C., organizer of the Amalgamated Meat Cutters and Butcher Workmen shot himself in the leg and died shortly afterwards. He was aiming at a worker member of the union, but was so drunk he shot himself.

" Workers in the Amalgamated Meat Cutters and Butcher Workmen should fight for honest rank and file workers as their leaders."

The contemptible cowardice and hypocrisy of ex-members is the theme of this letter which was published in the FAECT *Bulletin* (1935):

" One effect of the Politician-Planned rise in employment is the clearing out of DEAD-WOOD from the membership of FAECT.

" Strange as it may seem to many of our readers, a $20 per week job temporarily under the belt of such an individual will send him scurrying away from the LOGIC OF TECHNICAL UNIONISM like a burned rat. He slips back to the shaky position of playing vassal to some petty Bourbon employer. The usual excuse is that he hasn't had a job for over a year and is afraid to jeopardize it — that the Federation is a " leftist " group, etc.

" Now this automatic housecleaning has its good consequences in that it leaves a membership of stalwarts, intent on continuing the building up of the FAECT on an INDUSTRIAL UNION BASIS."

The shop papers constantly presented examples of heroic leadership of the working classes, and gradually introduced the optimistic symbols of the future which are part of Marxist doctrine. The function of this was to present targets of love as well as hate to the workers. To some extent the same result was attained by the use of humor, which not only attacks unfavorable features of the environment, but shows that " we " are good-natured. The following bit, called " Roaming the Alleys " is from the *Milkman* (October 1933):

3:30 a.m. — Cats, Dogs and Milkmen only to be seen.

4:00 a.m. — " Hands up! Give me all your dough! What only 30 cents! Why you . . . ?$#&X (a nice and gentle holdup).

4:30 a.m. — " Whoa — Halt — Whoa — Damn you — Whoa a a." (milkman chasing a runaway horse).

5:00 a.m. — " Get the hell away from here. You're making too much noise " (from a sunny dispositioned and light sleeper).

5:30 a.m. — " Shay can I have a bottlesh milsh. I sh dry " (from a 3.2 drunk).

6:00 a.m. — " Yoo-hoo milkman! Will you please sell me a quart of milk? " " Sure, lady. Watch out, lady, you're losing your skirt. You'll catch cold " (one of those happenings).

6:30 a.m. — " Come Seven — Come Eleven. Baby needs a pair of shoes!!! " ('nuff said).

7:00 a.m. — " What! Late again!!! Listen, milkman, I need my milk before breakfast. All the other drivers have been here hours ago. If this happens again . . ." (from a contented customer 3rd floor).

7:30 a.m. — Whew!!! Glad this night's over. Now for grub and collections.

The humorous dialogue as a channel is found in the *Armory News* (July–August 1934):

" Private Jones sez . . .

" Salutations, you marchin', calloused, foot-sore land lubbers of the infantry.

" Greetings, you horse washin', manure cleanin' devils of the Field Artillery.

" As for me-self I'm just Private Jones, the guy who says ' Yes, sir ' to the officers but thinks about the time when he can boot the officers in the can. I'm the kind of a guy who figgers if what the army pays us guys was women's dresses me goil could join a nudist camp. . . .

" By this time we were standing in front of the 8th regiment. All the men seemed to keep away from the Negro guardsmen. In a number of companies the men were told not to associate with them. Popoff and I walks over to a group who were receivin' instructions of the duties of a soldier from their Capt.

" ' Private Murphy,' asks the Capt., ' why should a soldier be ready to die for his country? '

" A smile lit up Murphy's face, ' Sure, captain, you're quite right, why should he? ' "

The public speech lends itself to modes of symbol development which are not congenial to printed media. The speaker, taking advantage of the high tension level of the audience, can rise to an intemperateness of expression which is usually inappropriate in print. Overdrawn language becomes acceptable which is impermissible out of the fully developed crowd situation. Only in general crises is the distinction between spoken and written discourse obliterated.

Representative of Communist speeches made during the early days of the Great Depression when insecurity was high are those delivered at a meeting held in the Coliseum of Chicago, on Friday, January 9, 1931, at 7.30 o'clock in the evening.[5]

A stench bomb had been released in the Coliseum just before the meeting was called to order, and the first presiding officer (Nels Kjar) seized the occasion for a sarcastic reference to a religious group. His opening sentence was:

" Comrades, please, a little order. Somebody threw a little holy water here. Maybe some good Catholics. I don't know. But I want to explain that we want all of you who can afford it to take for four months the *Labor Unity* for fifty cents."

[5] Quotations are from a stenographic transcript.

It was apparently assumed that the backbone of the meeting was composed of convinced " freethinkers " and ardent revolutionaries; hence the insult to the church and the immediate demand for an act of participation in organized effort by buying the organ of the Trade Union Unity League.

The chairman, who immediately took charge (Philip Frankenfeld) picked out another enemy:

" Already we have seen that the American Federation of Labor — "

(*Boos*)

" Its officialdom, but not its rank and file, tried to befoul this meeting with their own fair smell. So you know what happens when you meet a skunk, don't you? All right." [6]

(*Applause*)

An example of victorious action, and in this case of illegal action, was exalted:

" Several days ago in the State of Arkansas five hundred starving farmers came to the general store in that little town of Anderson, Arkansas, and said: ' We want food. We want milk for our children, and if you will not give it to us, we will take it ourselves.'

(*Applause*)

" And, fellow workers, the machinery of Congress, which usually is not so well greased and oiled, and which takes decades to decide on matters, worked so quickly that Saturday, the day on which the demonstration took place, and Monday fifteen million dollars were granted to the starving farmers." [7]

(*Applause*)

Now came an attack on local authorities, and incitement to action:

---

[6] The " other " smells bad. This style of reference fosters the projection of repulsiveness away from the self. Note also the distinctions made between " officials " and " rank and file," the former a negative and the latter a positive symbol of identification.

[7] This anecdote is Pro-Self (Worker) by Self; we win by asserting ourselves.

"Fellow workers, in the city of Chicago we will never get Big
Bull Thompson — [8]
(*Boos*)
— and the City Council, to grant one penny for relief, unless the
jobless, hungry, starving workers of Chicago will proceed in the
same fashion and manner, to say: 'Unless you give us relief, we
will go out and help ourselves to it.' [9]
(*Applause*)
"Comrades, millions of dollars are stolen annually from the
City Treasury from the workers of Chicago by these grafting politicians." [10]

Personal sarcasm:

"Why, even Commissioner Alcock told us the other day:
'There are 400,000 jobless in Chicago. We know that there is
hunger and misery, and why, Mr. Thompson and myself, out of
our own little pockets, are feeding six families.' Imagine that, feeding six families, when he admits there are 400,000 unemployed." [11]

Incitement to lawlessness crept out in speeches made by others. Nels Kjar, introduced as the Communist candidate for
mayor of the city of Chicago, declared:

"We, the Unemployed Council and the Trade Union Unity
League, we say, let us organize and fight, why should we starve?
Well, because they have got a lot of watchdogs around the food, so
we shall not get this food, but we say this, when a man is hungry,
he has a right to eat, regardless of the capitalist law.[12]
(*Applause*)
"We say this, necessity knows no law."

---

[8] The "other" is presented as both weak and hypocritical.

[9] The Anti-Self references (jobless workers) are promptly followed
by Pro-Self by Self references (expectations of indulgence procured by
defiant threats).

[10] Presentation of the other as guilty. This follows an incitement to
illegal action and projects guilt away from the self.

[11] The "other" is presented as stupid (weak) or hypocritical
(guilty).

[12] The use of the term "right" turns the conscience against itself —
the conscience which is accustomed to revere the "Law."

Toward the end of his speech the star orator of the evening, William Z. Foster, added:

" Comrades . . . why do you workers admire the farmers in Arkansas for the bold stand that they took? I will tell you why. I will tell you why the workers of this country admire that handful of farmers, because every worker in this country thinks the same thing in his heart, that is what the workers should do, not stand aside and calmly starve in the midst of plenty, but force them to give out of these stores."

Praise of the working class and attacks upon the " boss class " appeared early in the evening, notably in the speech of Brown Squires, Negro Communist who spoke with special reference to the TUUL and the importance of racial unity:

" The working class, not by color, or not by creed, produces everything that is produced, they manufacture everything that is being manufactured; and yet they enjoy none of it. The profiteers, the grafters and political profiteers have taken over all of the production that has been created by the working class." [13]

Another theme of Squires was the latent strength of the workers:

" Comrades and fellow workers, we do not realize our power, but the American Scaberation of Labor and its bureaucrats, they recognize it, because they want to put an unpleasant smell into this great audience. But we should realize our power, since we create everything, since we protect everything, and the only way by which the ruling class can keep us from food, from jobs, or even from controlling what we produce, is by using one laborer against another, one race against another." [14]

(*Applause*)

---

[13] Pro-Self: we are moral. Anti-Self by Other: we are made weak. Anti-Other by Self: they are immoral.

[14] Pro-Self: we are moral and strong. Pro-Self (asserted) by Other: they know we are strong. Anti-Other: they are weakening and resort to immoral measures.

The victory of the Russian workers was added to the example of the Arkansas farmers and re-emphasized throughout the evening. Kjar said:

"You know, fellow workers, there is one section of the world today controlled by the working class. This is the only place in the world today where there is no unemployment, and when some forty scoundrels tried to poison the food, tried to create starvation, they lined them up against the wall. That is what we have to do here.

(Applause)

"It is not only our right, but it is our duty." [15]

To William Z. Foster fell the main part of the task of depicting the present deprivations inflicted upon the workers, a picture relieved by the diagnosis of the "final crisis of capitalism," the success of the Soviet Union, and the tendency toward world revolution.

After the initial speakers, Foster was introduced and received with prolonged and loud applause. The chairman announced:

"A group of workers' children wish to present a flag which they made, to Comrade Foster, as the secretary of the Trade Union Unity League."

A little girl: "Dear Comrade Foster: The Chicago children in the Chicago Jewish schools are here to greet you. In our schools we have learned much about you, and your arrest for the workers' cause. We enjoy hearing that you are so brave to the bosses, and what you showed them. We are all glad to hear and see you today — tonight."

(Applause)

Amid the excitement of the audience Foster accepted the flag and added:

"And I think it may be said, perhaps these children do not realize it, but some of the rest of us do, that by the time they get to

---

[15] Note again the combination of counter-mores incitement with mores language: "right," "duty."

be as old as some of us are, they will have lived so long under the
Soviet Government that they will have practically forgotten all
about the capitalists." [16]

Foster began by depicting the plight of the workers:

" And what is the position of the workers in this crisis? Mass
starvation. Do you hear those words? Mass starvation is what the
American workers are confronted with at the present time."

He then drew pictures of the bread-lines, the overcrowded
jails (full of hungry workers), and the misery of evictions. The
picture of misery was relieved by a story of direct action:

" Evictions, evictions. The other day in Pittsburgh I was present when an eviction took place — that is, when they tried to make
it take place. A Negro woman, a woman with seven children, a
widow — they came down to evict her from her home, because
she could not pay the rent. Well, fortunately, we were able to stop
it. We gathered up a few of the neighbors, one hundred or two,
and they waited for this constable and this landlord. When they
came to make this eviction, they gathered around the constable and
the landlord, and they were damn glad to get out of there with
whole skins without evicting this woman.
(*Laughter and applause*)
" Workers, do not permit them to evict any workers in the city
of Chicago."
(*Applause*)

After this interlude there came more details about the deprivations afflicting the workers of America. Foster supplemented personal anecdote and general affirmation by the im-
personal language of statistics:

" Do you know, according to the standard statistics from a
capitalist organization, the income of American workers has de-
creased nine billion dollars in the past year. . . .

---

[16] These symbols of optimistic expectation (symbols of the " illusion
of victory ") — symbols of fact — are Pro-Self and stimulate active demands.

" Bread-lines, starvation, wholesale lynching of Negroes in the South, clubbing of unemployed, arresting of their leaders, and throwing them into jails wherever they dare to make a stand. These are the conditions in prosperous America! " [17]

Details about the crisis elsewhere:

" No, this is not a temporary sickness; this is the death sickness of the world capitalistic system. Capitalism is in decay. We are standing at the bedside of a dying system of society, the capitalist system. Do not worry, however; this system is not going to die of its own volition; we will have to give it a good push on the way." [18]

(*Applause*)

Foster then took up the growth of the Soviet Union, relying extensively on the testimony of the alarmed enemy, an article in the *Wall Street Journal*:

" But what is the Five-Year Plan? . . . According to this capitalist writer, ' Centuries compressed into five years ' . . . he goes on telling the tremendous doubling and tripling in every industry. How he rolls over the billions here! But there is one thing about these billions that they do not like exactly. Our crowd have got these particular billions, and Wall Street hasn't got them, and Wall Street isn't going to get them. . . . This capitalist writer . . . has on the front page here the picture of a steel mill, a blast furnace, and he has a very significant remark under that. He says: ' It looks like capitalism, but it isn't.' "

This adroitly indicated the weakness of capitalism (its writers were alarmed by the immense strides of the Soviet Union) and emphasized the authenticity of the claims made for the Five-Year Plan.

The hypocrisy of capitalism:

" A year and a half or so ago, about fourteen months ago, President Hoover announced an agreement there would be no wage

---

[17] The workers are not merely weak — they are unjustly weak.

[18] Symbols of " Fact " on a world scale reinforce symbols of " Demand " for action.

cuts in this United States. How has that agreement been kept? That agreement was a lie. That agreement was a fake."

The cynical and insolent exploitation of misery by the capitalists:

"I was in New York going along the street the other night [Notice again the use of the personal eyewitness technique of presenting material], and I saw a sight that disgusted me more than anything else I have seen in the course of the crisis. In Columbus Circle, New York, one of the big centers of the city, the *New York American* had a bread-line, right in this display section of the theater district, the great artery of New York. Why did the *New York American* have this bread-line there? Simply for a cheap advertisement for the Hearst paper, no more. Actually capitalizing the misery of the workers. It is about — it seems to me that the gall of doing something like this — is about on a par with the Bank of the United States in New York.

". . . This bank failed a couple of weeks before Christmas, and so you know what that bank did on Christmas? They hung up some wreaths in the windows wishing the depositors a Merry Christmas. Well, this is about the way they have been treating the workers."

Here Foster presents himself as stirred by human sympathy, a generous, outspoken, and courageous object of love and esteem.

The same indulgent attitude on the part of the leaders was exhibited in the appeal for funds to finance hunger marches and papers. After the well-worn pattern of fund-raising from congregations went the appeal of Kjar:

"Comrades, I have one more thing to perform. I am not going to beg here, but I am going to demand that you do your duty. You can do more than clap your hands tonight. We need money for this movement. We need money to organize the working class, and we are going to take a collection here tonight, and we are going to ask all of you who are still working, to hold up a dollar bill and help this movement. Let us see how many can hold up a dollar bill, those who are working. Comrades, we are going to send a delegation to

Washington, D.C., the 10th of January to present the unemployment bill to Congress, and we need some money to send the delegates. It is for your own benefit. They will go there to represent you, and you who still have a dollar, or a quarter, or a dime, you must help us to do this thing. You must help us so we can get somewhere. You know we are not going to get money from the City Council for that. It has all got to come out of your pockets. I see a lot of dollar bills here. . . . There are many workers who haven't got a penny left. Those who have only got carfare, keep it. We do not want to take your last cent."

As a means of preparing the workers to assert themselves despite obstacles, the speakers made occasional references to the sacrifices expected. The misery of the workers was not to be abolished all at once, but in the course of a long struggle, which would surely be crowned with victory, but which would endure many temporary reverses. Thus Kjar said:

" If we all get together, no power on earth can stop us, neither stink bombs or capitalist police or watchdogs, nothing can stop us.
(*Applause*)
" And that is why I am stressing organization here tonight. They might club some of us. Some of us might get worse than a clubbing, but we cannot stop. It is better to fight to eat something than to lie down and starve. It is better to fight for the working class than to go into another World War and have twenty million people killed for Morgan's profit."

Also in the tradition of referring to the reclaimed sinner, the chairman commented at one point:

" Comrades, I want to announce the fact that Comrade Squires in the last war fought for the glory and profit of Wall Street. Now he fights in the interest of the working class."
(*Applause*)

Through the media of the shop paper and the speech, besides other channels, Communist propaganda was able to elaborate the brief commands and assertions of the slogan and to wage war against the unity of the old conscience, which is the principal strategical task of revolutionary propaganda. By means of stirring anecdote and impressive statistics, by means of eyewitness accounts and enemy admissions, it was sought to arouse self-assertiveness against the established order, to foster the projection of weakness and guilt upon it, and to concentrate love and esteem upon the symbols and practices of the Communist movement.[19]

[19] Detailed comparison of the symbols prevalent in different channels of revolutionary propaganda will probably show that certain patterns have the maximum of skillfulness. The methods of symbol analysis which are developed in this report are capable of being expanded and applied to any symbol clusters and channels.

CHAPTER IX

The Technique of Demonstration

COMMUNIST Party leaders have given more thought and energy to political demonstrations than have the leaders of any other political party in the United States. There is nothing new for the American political scene in the mere fact that masses march: political campaigns in the nation have been famous for their parades, barbecues, and convention outbursts. The spectacular methods of the Ku Klux Klan have made history in the art of mass appeal. Coxey's "army of the unemployed" marched on Washington in the 1890's. No other political party, however, has systematically incited the masses to demonstrate in a variety of modes and for a variety of purposes, forming a gamut which ranges from electoral campaigns to protests against eviction, unemployment, and kindred deprivations. The Communist Party integrated all separate threads into a whole.

The term "demonstration" is a word of positive reference, a "plus" word of high rank in the Communist vocabulary. Less important gatherings are referred to as "meetings," possibly even as "mass meetings." The term "demonstration" is mostly reserved for important occasions in which there is a certain intensity of mass demand.

Skillfulness of demonstration technique means the establishment of a proper relationship between objectives and conditions facilitating or obstructing their achievement. There has been no effort in Chicago to stage a demonstration which would precipitate immediate revolutionary action for the seizure of power. Demonstrations were intended to achieve much more modest changes in the environment. Although we sometimes use the term " demonstration " to refer to ceremonial gatherings which are staged for the purpose of counter-identification only, and Communists occasionally slip into the same terminology, it is more common to restrict the word to mass actions which are focused exclusively upon immediate demands which the party believes to be shared or sharable by extra-party groups.

Chicago demonstrations have sought non-revolutionary goals during the entire period. The techniques applied have been modified as the obstructing and facilitating factors of the context are varied. If demonstrations arise spontaneously among the masses, the tactical problem is to guide them. The spontaneous demonstration spreads only in periods of high tension and affect. The symbols of demand utilized on such occasions usually refer to the immediate future, to very specific objectives, and to a limited area.[1] Such occasions demand the presence of strong leadership — that is, persons able to organize the reactivity of the moment into immediate activity.

There are many phases in the staging of a demonstration. The issue or occasion must be decided upon, and the type of gathering (parade, indoor or outdoor meeting, etc.) determined. The date must be selected, with consideration for competing events occurring in its proximity on the same day. If the demonstration is to be an indoor affair, a hall must be rented; if it is to be an outside demonstration or a parade, a permit must be secured from the proper police authorities. After these matters have been taken care of, efforts must be divided along two lines of activity: the careful financing and planning of the affair, and the recruiting of " mass " attendance. Usually both of these must be successfully accomplished if the demonstration is to be successful. The former includes

[1] Case studies are found in the next chapter.

the development of a well-balanced program of speakers, music, or entertainment; the planning of decorations for the hall in the case of indoor gatherings; the preparation of slogan placards to be hung on the walls or carried in the parade. Success in the planning of these matters requires imagination, a sense of dramatization necessary for effective mass appeal. In the recruitment of an audience, every available channel of eye and ear must be put to work within as large a circle of persons as possible: not only must the party be aroused to action down to the last member of every unit, but also the affiliated organizations must be stimulated into participation.

If the attendance is poor, if persons are sparsely scattered through a large hall or the " monster parade " dwindles in fact to a straggling few, the occasion has been lost at the outset. If the attendance is good, the success or failure of the affair rests upon the effectiveness of the program: the speakers, the ceremony, the color, the entire staging of the dramatic performance.

Demonstrations are very important items in the program of mass mobilization planned by the Communist Party. Yet for many years the party showed little skill in the handling of mass gatherings. Accounts of party demonstrations of pre-depression years showed attendance to be small and mostly composed of the " old reliables " of the Chicago radical movement. With the unrest which developed as the depression set in, the party was faced with the challenge of making this unrest articulate through the channel of mass demonstration. Favorable conditions for the realization of what had long been nothing more than the day-dream of organizing the American proletariat were at last at hand.

The Communist Party began by organizing many indoor meetings. This was a continued application of the type of gathering which had been prevalent for years. These occasions, like the issues presented, were more or less stereotyped, and also rather unattractive. There was no flare, no color, no imagination in the appeals made. In these meetings serious and intense pleas for organization determined the atmosphere.

During the first depression year the Communists were greatly handicapped in using the channel of mass demonstration by the restrictive measures taken by the police. Increased pressure from radical elements was anticipated when the Industrial Squad, popularly termed the " Red Squad," was created in the latter part of 1929.[2] From its date of organization the squad attended public radical meetings of any size or importance. During 1930, however, the squad attended a larger percentage of the Communist meetings held than it did in subsequent years. It also took more aggressive measures to thwart plans for the organization of public unrest. This attitude was part of the temper which sought to eliminate from the focus of public attention all facts pointing to the existence of a serious unemployment crisis.

As a means of checking Communist attempts to organize the general unrest into demonstrations, the Industrial Squad raided the headquarters of the Communist Party and its affiliated organizations, prevented the handing out of leaflets by arresting those distributing them, and broke up several indoor meetings where demonstrations were being planned. Thus a meeting held at Musicians' Hall at 777 West Adams Street for the purpose of organizing a huge unemployment march on the City Hall was broken up by the squad, who made 146 arrests, charging those taken into custody with " inciting to riot " and " disorderly conduct."

The Communist reaction to these aggressive police tactics was direct and outspoken. At indoor meetings police were requested to leave. On one occasion, on August 12, 1930, at a meeting in an Italian neighborhood, 900 South Paulina Street, not only were police asked to leave, but a resolution was drawn up and voted that the squad, if not acquiescing in

[2] The " radical bureau " of the Chicago Police Department which had been functioning prior to 1919 was abolished during that year and did not again operate until 1929, when it was reorganized as the Industrial Squad.

OT AT HUMBOLDT PARK RELIEF STATION, MARCH 11, 1932

RIOT IN FRONT OF THE JAPANESE CONSULATE, MARCH 12, 1932

the request, be forcibly ousted from the hall. Whereupon the police left, returning soon with reinforcements from the 23rd Street Station.

If indoor demonstrations met with difficulty, the few attempts at outdoor gatherings during 1930 met with outright failure. Thus the attempted outdoor meetings at Union Park on July 4, at Belmont and Wilton Streets on August 9, and at 33rd and Dearborn Streets on September 8 were all put down by the police authorities before there was time to make a public showing. The police sometimes used force in dispersing the crowds, and the tactic of mass arrest was frequently applied. The extent and type of violence used on these occasions is difficult to reconstruct, even from written accounts. Regarding a march of jobless men to the City Hall on November 24, 1930, demanding that immediate relief measures be taken, the *Daily Worker* reported: [3]

" The police were very brutal, hurling men and women alike down the stairs and beating them over the heads and faces with their sticks. One Negro worker was brutally beaten."

Wrote the *New York Times:* [4]

" Police ejected the demonstrators without much disturbance."

Whatever may have been the degree of coercion used, with one exception every attempted outdoor demonstration during 1930 was cut short. The single exception was a Communist funeral procession. On September 10, funeral services were held for Lee Mason, a Negro Communist and party candidate for Congress. The services were held at Odd Fellows' Hall, a Communist center at 3335 South State Street, followed by a funeral procession. Although leaflets had been distributed stating that Mason had died as a result of " police brutality," according to official figures less than one hundred persons

---

[3] *Daily Worker,* December 4, 1930, p. 4.
[4] *New York Times,* November 25, 1930, p. 5, column 2.

joined the funeral march. The idea of utilizing the funeral permit, however, was not forgotten, and it was in burying the dead of the eviction riot of August 3 that the Communists held their first successful parade in depression Chicago.

During the first half of 1931 the repressive police measures continued to cripple efforts of the Communists to use the channel of demonstrations. The elaborate instructions for the organization of masses on such occasions and the development of techniques for coping with police interference failed to operate in the face of police methods of choking demonstration plans through timely raids on headquarters, interference with meetings at which plans were being formulated, and confiscation of literature. In cases where mass demonstrations almost materialized, as on July 4 at Union Park, police tactics of mass arrest and violence cut short these potentially successful occasions.

It was in the face of this rigid pressure upon mass activity that the spontaneous demonstration developed. This type of demonstration sprang up first in connection with evictions. During the last part of 1930 the Unemployed Councils had established headquarters in many of the poorer sections of the city. These meeting-halls served as clubhouses where jobless men tired of tramping the streets in search of work came to rest and talk rather than face the trying tensions of the home. These men, establishing mutual relations of identification on the basis of their common misfortune, began to act together to prevent evictions. The demonstrations were entirely unplanned and could not be throttled at the source because the men themselves never knew in advance when or where they would next demonstrate. Someone might come into the hall and tell of a person blocks away who was at that moment being evicted. Their indignation aroused, the men would march in a group down the street, adding the sympathetic and the curious to their number as they marched, until, by the time they reached the scene of the eviction, the crowd would have grown in size and temper. The furniture of the unfortunate family would be replaced and the crowd, delighted with its success, would disperse gradually, in small groups.

The early relief-station demonstrations were of the same spontaneous nature. Hearing that some family had been refused relief or that some particularly needy case was being denied immediate attention, groups would gather and march on the relief stations, demanding action. Social workers in many of the offices, having intimate knowledge of the misery behind such demands, hesitated to call the police. The demands in many instances seemed justified, and the inadequacy of the relief administration — enormous case loads of four or five hundred families carried by a single worker — was often responsible for the situations which elicited protest. Hence at first the relief offices met the demands of the demonstrators, giving Mrs. Jones the food basket which she should have had a week earlier. With success, demonstrations of this sort increased in number and size. The relief stations found themselves unable to deal with this type of mass pressure. For example, on the afternoon of August 31, 1931, a group of 400 persons began to march on the United Charities offices located at 4500 South Prairie Avenue. By the time they reached the relief station, the number had grown to fifteen or sixteen hundred. A speaker addressed them in front of the station, and the tension grew so high that when Joel Hunter, Chief Administrator of the Charities, asked for the selection of a committee to present the grievances of the crowd, there was a move to storm the station. A police squad arrived, and a general riot ensued.

The success of these early eviction and relief demonstrations, made possible by their unpredictability, developed a sense of collective strength in the poorer neighborhoods where such events were most common. As the news of these collective victories spread, families began to bring their grievances, particularly relief and eviction difficulties, to the attention of the neighborhood Unemployed Councils. Thus through the medium of mass demonstration the unemployed committees became the private army of the unemployed.

Spontaneous outbreaks grew in size and frequency, and through them the accumulated tensions and affects resulting from economic deprivation and from newspaper neglect or criticism and police repression became " collectivized." Police forces were strengthened in an effort to continue the general repressive policy, but repression proved impossible because of the nature of these occurrences. After several critical clashes, the police chose a simpler alternative: instead of discouraging and interfering with planned demonstrations, they chose to allow them, requiring only that a permit be obtained for outside events, as was customary in the case of any group or organization desiring public meeting privileges. In this way the rising insecurities could be led into channels which were at once more harmless and more amenable to control.

This policy necessitated a further centralization of responsibility for the policing of Communist events. The arrest records of radicals had begun to be centrally reported to the Industrial Squad as of the 1st of January 1931. Now, about the middle of the second year of the depression, Lieutenant Mills, in charge of the Industrial Squad, was given the additional responsibility of recommending to the Commissioner of Police whether each permit request received should be issued or refused. The Industrial Squad Lieutenant made such recommendations only after investigating the site or the line of march proposed. If permits were granted, he then designated to the appropriate police district the specific extra detail which was held to be necessary to cope with each situation.

The release of general police pressure allowed the Communist Party fuller rein in the use of the channel of demonstration. At the same time it placed them under a more rigorous control, since Communist policy demanded that application for a permit be made in each case so that the demonstration could not be attacked as " illegal." By this means, if by no other, the police were informed of all planned events and could apply preventive methods which had previously been more difficult to use. The fact that general repression had been removed also induced the Communist Party to plan more of their demonstrations in advance, and the police were able, even if permits were not required, as in the case of indoor events, to anticipate these occasions by the leaflets circulated, copies of which readily found their way into police hands. The whole arrangement tended to put the relation between the police and the Communist Party on a more " organized " basis, allowing for peaceful adjustments in some situations and affording a legal justification for police violence in other instances — namely, those of " illegal " demonstration.

The first event of any size occurring under the new policy was a parade and demonstration organized by the Young Communist League in honor of National Youth Day, September 8, 1931. A permit was granted for a parade starting at 14th and Loomis Streets, which, following a devious route, ended at 19th and Allport, where an open-air meeting was held. The line of march was carefully patrolled by fifty-five uniformed police, in addition to the Industrial Squad, as the twelve to fifteen hundred people paraded, some carrying banners reading " Against Bosses War " and " Bread for the Children of Unemployed Workers."

The Communists adapted themselves to the new type of control in several ways. First of all, they took advantage of the new freedom by demonstrating more frequently. The number of demonstrations increased from 408 in 1931 to 566 in 1932, an increase larger than that found in other channels of propaganda during that year. Second, the change in policy marked a new period in the development of the technique of demonstration in Chicago. The possibility of holding more demonstrations with less police interference gave opportunity for the development of skill in the dramatization of mass events. The contents of the demonstrations held became more varied: double and triple parades were held, and combinations of parades with other forms of demonstration were worked out.

The legalization of the mass demonstration did not lessen the amount of police control of Communist activities, however, but made possible a preventive type of control. The police could forbid demonstrations when tensions were high or when the location or the issue seemed dangerous, could modify the place or time, and could by virtue of advance notification thwart at the point of assembly a situation which developed in defiance of the regulations. The Communists found that permits were frequently refused. Reasons for refusal were usually stated by the police. Confronted by this policy, the Communists remained inclined to look upon demonstration as a right rather than a privilege. For some time the Communist Party ignored refusals for demonstrations and proceeded to hold meetings despite the fact that police interference was inevitable. The tactics of mass arrest and the application of clubs and rubber hose, which had been used by the police in 1930, were continued for the purpose of preventing demonstrators from assembling on such occasions. Thus the demonstration in front of the Polish Consulate, 844 Rush Street, on September 19, 1931, for which no permit had been obtained, was prevented by dispersing the crowds as quickly as they gathered and by the arrest of thirty demonstrators.

To defeat these tactics a completely new technique was initiated on January 11, 1932, when simultaneous demonstrations were held at all the relief stations of Chicago. This method of circumventing police control was in some sense analogous to the spontaneous demonstration. Passed along by word of mouth and made known in advance through branches of the various protest organizations, it was meant to be a " surprise attack." It was frequently tried in instances where it was anticipated that police would refuse to grant a permit. Thus on December 5, 1932, while the delegates of the Hunger March were presumably presenting their demands in Washington, D.C., unemployed demonstrations were called.

These were to be held in front of all relief stations and aldermen's homes throughout the city. Comparatively few materialized, and the police, who usually managed to receive such information beforehand, were prepared for any eventuality.

Although the simultaneous demonstration proved effective to a certain degree against police restrictions, the most direct defense against, and retaliation to, the repressive control exercised by the authorities was the use of violence by the demonstrators. When illegal demonstrations were held at which violence was expected, the demonstrators sometimes armed themselves with sticks and clubs and filled their pockets with stones. In case of a general riot these were used to battle the police. Certain Unemployed Council branches even organized Defense Corps to combat in demonstrations. The following document is an example of the type of instructions issued to such defense groups:

" Members of the Defense Corps, in action at demonstrations, must be divided into groups to surround the Communist speakers. In the past, the defense corps, when surrounding the speaker have faced the speaker instead of facing outward. This plan is changed and the defense corps members must hereafter always face outward as they surround the speaker as they can be more effective in combatting the action of police officers trying to get to the speaker.

" Members, familiar with the use of clubs and brickbats are to arm themselves with these and other blunt weapons but all members not experienced in the use of such weapons are not to attempt to arm themselves but use their fists instead and should try to take the clubs away from the police officers and use them on the police.

" Particular stress is laid on the fact that under no circumstances are clubs to be used in an ' individualistic or terroristic manner,' their sole use being for the defense of the speaker.

" Relative to the speaker, when the members are hoisting him to their shoulders, they should see that they are close to a wall or some background that would leave one side less to defend. Also, the defense members are instructed to divide themselves into two groups, one directly circling the speaker and the other circling around the speaker at a little distance, the objective being to work as many of the workers in between the two defense groups as possible to form a sort of cushion and force these workers into action. The moment the police make an attempt to break up the meeting and seize the speaker, the defense corps members are instructed to shout and yell, it being their duty to pick the proper slogan, such as ' Down with the Police,' and stimulate a general repetition of the slogan by the masses.

"Also if one group of police consisting of, say, six officers, makes an attack upon a speaker, a cordon of workers are supposed to stop the police group by getting them sandwiched in between defense corps members."

The technique of defense against the police at demonstrations was also frequently discussed at closed meetings of the Communist Party during this period. At a meeting of section organizers held during December 1931, the failure of a demonstration which had been broken up by six police officers was discussed and criticized. It was decided that a defense committee of ten under the direction of a " captain " would be organized prior to each demonstration to resist police attempts to break up the crowds. One of the organizers is reported to have said in closing:

"From now on we are going to demonstrate, permit or no, expecting to give them [the police] a battle. And I can assure you that in the future no six or seven police are going to be able to break up a parade of six hundred as they did yesterday." [5]

There were many instances of violence between police and demonstrators during the following year. On numerous occasions demonstrators appeared armed for defense. During

[5] This determination to demonstrate resulted in the following occurrence, reported by the Communists. Herbert Newton, a Negro organizer, was addressing a crowd in Ellis Park when police arrived and requested the group to disperse. The speaker hastily climbed a tree and continued to address the throng, urging them to remain. It was reported that Newton was silenced only after the fire department had supplied the police with several ladders with which to reach him as he was " swinging from limb to limb."

one demonstration before the Japanese Consulate at the Tribune Tower on March 12, 1932, shots were fired by one of the participants, Stephen Chuk, when the police charged on the crowd. The use of firearms by the police, however, was more common. Police " terror " and " brutality " were bitterly protested. Workers claimed that not only were clubs and rubber hose used on them when police were dispersing a meeting, but after arrest they were mercilessly beaten and maltreated. Particularly on the south side it was claimed that terroristic activities of the police were flagrant. On January 13, 1932 a resolution was drawn up demanding the " withdrawal of Stege and Barker and the Red Squad from the south side, where they are being used to brutally break down every protest of the workers against starvation." Special demonstrations were held against " police terror." For example, on September 21, 1932, demonstrators gathered in protest against " police brutality " at 46th and Gross Streets. No permit had been received for the occasion, and some of the demonstrators came armed with pieces of hardwood flooring with which to protect themselves. Sixteen were arrested on this occasion.

Since in general the police policy in Chicago with regard to radicals has consciously sought to limit the number of violent outbreaks between police and demonstrators, the police in some instances tried to accommodate themselves to the changing state of tension. This policy developed in 1931, and the first example was given on the occasion of the October Hunger March of that year. With the Youth Day success freshly in mind, a convention of the Unemployed Councils held in the People's Auditorium, 2457 West Chicago Avenue, on September 13, launched the organization of a Cook County Hunger March to take place in October. This march was to be a build-up in preparation for the state and national hunger marches planned for the following months. Representing 159 workers' organizations, 291 delegates assembled and a series of demands for relief of the unemployed were adopted. These demands were to be presented to the County Board of Commissioners on Saturday, October 31, and their presentation was to be reinforced by a Hunger March parade past the Commissioner's office. A letter was sent to the Police Commissioner's office stating that a committee would be at his office on September 30 at 11.00 a.m. and that they would like to have him consider the proposed line of march so that a proper permit could be obtained. The line of march requested was not granted, but instead of giving a flat refusal to a demonstration which had been in the process of planning for two months and which they knew would be held in spite of police orders to the contrary, the police redefined the line of march and the party agreed to compromise. No parade went past the City Hall on October 31, but two parades, one starting at Damen and North Avenues, the other at Canal and Monroe, both emptied into Union Park, where the mass demonstration was held. Over two hundred uniformed police, eight of whom were mounted patrolmen, watched the fifteen hundred to two thousand marchers [6] to see that no last-minute shifts were made in the routing of the parade and that no trouble broke out. A precautionary detail was also stationed at the City Hall.

Although the Communists showed themselves willing to accept what they considered to be reasonable compromises offered by the police, in many instances both parties were adamant and there was little room for peaceable adjustment. Permits for certain types of demonstrations were constantly refused, so that within a short time the Communists learned correctly to predict police response in such cases. Thus, for example, permits for demonstrations before consulates of foreign nations were never granted, as they were considered an insult to the nation involved. Several times during 1931 and 1932 no permits were requested when such affairs were planned. Violence usually resulted on such occasions. Later, when party policy became more legalistic and tension was less high, requests for permits in the case of consulate demon-

[6] These are official figures. The *Daily Worker*, on November 2, 1931, estimated 11,000 marchers.

strations were entered as a matter of form, even though it was well understood in advance that they would not be granted and that the demonstrations would be held in spite of police refusal of permit.

It was likewise a police tactic to deny permits for demonstrations planned for the scene where a recent riot had occurred. For example, on July 20, 1932 a clash took place at 1701 String Street. The account of this event submitted by the Chicago Civil Liberties Committee was as follows:

" No permit had been issued. Handbills had been distributed in advance. Toward 11:00 a.m. a fair-sized crowd had congregated. Speeches were made and a delegation of about 12 men and women was selected and approved by the crowd. This delegation was to present the written demands of the group to the supervisor of the relief station. A number of uniformed police were at hand but made no attempt to interfere with the meeting. The delegation crossed the street to the relief station. However, the police entered the station before they got there and closed and locked the door. For a few moments the delegation stood at the door and calmly requested that it be admitted, then these requests turned to threats. People began to pound the door. A glass in the window of a door was broken. At about this time the police reinforcements arrived. They demanded of the crowd that it cross back to the other side of the street. The crowd did so without offering any resistance. Then members of the industrial squad told the crowd to disperse. The crowd did so. No reports of physical injury sustained by police or others on the scene of the disturbance have come to the attention of the committee. Four witnesses interviewed state that they believe there were no casualties. However, two of those arrested reported that they were beaten by members of the Industrial Squad after they had been arrested."

The week following this event a mimeographed notice was issued announcing a demonstration to be held in the same place. As was frequently the case during that time, the call to demonstrate was circulated before a permit had been issued. The permit was flatly refused on the grounds that such an assemblage so shortly after the "rioting" of July 20 would probably be an occasion for another disturbance. The Communists, however, persisted in attempting to hold meetings at 1701 String Street. Special resolutions were passed requesting permits and demanding a withdrawal of "police interference" in demonstrating activities. The police declined to make any change in their policy, and riots at this spot continued. During one demonstration in October 1932 Joseph Sposob, one of the demonstrators, was shot and killed by the police. The police continued to deny demonstration at this spot for over a year after this shooting occurred.

Permits for relief demonstrations were granted with the understanding that a small number of persons be selected to present the demands and resolutions of the demonstrators to the officials at the relief station. The officials of the various relief organizations in Chicago expressed their willingness to give these groups opportunity to express themselves. Occasionally, however, committees of unemployed, doubting the promises of relief supervisors or questioning decisions made by them, planted themselves at the station, declaring that they would remain until their demands were met. The relief stations frequently called on the police to eject these "sit-down" committees.[7]

The rule of committee presentation of grievances was enforced with increasing rigor throughout 1932. Finally relief authorities, claiming that the pressure of organized groups was so great that it slowed up work at the stations, informed the police authorities that a central complaint office would be established in the downtown district where committees from unemployed organizations could enter their complaints. This Public Relations Bureau was set up at 310 West Madison Street, and it was announced that, as of January 1, 1933, no complaints

[7] It was the policy of the public relief administration to call on the police only when it was believed that life or property was in danger, or when the presence of individuals or groups seriously crippled the work of the service.

would be received from committees at the outlying relief stations themselves.

This ban placed upon relief-station demonstrations was met with bitter denunciations from the Communists. Demonstrations were held at the relief stations in defiance of the new ruling, demanding recognition of the committees of the unemployed. The ban was strictly reinforced by police measures, however, and several violent outbreaks between the police and the unemployed occurred. On January 18, several persons were wounded in a riot at the Lawndale relief station at 2133 South Kedzie Street. The demonstrators retaliated to police clubbing by hurling rocks and stones, and four workers were hurt by buckshot fired by one of the patrolmen. Another riot occurred at the Humboldt relief station. After a few outbreaks the police modified the policy of flatly refusing permits for relief-station demonstrations and instead offered an alternative location near by. Thus a request to demonstrate on January 23 at the Flop House at 89th and Strand Streets was granted, provided that the meeting would be held instead at Mackinaw Avenue near 90th Street. A request for a demonstration at the relief station at 109th Street and Michigan was granted provided the scene of the demonstration be changed to 109th Street east of Indiana Avenue.[8] As has been shown, this tactic of shifting the point of demonstration or the routing of a parade had been employed as early as 1931, and it was applied with increasing frequency by the police during 1933 and 1934.

The cutting off of the possibility for demonstration at the relief stations was a great blow to the Unemployed Councils. Such demonstrations had been a convincing and dramatic method of illustrating to the community the importance of collective pressure. With the complaint office set up at a cen-

[8] Sometimes permits were granted with specific stipulations appended referring to details other than the location. Thus the permit for a demonstration on the corner of 16th and String Streets, June 30, 1933, which carried the provision that no delegation be allowed to go to the relief station at 1701 String Street.

tral point, all negotiations were carried forward in a routinized manner without the reinforcement of mass demonstration, and the Unemployed Councils were decidedly limited in their appeal.

It was at this time that changing conditions necessitated a revision of policy on the part of Communist organizations. Although unemployed workers had previously been willing to demonstrate even in situations where violence was inevitable, after a few demonstrations protesting the ban had met with rigorous police offensive, leaders of protest groups found they were no longer able to arouse this form of " illegal " activity. The advent of the new administration in Washington, with its many reassurances to disaffected groups, had lowered the level of insecurity and made the mobilization of mass protest activity increasingly difficult.

Adapting to the shifting levels of tension, Communist groups held fewer illegal demonstrations. For example, when the issue required protest to the consul of a foreign nation, the demonstration was often called for some location permitted by the police, rather than in front of the consulate. Thus when the American League Against War and Fascism issued the call for a protest against the suppression of Socialist and Communist risings in Vienna in February 1934, the gathering was held under permit at the Congress Plaza instead of at the Austrian Consulate. A delegation elected at the beginning of the meeting was sent to the Austrian Consul and reported back before the gathering had dispersed.

The Communist Party itself, however, was slower to refrain from illegal demonstrations, than some of its affiliated groups. As a result of their long experience, the police had perfected several techniques for preventing unauthorized demonstrations. Certain of these which were important during the period in which the levels of tension and affect were high have already been discussed. During 1933 and 1934, when, as an outcome of changes in the environment, these levels were considerably diminished, other less rigorous techniques for preventing assembly came to the foreground. One of the most common of these was the "keep moving" method, whereby members of a police detail were scattered at intervals within a block or two of the spot where the unpermitted demonstration was to occur, and as people began to assemble, told all "loiterers" to "keep moving." Any who resisted were taken into custody. Very often merely temporary arrests were made on such occasions, and after the demonstration had been prevented, such people were released without being booked. Arresting the leaders, who were usually well known to the squad, as soon as they appeared at the scene of the demonstration was another common tactic used to great effect.

The Communist Party attempted to counteract these police tactics at the unpermitted demonstrations by various tactics planned in advance. This defense always included the risk of relevant information reaching the ear of the police through spies or "stool-pigeons" active in party ranks. As early as 1932, however, demonstrators came to the designated place in small groups, thus hoping to increase their ability to resist police efforts to prevent assembly. A contrast to this tactic was used in 1934 when great numbers assembled a few blocks away and approached the scene simultaneously (*en masse*) from several directions. This tactic was attempted in a demonstration before the German Consulate in July 1934, but was unsuccessful because the police broke up the congregated groups before they had time to march on the Consulate.

On the whole, however, the trend after January 1933 was to move away from outright defiance of police orders and toward the use of legal methods for combating police refusals of permit. During 1933 and 1934 police refusals to issue demonstration permits were fought mainly through the mobilization of public sentiment in the name of civil liberties. The constitutional right of demonstration was stressed. For example, a request for a permit which it was anticipated would be refused because a riot had previously occurred at the place indicated read as follows:

To Police Commissioner Allman:

Greetings:

We, the undersigned hereby support the Mid City District Unemployed Councils in requesting that a permit be granted for a demonstration and street meeting on Friday, June 30th, 1933, at 1 p.m. at 1701 String Street.

Which is also our constitutional right inasmuch as the conditions of the workers are unbearable in this territory and warrant protest.

The Communists were persistent in their demands upon police authorities. The Commissioner of Police and the Mayor of the city were deluged by resolutions, letters, and telegrams, and city officials were harassed by telephone campaigns demanding that Communist groups be allowed their "constitutional rights" in the form of permits for this or that occasion. A permit for demonstration once refused might be six or eight times requested over a period of several weeks or months amid as extensive and intensive a protest as could be organized. Although concessions were rarely, if ever, made by the police in such instances, the policy of protest continued. Communist groups even sought to line up other political groups in their favor. Thus Alderman Sheldon Govier of the 9th Ward on July 25, 1933 received the following request:

"We the Unemployed of the Unemployed Councils in the 9th Ward ask you as our Ward Alderman to secure a permit to have the right to hold a demonstration at our relief station located at 50 East 109th Street to demand the right to live."

Instances in which permits were granted but the line of march had been revised by the police were similarly protested. For example, the United Front May Day Conference of Roseland protested against the route assigned in the following resolution:

Resolution of Protest

Whereas, we, the duly elected delegation of the United Front May Day Conference of Roseland and surrounding territories representing 38 various organizations, protest the route given us under your permit No. 14690 under the date of April 17th, 1933.

We demand that the route we originally asked for be granted which is as follows: On State Street from 108th Place to 111th Street, then east on 111th Street to Michigan Avenue, and south on Michigan Avenue to Kensington Avenue, because we feel that our constitutional rights are being violated by your refusal to our request of the above route.

During 1933, 55 permits for demonstration were refused Communist organizations by the police. In 28 instances refusal was stated to be due to traffic considerations, and in 14 instances to the fact that riots had previously occurred on the sites requested. In 1934, 50 permits were refused, 26 of these for reasons of traffic management.[9] Many new rules were developed restricting more than before the circumstances under which demonstrations were allowed. For example, permits were not granted when complaints had been received from citizens regarding earlier Communist demonstrations held in their locality; nor were permits granted in the neighborhood of factories where strikes were occurring or where there was danger of industrial unrest for other reasons. Demonstrations were likewise forbidden in front of public institutions, or on corners where a demonstration had already been held less than a week before. The expectation of violence having been practically removed from demonstrations, it was possible for the police to make and enforce rules regarding demonstrating practices which would at an earlier time have led to bloodshed.

[9] In requesting permit for a May Day parade through Chicago's Loop, Secretary Newhoff of the International Labor Defense thought to put force behind his request by stating that he represented 220 organizations and that more than 50,000 Chicago workers would march in the parade. Replying that he had no reason to disbelieve this statement, Lieutenant Mills pointed out that it takes seven minutes for every 1,000 marchers in close mass formation to pass a given point, and that it would be a physical impossibility to tie up the Loop for five hours and fifty minutes, and that thus the permit could not be granted for reason of traffic considerations.

The technique of advertising and staging demonstrations developed rapidly in 1933 and 1934 as less tension became associated with the act itself. Parades of colorful signboards on trucks were sometimes used to advertise coming events. Special build-ups, analogous to " pep-meetings," were held prior to important demonstrations in order to assure good attendance. In addition to the general call to demonstrate, special leaflets were often addressed to the workers of particular factories, thus localizing the importance of the occasion.

The actual staging of the demonstration was given more careful thought. Attempts were made in many instances to secure a permit for a line of march in working-class sections of the city, so that the occasion might become a topic of discussion among such groups. On several occasions when parades were planned, a crew of men were sent out the night before to put up posters along the line of march and paint slogans against whitewashed fences and walls. As tension diminished, programs for each occasion were carefully planned to hold the attention of those in attendance. A city-wide English-singing chorus was organized (October 1933) to sing at mass meetings, thereby to popularize the songs of the Left movement. In 1931 and 1932 workers had paraded without rehearsal; the spirit rather than the form of protest had been uppermost. In 1933 and 1934, however, many more organizations participated in a single parade, and there was a complex division of responsibility, every detail being worked out in advance by a joint committee. Workers marched eight abreast according to organization and filed through the streets in an orderly and impressive manner.

This increased degree of organization in the staging of demonstrations and parades was accompanied — as we remarked above — by an increased elaborateness of the events themselves. In some cases parades starting in three different sections of the city (west, north, and south) converged just west of Chicago's Loop and poured through Randolph Street to demonstrate in Grant Park on the lake front. On another occasion, simultaneous open-air meetings were held at four or five corners in a single section of the city, a parade finally joining the points of demonstration. These are two of the many combinations made in later years.

CHAPTER X

Representative Demonstrations

THE PREVIOUS chapter outlined the technique of demonstration developed by Communist organizations. The present chapter presents accounts of particular demonstrations. The demonstrations here summarized are at once important in themselves and representative of many others.

1927: Sacco-Vanzetti Demonstrations

The Sacco-Vanzetti mass demonstrations held in Chicago during the year when agitation regarding this case was at its height are among the best demonstrations held during the few years preceding the depression.

The Sacco-Vanzetti case had for six years attracted worldwide attention. Efforts had been made by organizations in the United States and abroad to obtain the liberation of the defendants by pardon or by setting aside the findings of the jury which had convicted them of murder. The two Italians, one a worker in a shoe factory at Stoughton, Massachusetts, the other a fish trader at Plymouth, were convicted in 1921 for the murder of a paymaster at a shoe factory in Braintree, Massachusetts. The labor groups contended that the defendants had been clearly proved not guilty of the crime, but had been convicted because of prejudice against them as reputed "radicals." A "Sacco-Vanzetti Defense Committee" was organized, and a defense fund started which eventually amounted to several hundred thousand dollars. Propaganda spread to foreign countries, and the case became an internationally important labor issue. Indeed, one of the first to mobilize agitation had been a labor organization in Milan, Italy.

On August 3, 1927 the report of the Special Committee, which had been appointed by the Governor of Massachusetts to make an investigation of the case, was made public. The last hope for a pardon for Sacco and Vanzetti was blasted; electrocution had been set for August 22.

During the first three weeks of August sentiment in Chicago ran high. Many meetings were held in protest and these were regularly attended by the police. On August 9 about 4,000 people were present at Carmens' Hall, at Van Buren Street and Ashland Avenue. The meeting proceeded peacefully, but the audience was tense, over-responsive, restless. As the meeting closed, a young Italian woman named Aurora d'Angelo sprang to the stage and began to address a highly excited appeal to the audience. The police rushed to the stage and forcibly escorted her from the hall. The overwrought crowd followed into the streets and gathered about her. Climbing onto a parked automobile, she continued to address them. The police attempted to disperse the crowd, but unsuccessfully. Forming a parade with the young Italian woman in their midst, the demonstrators marched down Van Buren Street. Once more the police interceded, breaking up the marching ranks and insisting that the groups move on their way. There was no violence, only a determined stubbornness on the part of the police and an unquenchable enthusiasm on the part of the crowd.

Days passed, and as the date set for the execution of Sacco and Vanzetti drew near, the police sought to prevent any mass demonstration on the part of the Communists. Headquarters of the Sacco-Vanzetti Defense Committee at 23 South Lincoln Street were closely watched. In this way the police obtained information regarding plans for meetings. As soon as a hall or auditorium for the demonstration had been decided on, the police approached the owner or agent and warned him against renting the hall. Hanging posters or distributing literature regarding the case was forbidden.

Despite great efforts made by the police to avert all collective protest regarding this highly charged issue, a leaflet was distributed giving the call to a demonstration to be held on Friday, August 19, at 8 p.m. at the Ashland Auditorium.

The officials of the Auditorium were visited by the police. The agent of the building explained that although the Defense Committee had requested to rent the hall for the demonstration, it had not yet been rented. Since the leaflets had already been distributed, however, it was requested that the police department concentrate ample forces.

On August 19 the neighborhood of the Ashland Auditorium was heavily policed. The crowds were dispersed as quickly as they gathered. International Labor Defense leaders mingled among the crowds, passing out leaflets urging a strike on August 22, the execution date. Although there were no serious clashes with the police, Aurora d'Angelo and other leaders were arrested and the leaflets confiscated by the police.

After the execution tension ran even higher, particularly in Italian communities of Chicago. The headquarters of the Defense Committee were draped in black and red bunting in mourning for Sacco and Vanzetti. Vainly the Communists tried to obtain a hall so that Luggie, the sister of Vanzetti, and Mrs. Rose Sacco could speak. A small committee was formed to see the Superintendent of Police regarding the holding of a meeting; if this measure failed, the plan was to see Mayor Thompson himself. The committee calling on the Superintendent of Police were informed that they would be permitted to hold the meeting only after the burial of Sacco and Vanzetti.

A memorial meeting was finally held, but only after a lapse of time which allowed the tension of the community to be dissipated. Subsequent meetings were also held by the committee, but the psychological moment for mass demonstration had been lost, owing to the tactics of the police.

1930: *Unemployment Demonstration*

The second month of the first year of depression in the United States was the date set by the Communist International for a world-wide demonstration against unemployment. It was the first attempt to organize a large-scale protest since the stock-market crash which had presaged the downward trend in business. The rumbling of the crash could still be heard beneath the cheerful chatter of a press which promised quick recovery and happy days.

The demonstration was originally set for February 26. A week or two before this date, however, the Executive Committee of the Communist International in Moscow sent the following cable to the Executive Committee of the Communist Party in America, with headquarters in New York:

THE EXECUTIVE COMMITTEE OF THE COMMUNIST INTERNATIONAL HAS DECIDED TO POSTPONE THE INTERNATIONAL DAY FOR STRUGGLE AGAINST UNEMPLOYMENT THE DATE PREVIOUSLY DECIDED UPON WAS FEBRUARY 26TH.

TO ENABLE ALL PARTIES TO THOROUGHLY PREPARE FOR REAL DEMONSTRATIONS AND TO CARRY ON A BROADER PREPARATION CAMPAIGN THE ECCI HAS DECIDED TO POSTPONE IT UNTIL MARCH 6TH.

THE COMMUNIST PARTY OF AMERICA MUST UTILIZE THE ADDITIONAL EIGHT DAYS FOR A MOST ENERGETIC CAMPAIGN AND ORGANIZATIONAL PREPARATIONS, SO THAT GREAT MASSES WILL BE MOBILIZED.

THE COMMITTEES OF ACTION MUST BE ORGANIZED EVERYWHERE TO GUARANTEE THE BEST CO-OPERATION BETWEEN THE EMPLOYED AND UNEMPLOYED WORKERS.

The message continued by pointing out that the party must give every assistance to the Trade Union Unity League in organizing Unemployed Councils. It directed that demonstrations must be held outside the factories, and small meetings of every character among the unemployed themselves in leading up to the mass demonstration of March 6. Employed workers, it declared, must strike on the day of the demonstration, so that employed and unemployed might demonstrate side by side. It then continued:

THE DEMONSTRATION MUST BE THOROUGHLY PLANNED AND PRE-PARED AND EVERY MEMBER MUST KNOW HIS DUTY AND PLACE.

DEFENSE OF THIS DEMONSTRATION AGAINST POLICE ATTACK MUST BE WELL ORGANIZED AND IN EVERY INDUSTRIAL CITY THERE MUST BE AN AGGRESSIVE MASS DEMONSTRATION OF THE UNEMPLOYED.

WORK OR WAGES MUST BE OUR DEMAND, AND A TREMENDOUS MASS PROTEST MUST BE ORGANIZED AGAINST THE CAPITALISTIC STATE DEMAND-ING INSURANCE AND RELIEF TO BE UNDER THE DIRECT CONTROL OF THE WORKERS THEMSELVES.

The cable closed with the following command:

FORWARD IN MASS ACTION AGAINST UNEMPLOYMENT DEMONSTRATE AND STRIKE ORGANIZE LARGE MASS MEETINGS OF THE EMPLOYED AND UNEMPLOYED WORKERS ON MARCH 6TH.

The Communist Party in the United States moved into action, as the first opportunity to gear itself for large-scale action seemed at hand. Instructions began to flow from the Central Committee of the party, which were transmitted through the districts to the sections, and through the sections to the life-cells of the party, the street and shop units.

The Agitprop Department of the Eighth District in Chicago issued instructions similar to those released in every district of the country. The final set of instructions released one week prior to the event read in part as follows:

" Tasks that must be carried through this week.

a. We are printing 200,000 leaflets.

b. We are printing 50,000 stickers.

c. We are printing 50,000 shop papers.

" 1. All of this literature must be distributed and posters stuck up all over the city. This requires the participation of every Party member.

" 2. Every comrade must, during this week, report daily to the place that is assigned for distribution or any other tasks that may be assigned.

" 3. Comrades who are unemployed are to report early in the morning for shop gate meetings.

" 4. Sections will arrange before each factory gate, one meeting in the morning at the employment office and one noon day meeting for the workers in the Plant.

" 5. Every Street Nucleus is to arrange at least one open air meeting during the week for the mobilization of the workers in the neighborhood.

" 6. The distribution will take place in an organized manner and therefore requires that all comrades carry out instructions."

It was at first reported in the press that the unemployment meeting would not be permitted because the authorities had been told that " the paraders have been asked to arm themselves with knives and blackjacks to attack the police." It was also rumored that thirteen men were coming from New York to kill the Deputy Police Commissioner and John P. Stege.[1]

Under the heading of " Discipline and Preparation," Communist Party directives warned:

" We must be prepared to guard ourselves against provocation of the Government. We have already seen for the past 2 weeks daily reports in the bosses' press about ' bomb plots,' etc. During the last few days, no doubt, efforts will be made to issue alarming statements. We must be prepared to expose these provocative actions and point out that the Communist Party does not believe in individual terror but in mass action of the working classes.

" Above all we must keep contact with the masses all through the demonstration, remaining on the front lines and leading them. Only then will we really be able to show that we as Communists are the leaders of the working classes."

The negotiations for permission to parade were carried on through a committee of the American Civil Liberties Union. Requests to parade past the City Hall were denied. The per-

[1] *New York Times,* March 6, 1930.

mit was granted for a parade on west-side streets with the stipulation that there be no interference with traffic or business and no violence. Flags, slogans, and other Communist insignia were likewise banned. From the beginning, however, the party anticipated that police would attempt to break up the demonstration, and instructions to the nuclei gave full directions for meeting police interference:

" As soon as the place for demonstration has been definitely fixed, the comrades in charge must make a careful study of the locale. All approaches to the place must be carefully noted. It is necessary to determine in advance in so far as possible, what the strategy and tactics of the police will be and arrangements made *to circumvent the police strategy.* Thus, it is necessary to provide for an approach from several different directions, so that if one section of the demonstration is attacked, another section can come forward from another direction. If the speakers' stand is demolished and one speaker is pulled down *another must be prepared to take his place in another section of the demonstration.* Each comrade who is to speak is to be surrounded by a considerable group of comrades who can lift him up on their shoulders and hold him while he speaks and at the same time *prevent the police from reaching him as long as possible.* Similarly, the comrades who carry the banners and placards must be *surrounded and protected,* a reserve of banners and placards must be provided for, so that when the police succeed in destroying one set, another set may be raised and exhibited.

" The comrades should be organized in detachments according to sections or units as the case may be. The section organizer or another responsible comrade must act as marshal for a detachment and a unit organizer or other responsible comrade as captain of each group. Each Party group, speakers, banner bearers, etc. must be provided from each detachment or group. Each Party group should serve as center for non-Party workers who participate individually or as organizations.

" *Liaison is very important.* Comrades should be especially selected in advance, to maintain contact between the leaders of the demonstration and leaders of the detachments and groups.

" The tactic of the police is to rush into the crowd with clubs drawn and to divide the workers into small groups whom they proceed to beat and arrest. Thus far our comrades have tended to give way before the onrush. If the demonstrants *will keep surging forward,* the police will *find themselves surrounded in a difficult position where our comrades can prevent them from using their clubs.* If divided, however, it is necessary that we know definitely our object and keep returning to it as often as necessary until the demonstration has been consummated.

"Often the police will try to scatter the mass by appearing to chase after someone. Our comrades thinking that workers are being attacked in that quarter run after the police and leave the main body of the demonstration to be handled by the remaining police. These and other tactics of the police can be *defeated* if our comrades are *disciplined* and have experience and leadership which does not permit of each comrade deciding for himself where and what to do.

"The greatest difficulty and number of casualties occur when the demonstration is apparently over. The tendency then is for the ranks to break and for groups to become isolated. This is taken advantage of by the police who then do most of the slugging. The return or retreat from the demonstration must be made in an organized and orderly manner. The leadership of the demonstration must select the proper time for such a retreat or return, and the liaison must inform all detachment and group leaders and all must undertake to move together. Here, as throughout, the need for a *trained workers' defense corps* becomes most clear. Such a corps would be able to cover the retreat, *engage the police,* surround the demonstrants and give them the necessary protection.

"During all the process of the demonstration, the comrades must be aware of the importance of singing, shouting slogans, booing, and otherwise engaging in activities which tend to maintain the morale of the mass. Here too the leaders must set the example.

"Time is an important element, the comrades must realize the importance of promptness. If Comrades come late, the demonstration can be broken up before it is started. The time for concluding must also be set and so far as possible adhered to. The latter is important in order to prevent a demoralized retreat."

The technique of demonstration was much too undeveloped at that time to make possible the application of any such elaborate set of instructions. Furthermore, the police were completely informed regarding all party directives and made plans accordingly. Despite the preparations for trouble which were made by both police and party, however, the parade was an orderly, uneventful affair. Close to four thousand people marched down Halsted and Lake Streets. A committee of fifteen, headed by Nels Kjar, presented a petition at Mayor Thompson's office. The demands were made in the form of Communist slogans of the day: " WORK OR WAGES," " A 35 HOUR WORKING WEEK," " RECOGNITION OF THE SOVIET UNION," " ABOLITION OF ALL VAGRANCY LAWS," and others.

The demonstration was successful as judged by the turn-out. But the enforcement of rigid police restrictions upon methods of dramatizing it meant that many potentialities in the situation could not be turned to full account by the Communist Party.

1931: Eviction Demonstration

On Monday afternoon, August 3, a crowd composed mostly of Negroes were gathered at the Washington Park forum listening to a speaker address them on the unemployment situation. He decried the jobless condition of the Negroes, the little that was being done for them in the way of relief, the hundreds of families who were evicted from their homes because of their inability to pay rent.

The gathering was typical of the groups which met at the Washington Park forum on sultry afternoons to listen to such speakers from the Unemployed Councils. The group consisted mainly of rather poorly dressed unemployed men come to hear their problems discussed, to learn what others thought would come of it all and what could be done to alleviate their situation. It was heartening for the unemployed man to be able to meet with others in a similar situation, to find solace in the realization that his was not an isolated trouble.

The speaker was telling of an eviction which was taking place that very afternoon. Rose Warrick, an unemployed Negro woman living a few blocks away, was being evicted from her home. With rising sympathy and indignation the crowd listened to the account of the woman's situation. When the question was raised, the crowd cheered its approval of the motion that the entire forum proceed to the site of the eviction and replace the furniture.

En masse the crowd began its march through the streets. Eviction demonstrations had become a commonplace in the Negro community, so as the march advanced, hundreds more joined the ranks. By the time the marchers drew near Dearborn Street, their number had grown to several thousand.

Meanwhile reports of the advance had reached the Wabash Avenue police station, where for several days an emergency squad of police had been stationed because of the increasing number of violent incidents occurring in the neighborhood. Several police hastened in the patrol wagon to the scene of the demonstration. As the crowd marched down Dearborn Street, some officers stepped out of the wagon and, arresting several of the men heading the marching column, left to secure reinforcements. It was but a few moments before their return. Two patrol wagons blocked the street ahead of the advancing crowds. Some twenty-five police under Lieutenant Hardy made an effort to disperse the steadily swelling crowds. Shouts of protest went up from the angry demonstrators even as many of their number began to retreat. The police drew revolvers and fired into the crowd. General confusion and tumult ensued. Thousands of terrified people scattered, rushing for their lives, tripping, stumbling, stepping on one another. Others fought, slugging with fists, hurling sticks and stones at the police. It was but a few minutes before the scene was cleared. The police had shoved twenty or more men into the patrol wagons. Three Negroes had been killed by the police gunfire; many demonstrators and bystanders, as well as three policemen, had been injured in the riot.

News of the eviction riot screamed in the headlines of the evening press. The realization of the extent of unrest in the Negro district threw Chicago into panic. The fact that the clash had taken place in a Negro neighborhood of the city aroused the double fear of Communist and race riots. Chicago police authorities ordered scores of squad cars to patrol the district, immediately dispersing crowds wherever they attempted to gather. One hundred police were held in reserve at the Wabash Avenue police station. It was reported at the time that several National Guard units were held in readiness for any violent outbreak. Mayor Cermak himself was away on a yachting trip at the time, but his secretary, State Senator Henry Sonnenschein, sent a stenographer to Washington Park to take down all orations delivered to the large Negro audiences which gathered there during the following week protesting the shooting of the three Negroes. These meetings were heavily policed. Tensions which for many months had been brewing had finally burst wide open. Unrest in the Negro community continued to increase.

The Communist Party, backing the Unemployed Councils, pushed on in its effort to organize the unrest uncovered by the events of August 3. A plea for " mass struggle against starvation and evictions " was made to the Negro population from soap-boxes on street corners as well as from the speakers' stand at the Washington Park forum. Fifty thousand copies of an appeal signed by District Eight of the Communist Party and addressed to "The Workers of Chicago " were distributed throughout the city, mostly in the south-side sections. The slogan printed across the head of the leaflet was: " DEMAND DEATH PENALTY FOR THE MURDERERS OF THE WORKERS."

The party interpreted the riot in the following words:

" This massacre of defenseless Negro and white workers who protested the eviction of the unemployed woman and put the furniture back must arouse the whole working class of Chicago and bring to the forefront the role of the police as the instrument of the bosses' suppression and murder of the workers. Not satisfied with killing 3 workers and wounding many others, tens of innocent workers have been arrested and thrown into jails. This massacre of workers in the streets of Chicago was preceded by a reign of terror on the part of the police against the workers in different parts of the city, who demonstrated against evictions and demanded immediate relief. . . . Acting Commissioner John H. Alcock declared the other day ' we are going to have serious trouble any day now perhaps.' This statement clearly indicates that the police were prepared for what happened on South Dearborn Street on Monday afternoon.

" This massacre of the workers in Chicago is a part of the attack of the boss class throughout the country. Striking miners in Pennsylvania, Ohio, are being shot by the coal and iron police; in Camp Hill, Alabama, Negro farmers [share croppers] have been attacked and killed because they too dared to organize themselves to fight for better conditions; nine Negro boys [Scottsboro case] are being held in Alabama waiting legal lynchings and the electric chair; a reign of terror prevails in Rhode Island; only yesterday in Southern Illinois meetings have been broken up and workers arrested because they dared to organize to fight against mass starvation. Bullets, clubs, jailing is the answer of the ruling capitalist class, the Republican, Democratic and Socialist Party administrations throughout the country for demands of the masses for bread or work. Wages are being cut and the army of the unemployed grows daily. There are more than half a million unemployed in Chicago, and more than Ten Million in the country, and the only answer the boss class and their government have to the demands of the workers is increased terror.

" Workers of Chicago have been attacked in the past, but never was the attack so open, so brutal as this murder of three workers by the Chicago police under the administration of the Democratic Mayor Cermak, who promised in the election campaign that he would solve the problem of unemployment."

This account was followed by the appeal of the Communist Party that the workers of Chicago unite under its leadership. Demands were presented, beginning with those specifically related to the occasion and leading up to general slogans current in party propaganda at the time:

" The Communist Party, the only political party of the working class, the Party that supports and leads every struggle of the employed and unemployed, fights for full rights of the Negroes, for self-determination of the Negro masses, calls upon the workers of Chicago to unite and demand:

"1) Arrest of the policemen and Lieutenant Hardy who shot the workers, demanding death penalty for the murderers.

"2) Release of all arrested workers.

"3) Right of the workers to defend themselves against the murderous attack of the police, gangsters, etc.

"4) Stop eviction of the unemployed.

"5) For immediate relief of the unemployed.

"6) For social insurance to the amount of $15. per week for the unemployed.

"7) For full rights of the Negroes.

"8) For right of the workers to organize and hold meetings."

The issue was made one of nation-wide importance. A plea for " solidarity " as an answer to the " Chicago massacre " was issued by the Central Committee of the Communist Party of America. This appeal, published on the front page of the *Daily Worker* of August 6, read:

TO ALL DISTRICT ORGANIZATIONS:

HOLD SOLIDARITY DEMONSTRATIONS AGAINST THE CHICAGO MASSACRE
OF OUR UNEMPLOYED COMRADES

The barbarous murder of our three class comrades by the Chicago bosses, Negro and white, must be answered by the sternest pledge of revolutionary solidarity and fighting strength; by the mobilization of large masses of Negro and white workers who must take the streets in tremendous solidarity demonstrations. The ultimate sacrifices of our three unemployed comrades must be the signal for the intensification of the unemployed movement. These demonstrations must mark the crossroads at which the millions of unemployed workers, under our leadership, must break the fetters of capitalist illusions (prosperity over the hill) and must forge in struggle a powerful mass unemployment movement to force the ruling class to grant immediate relief and unemployment insurance. . . .

It is the revolutionary duty of every district to hold immense solidarity demonstrations linking up the struggle of the unemployed in Chicago with the national and class oppression of the

Negro masses as exemplified in the Scottsboro and Camp Hill, Alabama cases; with the struggles of the miners against starvation, and with the struggles of the textile workers against wage-cuts and wretched working conditions.

Every available force must be mobilized for participation in these demonstrations!

CENTRAL COMMITTEE, CP, USA.

As a precaution against further outbreaks a temporary suspension of evictions was ordered and increased attention was given to the problem of relief resources. With the moratorium on court eviction orders, the fatal eviction demonstration was hailed as a victory by a Communist speaker at one of the huge open-air meetings held during the week of August 3:

"For the past ten weeks we have been fighting for just this thing, but not until this violent clash occurred have the city and county officials taken proper notice of the suffering caused among jobless families by landlords who put them out into the streets because they cannot pay their rent through no fault of their own. With the suspension of eviction orders, hundreds of poverty-stricken families, white and black, in all parts of the city are now relieved of the specter of being heartlessly shoved out into the street."

1931: Funeral Demonstration

The Unemployed Council planned that the three dead of the August 3 demonstration be given a mass funeral. It was decided that the bodies should lie in state at Odd Fellows' Hall, a Negro Communist center, at 3335 South State Street, so as " to give the outraged masses an opportunity to view the bodies." In the center of the back wall of the stage on which the bodies were to lie in state was a huge photograph of Lenin, a spotlight focused upon it. On either side of the platform were large paintings of a white and a Negro worker, hand in hand, and under these were inscribed the slogan: " NEGRO AND WHITE WORKERS, UNITE TOGETHER! " The stage itself was crowded with floral pieces furnished by numerous organizations affiliated with the Communist Party. The largest wreath, a horseshoe made with red flowers, was sent by the Young Communist League. All together there were about forty floral pieces. The revolutionary color, in a profusion of red flowers and red flags and bunting, dominated the scene. On the side walls of the hall were enormous pictures of upraised fists and arms of workers. The colored lights played upon these paintings and gave them a natural glow.

Into this impressive setting the bodies of Abe Gray and John O'Neal were moved. The caskets, gray with silver mountings, were moved to the hall on the evening of August 6. A committee of twenty people had been appointed to receive and guard the bodies. Throughout the evening on either side of the two bodies, three of the committee stood at attention. From early in the evening the hall was crowded with hundreds of curious and sympathetic people, Negro and white. Many stood talking for hours about the riot, eyewitness accounts were related, and innumerable versions of the shootings were told and retold. The first of the bodies was brought to the hall about eight-thirty. By one-thirty, when the hall was closed, approximately twelve thousand people had filed past the coffins. Men were left to guard the bodies during the night.

The ten Negroes remaining with the bodies sat up for a long while discussing the riot. Several of them had been present and one of them complimented " the old man," one of the dead, on how brave he had been. " He had been wounded three times, but he took the revolver away from the copper who was doing the shooting and then used the two remaining bullets on another copper." It was at this moment, they agreed, that the Cadillac squad had arrived and a bunch of " dicks " had jumped out armed with machine-guns, " sawed-off shotguns," and revolvers. When they saw their three comrades lying on the sidewalk, they retreated to the alley toward Dearborn Street. The men argued about the details of the conflict, and described their getaways.

The following day and night the bodies continued to lie in state while thousands more came to the hall. All together during the two days, it was estimated that over twenty-five thousand people viewed the bodies.

Meanwhile plans for the mass funeral progressed. Representatives from all the mass organizations met on Thursday afternoon to work out the detailed plans for the Saturday funeral. A small committee was appointed to make application to the Commissioner of Police for a permit for the funeral parade. Each organization was made responsible for the distribution of leaflets. The Communist Party distributed 50,000 leaflets, the League of Struggle for Negro Rights 20,000, the Unemployed Council and the International Labor Defense each an additional 20,000. Between August 3 and the day of the funeral approximately 160,000 leaflets were distributed throughout the city, mostly on the south side. In addition announcements of the impending event were made each day to the record-breaking crowds which flocked to the Washington Park open-air meetings during the week following the riot.

On Saturday afternoon, August 8, from twelve to fifteen thousand people crowded State Street between 33rd and 47th Streets.[2] Only a limited number could gain access to the public funeral held within the hall at 3335 South State, but thousands filed by to look at the bodies, while thousands more stood about in front of the place unable to gain entrance to the overcrowded hall. Finally the coffins were carried out and the procession began to move slowly down State Street. Many red banners, kerchiefs, and bright sashes dotted the ranks which stretched from the hall to 41st Street, blocking streetcars and holding up all traffic for nearly an hour. Throughout the length of the parade were generously scattered slogan placards:

" THEY DIED FOR US! WE MUST KEEP FIGHTING! "
" FIGHT AGAINST LYNCHING — EQUAL RIGHTS FOR NEGROES! "
" NEGRO MISLEADERS INCITED THESE MURDERS! "

There were many other slogans in a similar vein.

[2] The *Chicago Daily News* estimated " over 15,000."

The funeral procession moved slowly and in orderly fashion. In addition to the marchers, thousands of people lined the streets, the sidewalks, the tops of buildings. Many of the spectators joined the cheers, the jeers, and the songs of the marchers. Over three hundred police on foot, on motorcycles, and in squad cars acted as escort to the funeral cortège. The parade marched south on State to 47th Street, turning west at Stewart to the railway station, where the bodies of Abe Gray and John O'Neal were to be put aboard trains bound for their places of birth in Mississippi and Arkansas.

In the three weeks following the August 3 riot and the mass funeral the Unemployed Councils in the south-side Negro district received 5,500 new applications for membership; the Communist Party, over 500.

1932: Relief Demonstrations

On January 10, 1932 the Unemployed Council issued a notice that simultaneous demonstrations would be held at relief stations all over the city at one o'clock on Monday, January 12. The purpose of the demonstrations was to demand that proposed relief cuts be abandoned.

At noon that day about fifty police were stationed in and around the Oakwood Emmerson relief station in the Negro section of the south side. Shortly before one o'clock the crowd began to gather at Oakwood and Langley Avenues. The assemblage was well timed. People came quickly and from all directions: out of houses, down alleys, down the streets — men, women and children — singly, in groups of threes and fours, or in ranks of greater number. The crowd congregated mostly around the Langley Avenue side of the building, where someone had placed a soap-box beneath the window of the relief office.

Although the primary issue was the relief cut, at this station the Communists took up an added grievance. It was alleged that a few days earlier one of the social workers of the Oakwood station had struck one of the clients in the face when he applied for relief. The man thus offended had taken the blow without protest, but several members of the local Unemployed Council had been present and the incident was played up at the demonstration. After a few preliminary remarks on the official issue of the occasion, another speaker mounted the soap-box and addressed the crowd.

" Are we going inside? " he asked the crowd.

" *Sure we're going inside!* " came the prompt reply.

"What are we gonna do inside? " (This with rising pitch of tone.) " Are we gonna slap their faces? "

The crowd responded with enthusiasm: " SURE, *we're gonna slap their faces!* "

There was a group which at first led the responses, but by the second or third occasion the crowd responded as one. Several speakers took to the soap-box, and the demonstration proceeded. A delegation had been selected and sent into the station to present the demands of the crowd, and at first it seemed that nothing spectacular was to happen. Within a few minutes, however, the news spread from mouth to mouth that Madden, the leader of the delegation, had been arrested by the police. The now steadily increasing crowd outside the station clamored for his release. Shouting, shoving, they crowded the broad doorstep of Lincoln Center until they forced an entrance into the building. The scene was one of general confusion. Jammed in the hollowed-out entrance of the building, the crowd battled in close quarters with the police. The police used their clubs freely. Dozens of demonstrators were injured, and several were wounded when one policeman fired into the crowd. The demonstrators bombarded the police with bricks, bottles, and stones. Two police were shot, one stabbed in the back, and another smashed on the head with a milk bottle. The police made many arrests.

In the face of police casualties the temper of the police against the Communist demonstrators ran high. From the scene of the demonstration one of the squads went to the south-side Unemployed Council Headquarters, at 4000 Federal

Street, turned the place upside down, and made several more arrests.

Thirty-two of those arrested were held on charges of inciting to riot, for unlawful assembly, and for disorderly conduct. Early on Tuesday morning, the day following the demonstration, several hundred persons gathered in front of the police station where the arrested workers were presumably being held, and demanded their release.

The Unemployed Council, the League of Struggle for Negro Rights, and the International Labor Defense issued 50,000 leaflets calling for further mass demonstration to protest this " new attack which is part of the general terror being carried on against the Negro masses of the south side by the notorious police, Captain Stege and his assistant Barker, together with the Chicago Red Squad." The Communist Party itself issued another 50,000 leaflets which were distributed throughout the city calling for city-wide mobilization in a meeting to " SMASH POLICE TERROR ON THE SOUTH SIDE OF CHICAGO! " Violent demonstrations continued during the following months, and this year may be regarded as the period of sharpest conflict between Communist organizations and established authorities.

Another serious outbreak occurred on October 6 of the same year. At about 7.30 a.m. the Lieutenant assigned to the midnight watch at the 22nd Police District notified the Sergeant on day duty that a Communist demonstration was anticipated in front of the relief station at 1701 South String Street some time during that morning. Early the same morning information of the proposed demonstration came to the attention of the Industrial Squad, and this intelligence was forwarded to the 22nd District. Handbills advertising the demonstration had been put into all doorways in the neighborhood surrounding the relief station. These announcements listed the demands of the Unemployed Councils of the Central District (headquarters at 1237 West 14th Street). The relief station had previously been the scene of several riots, and permits for demonstrations at this spot had repeatedly been refused. The squad of the dis-

trict was directed to notify the station at once if anything un-
usual occurred in the neighborhood of the relief center.

The demonstration formed by means of several groups of
about one hundred people approaching the site of the demonstration from all directions. Several of these crowds were
broken up by squads patrolling the district, but they re-formed
at other points and resumed their march on the station.

At about 10.15 a.m. calls were received from the Central
Complaint Room of Police Headquarters, and at the 23rd
District as well, that the police detailed at 1701 South String
Street were unable to handle the situation and were calling for
help as a riot had broken out. The Sergeant of the district directed all available police officers and squads to proceed to the
point of trouble at once. The Captain of the 4th Division was
notified.

A radio call was issued, and the first squad arriving on the
scene found a crowd of some three hundred people gathered
in the street listening to a colored woman addressing them
from a raised platform. To disperse the crowd, the police attempted to drive their squad car through it, but the car was
at once surrounded. Several demonstrators jumped on the
running board of the machine. A brick was thrown through
the window. The two officers jumped out of the car and found
themselves surrounded by the hostile mob. One of the officers
drew his revolver and fired. Other policemen arriving on the
scene helped to disperse the crowd.

Joe Sposob, suffering from a gunshot, was found by the
police lying on the porch at 729 West 16th Street. He was
removed by the patrol wagon to the Bridewell Hospital, where
it was found that he was carrying a gunshot wound under the
heart. He died about 11.15 the same day.

Another man, who later gave his name as Mike Lachobich,
was shot through the left ribs. Although this man made his
getaway from the scene of the trouble, an order was issued
for his arrest.

The following statement was given by a woman living at

641 West 16th Street, who was an eyewitness of the riot. The statement was taken by one of the officers of the 22nd Police District in the squad room of the station at 943 West Maxwell Street a day or two after the demonstration:

" I was going down to our shed to get some coal when I saw some men gathering in front of our house [641 West 16th Street] and on the corner of Ruble and 16th Street. I went upstairs to where I live with the coal and then I went to the front window. I called my sister [Mrs. Mildred Chalchoff] who was in my flat at the time, to come to the window and see the excitement. At first there was about fifty men gathered out in the front of my house and on String and 16th Street. We noticed several policemen in uniforms dispersing men. Some of the men went east to Jefferson Street and some were in front of my house and on the corner of 16th and Ruble. These men and a few colored women stood around on the sidewalk for about fifteen minutes. Our windows were open and we heard them say, ' Let's stand around until our communist leaders get here to speak, we can't do anything until they come.'

" All this time we were watching more men were gathering in front of the house in groups. I would judge that about two or three hundred men and women were gathered on 16th Street in front of my house. A heavy set man with a brown suit and khaki shirt and a blue tie was waving his arms and telling the crowd to come across the street where he was going to make a speech. We noticed this man walk across 16th Street, about opposite our house and jump up into the doorway of the C. B. & Q. Freight House. Immediately he started to make a speech and spoke about ten minutes. When he finished his speech a colored woman with a brown coat and a green hat was helped up onto this doorway. She also made a speech for about fifteen minutes. The man was speaking about being citizens and fighting for their rights saying that ' they are going to take away our free gas, electric light and rents.' The colored woman in her speech said about the same as the man about the free electric lights and gas and free rents.

" While the colored woman was still speaking the police squad came on the scene. The Green squad car #174 and a black squad car #115 came from Ruble Street and another squad car, black color, #146 came from String Street. These cars tried to go slow through the crowd, and the men and women tried to hold the cars back by pushing on the radiators and on the sides of the cars. The other policemen that we noticed on the corner in uniform were coming toward the squad cars at this time. The officers started to get out of the cars that were standing on the north side of 16th Street at this time. When the policeman in civilian clothes got out of the green car #174 the crowd started to push him against the freight house and started to strike him with their fists and clubs some of them kicking him while he was bending over. One of these men had a large rope beating this policeman with the coat on. He took it out from under his gray coat that he was wearing. Another tall man with a gray suit smashed the rear window of the green squad car #174 with something wrapped in pink newspaper. He walked away to the west toward Halsted Street and dropped this paper on the street about twenty-five feet west of where the fight took place near the freight house. All the three squad cars were near each other and they were trying with the aid of the other policemen that came from the corner to disperse the crowd. The policemen were telling the crowd to move on and all the time the crowd was pushing the policemen toward the freight house. I noticed one of the policemen with a club in his hand and several men took the club away from him and it fell to the ground and some other policemen picked it up. I heard a shot and looking toward where I thought it came from I saw the police officer with the brown coat down on his knees near the freight house, and the man that was making the speech dressed in khaki and brown suit and blue tie, standing near this officer holding his stomach. Two other men helped him across to the south side of 16th Street and walked with him west in the direction of Halsted Street. All the people started to leave immediately after the shot was fired. They all went different ways, most of them towards Halsted Street."

Protests against the police shooting of Joseph Sposob were sent to Mayor Cermak, to Governor Emmerson, and to the President of the Cook County Board. Protests from the many Communist affiliated groups were made in the following form:

TO: Mayor Cermak — Chicago, Illinois
     Governor Emmerson — Springfield, Illinois
     President of the Cook County Board, Whealan — Chicago, Illinois

We, _____ workers assembled at _____ protest against the murder of Joseph Sposob, the shooting of one other worker, the jailing of six others, and the raids and subsequent arrest of other unemployed workers in their homes.

We condemn this program of terror, designed to enforce the 50% cut in unemployment relief and the denial of cash relief to the single unemployed workers, as part and parcel of the Hoover program of enforcing a reduced living standard on the producing classes by means of clubbing, gassing, jailing, and shooting protesting workers — all to maintain the profits of the ruling classes.

We demand the immediate unconditional release of all arrested workers. We demand that the 50% cut in relief be withdrawn.

Adopted on this _____ day of October, 1932.

Signed: _____
    (Chairman)

_____
    (Secretary)

Joseph Sposob was given a mass funeral by the Communist Party. The leaflets widely distributed through the city calling people to his funeral read: " PROTEST AGAINST THE MURDER OF JOSEPH SPOSOB   JOIN THE MASS FUNERAL DEMONSTRATION — ALL OUT! "

1933: May Day

The May First demonstration of 1933 was organized by the International May Day United Front Committee. Permits for the parades and demonstration were duly applied for, and granted by the police authorities, with only slight changes from the route requested. The letter asking for a permit for the south-side parade stated:

" The parade will symbolize the solidarity of the workers of this section with the revolutionary proletariat of all other sections of the United States and the world who will carry on similar activities on this day. These activities are under the auspices of the International May Day United Front Committee's delegated representatives of all mass organizations on the south side which includes all labor unions, language societies and political organizations."

All of the organizations co-operating in the celebration issued special leaflets calling " All Out " to demonstrate on the 1st of May. The leaflets were circulated by the Unemployed Council branches, by the Stockyard Workers' Industrial Union, by a score of other affiliated organizations, as well as by the party itself. The fact that the Tom Mooney Congress would open in Chicago on April 30, with representatives from organizations all over the country, promised to give added importance to Chicago's May Day festivities.

May Day dawned gray and clouded in Chicago. Of the three parades which had been planned, the largest assembled at the intersection of Ogden and Randolph Streets at about 4 p.m. By five o'clock, when the parade began to move, the marchers numbered about six thousand. In the face of a terrific rainstorm which had broken over the city, the thousands of marchers held their ranks, singing revolutionary songs and shouting the slogan of the day: " FREE TOM MOONEY! " Following the line of march planned, north on Ogden to Lake Street, west on Lake to Ashland, the parade marched on headed by an automobile bearing Mrs. Spies and Mrs. Parsons, widows of the anarchists executed after the Haymarket riot. Slushing along in the pouring rain, singing, shouting, carrying their sloganed banners, the paraders first appeared not to be disturbed by the rain. But the route was long and devious. The dwindling ranks finally poured into the Chicago Stadium. About one thousand marchers had been lost from the number during the march.

The meeting at the Stadium opened at 7.45 p.m. with the singing of the *Internationale,* which was played on the pipe-organ. The hall was colorfully decorated with slogans of the day. There were no less than twelve speakers on the program,

but each of these spoke briefly. The meeting was adjourned
at 10.30.

Parades held in other sections of the city were less successfully attended.

1934: Lenin Memorial

The Lenin Memorial of 1934 was held on January 21 in the
large hall of the Coliseum. It was a Sunday evening meeting. By 8.15 the hall was about three-fifths filled. When
the meeting opened, the audience numbered some 6,000, almost half of whom were Negroes. Around the sides of the
balcony which runs all the way around the hall were hung
an array of Communist Party demands: "DOWN WITH IM-
PERIALIST WAR," "DEFEND THE USSR AND THE CHINESE PEOPLE."
There were a few new slogans among the many old: " HAIL
THE GERMAN COMMUNIST PARTY — BRAVE FIGHTER AGAINST
FASCISM "; another one read " HAIL DIMITROFF — LENINIST
FIGHTER FOR THE WORKING CLASS."

At the rear of the stage and covering the entire back of the
platform, suspended from the balcony above, were four enormous posters related, as was indicated in the program, to the
mass pageant scheduled for the evening. The first, marked:
"1917" in large red figures, showed Lenin leading the peas-
ants, workers, and soldiers in the Proletarian Revolution. The
second, an anti-war poster, presented a skull wearing a war
helmet, a cannon, several mangled corpses lying in the foreground; slightly above was painted a transparent blue eagle
of New Deal parentage. The third poster pictured a group of
workers. The fourth illustrated the united cause of farmers
and city workers by showing these two shaking hands. The
motif of this final poster was represented in a style similar to
that of the second: the hammer and sickle, in bright red, was
shown above the worker-farmer handclasp.

The hall was dotted with red flags, large and small, and with
many other banners. The east balcony was filled with young
people who gave cheers throughout the evening in the style

familiar to spectators at college football or basketball games.

The meeting opened with a selection from the Hungarian Workers' Orchestra, after which the Young Pioneers began a parade through the hall. The smallest children, many in red or red and blue suits and dresses, marched first, each carrying a red flag over his shoulder. The parade was led by the young drummers, beating the march for the ranks. Up one aisle of the hall, down another, then onto the stage marched the Young Pioneers, five hundred in number. When assembled upon the stage, the group gave a salute-recitation and sang several songs.

The meeting proceeded without much spontaneous enthusiasm. The program was carefully planned, with occasional selections by the chorus or orchestra. An appeal for funds was made by District Organizer Gebert and the collection was large. Attention lagged somewhat until Clarence Hathaway took the speaker's microphone. Speaking clearly, loudly, in contrast to the chairman, who could hardly be understood in the balcony, Hathaway declared that the day of revolution was close at hand.

" The membership of the Communist Party last December was 27,000. This has almost doubled in the past year. The Chicago Communists will be called upon to play a very decisive role in the coming revolution. Chicago is a central industrial city. There are many basic industries in Chicago. . . .

" The problem of revolution is not a problem of many years. It is already in sight. The policy of the United States is leading to imperialist war and fascism. . . . There is a need for unification against the attacks on the living standards of American workers."

Hathaway spoke of Lenin, moving the crowd to cheers in response to his words.

" The program of Lenin is in contradiction with the A. F. of L. program and that of the Socialist movement [boos]. In behalf of the American Communist Party, I say that the one program which will bring unity to the American people is the program of Lenin.

The A. F. of L. say Lenin only knew about workers of Russia. Their leaders say: ' It is a Russian program — not one for the United States.' But *we* say that the program of Lenin is *the* program of the working class [cheers] — precisely because Lenin studied the *world* working class — Lenin was *the* person who took the teachings of Karl Marx and applied them to the modern epoch. . . . He studied the revolution of the world! "

For over an hour Hathaway held the attention of his audience; his speech was received with tumultuous applause.

The final number on the program was a mass pageant depicting the role of Lenin as a leader of the working classes of the world and portraying the lives and struggles of the American workers against capitalism.

After several announcements about future meetings, the memorial demonstration officially adjourned at 11 p.m. Some time before this hour people had begun to leave the hall.

PART FOUR

THE VOLUME OF
PROPAGANDA

CHAPTER XI

Volume of Propaganda:

Promotion

FROM the birth of the American Communist Party in Chicago in 1919 Chicago has been one of the chief radiating centers for Communist propaganda in the United States. Although the political capital of the party was removed to New York about 1924, and the Midwest center declined in national importance, it has always remained a stronghold of the party. During the period with which we are concerned, Chicago continued to be an active relay center for propaganda directed from Moscow, and an important congregating center for party specialists.

Chicago's peak as a consumer of Communist propaganda originating either locally or externally was in 1932. This statement rests upon the data which are critically summarized in the present section of this book. Since there are no accepted methods of measuring the volume of propaganda, it has been necessary to invent procedures for this purpose.

We have defined propaganda as the manipulation of symbols to influence controversial attitudes. In accordance with such a definition, the propagandist may be defined as one who spends at least a certain quota of his time in the deliberate dissemination of contentious symbols. It must be emphasized that this excludes all who unwittingly transmit these symbols.

Within a given area and period, there is mostly a positive correlation between the volume of propaganda circulated and the number of persons engaged in circulating controversial symbols. In addition, there is an even closer correlation between volume of propaganda and the total amount of time spent in the circulation of these symbols. In the present chapter we shall attempt to discover the changes in the volume of Communist propaganda circulated in Chicago between 1930 and 1934 by an examination of changes of the two factors just mentioned.

These factors will be presented by two indices: the *Promotion Index* and the *Promotion Hour Index*.

The Promotion Index represents the number of persons, in proportion to the entire number in the community in question, who spend at least a certain quota of their time in propaganda.

The Promotion Hour Index represents the number of hours, in proportion to the total number of waking hours lived by the population of the community, which are devoted to propaganda.

It is out of the question to expect to arrive at thoroughly accurate magnitudes of the volume of Communist propaganda in Chicago. Nothing is to be gained by minimizing the discrepancy between what is most desirable and what is available. What is too easily and too often done is to give the *impression* of exact knowledge about the size of propaganda operations by assembling an imposing exhibit of details. But details may be voluminous without being informative. They bear on the question of propaganda volume only when they are relevant for the determination of *how many people* spend *how much time* and *how many resources* spreading symbols which come to the attention of *how many persons* during *how much time*. In the present chapter we shall seek to construct a Promotion Index and a Promotion Hour Index which will answer the first two questions.

Promotion Index

In order to measure the quantity of Communist propaganda circulated in Chicago during depression years, it is imperative that we ascertain the number of persons deliberately engaged in the circulation of Communist symbols. After having determined the number of persons so engaged for each year, we can compute the annual promotion index by weighting these figures with the yearly population estimates for the city. In this way it will be possible to obtain an index whose fluctuations are presumably positively correlated with the fluctuations of the volume of propaganda in Chicago.

In determining the number of promoters of Communist propaganda, we have arrived at two possible sets of figures. These we have called the *Crude Promotion Index* and the *Refined Promotion Index*. The former is based upon the total membership of the party, on the assumption that every member is a deliberate disseminator of Communist propaganda. The latter, on the other hand, is refined to include only those members who hold positions which would require their extensive participation in propaganda activities. These latter figures include officers of the units, sections, and district, as well as non-functionaries engaged in writing, speaking, or teaching Communism.

The promotion indices thus computed reveal the small proportion of the population which was engaged in the promotion of Communist propaganda during the years in question:

	1930	1931	1932	1933	1934
Crude Promotion Index ...	22.5	39.2	63.8	50.3	67.4
Refined Promotion Index ..	9.7	11.9	26.5	23.0	31.2

As indicated by the figures, 1932 was the year of greatest increase, and 1934 was the year of maximum participation. The rise in the number of party members and functionaries in 1934, which is reflected in the above indices, was due largely to the broadening of Communist policy as the line associated with the theory of " social Fascism " was abandoned.

As stated above, the Crude Promotion Index is based upon party membership. The importance of this index is indicated by the fact that the Communists considered every member as an agent of Communist propaganda. The pamphlet *Revolutionary Greetings,* distributed to each new party member, read in part as follows:

"Now that you become a member of the Communist Party, the Party of Lenin, you have become the interpreter of the theory and program of the Party through your every day activities as a Communist. You become an agitator and organizer of the workers you come in contact with on the job. Your activity becomes representative of the Communist Party and its principles."

Communist Party membership in the Chicago District fluctuated greatly throughout the depression.[1] The greatest in-

[1] Figures of membership in the Communist Party are not to be taken too literally, particularly for the earlier years. The Organization Department of the Communist International made the following statement to the Sixth World Congress (of 1928):

"With regard to these figures [for 1924] it should be stated that at the time of the 5th Congress, and in general before the re-organization on the factory group basis, not a single Communist Party, except the Communist Party of the Soviet Union, had any more or less satisfactory statistics on the fluctuations of membership. Thus, the figures characterizing the Communist membership at the time of the Fifth Congress are inaccurate and in all cases they are rather exaggerated."

In 1919 two groups which split off from the American Socialist Party christened themselves "Communist": the Communist Party, with about 27,000 members (26,680 reported in 1920), and the Communist Labor Party, with approximately 10,000 members. In 1920 a group which was expelled from the Communist Party organized the Proletarian Party, which presumably had only a few thousand (and perhaps only a few hundred) members. In an effort to unify the several Communist groups a United Communist Party was launched in 1920, but a split soon occurred, and another Communist Party was founded (with between 3,000 and 4,000 members). In 1921 a great many new organizations were set up. Finally in December 1921 a Workers' Party was established, with something over 12,000 members. An underground opposition group remained aloof and tried to create the United Toilers (party) of America; but this failed, and the opposition group itself disbanded after 1922. By October 1923 the Workers' Party numbered 15,233 members; at the end of 1924 the figure was 17,363. The next years were years of gradual decline, and at the end of 1928 there were between 12,000 and

crease was in 1932, an increase which outstripped the rate of growth of the party in the United States for that year. In general, however, the membership of the party in Chicago constituted approximately 10 per cent of the national membership:

	1930	1931	1932	1933	1934
Chicago C.P.	761	1,356	2,249	1,756	2,381
U. S. C.P.	7,500	9,257	14,475	19,165	23,536
Percentage ..	10.1%	14.6%	15.5%	9.2%	10.1%

Although the number of party members may serve for a Crude Promotion Index, it is readily admitted by party leaders that the nominal membership is many times greater than the active group. This condition is sharply reflected in the large turnover which has constituted a major organizational problem in the party. For this reason we have refined the index by an analysis of the party organization.

A study of the party organization revealed that party functionaries were found at three levels of organization: the district (which embraces Chicago), the sections (subdivisions of the district), and the units (basic divisions of the sections). The district organization as outlined in the Party Handbook of 1935 consisted of four bureaus, three committees, and two commissions. The section organization included one committee, one bureau, and one commission; whereas the units each main-

---

14,000 members, 9,300 of whom had paid their dues. In November 1928 a small Communist League of America (opposition) had split off. In 1929 the Workers' Party renamed itself the Communist Party of America. Another split led to the formation of the Communist Party of the U.S.A. (majority group), which claimed 1,000 members. In November 1931 a small Communist League of Struggle was built by a dissenting faction.

In 1919–20 the American Socialist Party was itself in favor of joining the Third International, and thus of becoming a Communist Party. Before the splits of 1919 the Socialists had 108,504 members.

Taking all of these facts into consideration, it appears that the high-water marks of Communist membership before the depression were the years 1919–20 and 1924–5.

tained a separate bureau. This constituted the formal structure.

It is therefore possible to compute the number of offices on
the basis of the party's own estimates of the size of party organs
as various levels:

	Av. No. Members	1930		1931		1932		1933		1934	
		No. groups	Offices	No. groups	Offices	No. groups	Offices	No. groups	Offices	No. groups	Offices
Unit bureaus	4	75	300	99	396	221	884	187	748	280	1,120
Sect. Bur.	5	14	70	14	70	17	85	18	90	21	105
Sect. Comm.	10	14	140	14	140	17	170	18	180	21	210
Sect. Com'sn	3	84	252	84	252	102	306	108	324	126	378
Dist. Bur.	8	1	8	1	8	1	8	1	8	1	8
Dist. Comm.	17	1	17	1	17	1	17	1	17	1	17
Dist. Com'sn.	5	6	30	6	30	6	30	6	30	6	30
Pol. Bureau	8	1	8	1	8	1	8	1	8	1	8
Cent. Comm......	33	1	33	1	33	1	33	1	33	1	33
TOTALS			858		954		1,541		1,438		1,909

It is pertinent to note that the number of offices in this formal
blue-print of the party was far greater than the number of active party members and in 1930 even exceeded the total membership. This relationship is clearly demonstrated by the following Office-Membership proportion:

	1930	1931	1932	1933	1934
Membership	761	1,356	2,249	1,756	2,381
Offices	858	954	1,541	1,438	1,909
Percentage	113%	70%	69%	82%	80%

The high Office-Member Index indicates the elaborateness of
the structure of the organization.

The limited number of active members required that they
occupy more than one position of responsibility at the same
time. Communist policy allowed and encouraged members
to hold office simultaneously at each of the three levels of organization, and to hold two or more offices at the same level.
It is extremely difficult to arrive at an accurate estimate of the

amount of plural office-holding during any given year. However, on the basis of a number of documents giving the composition of committees at various levels, we are able to compute an index which probably closely approximates the
amount of plural office-holding. This index shows for each of
the years in question the probable average number of officers
per 100 offices in the party:

	1930	1931	1932	1933	1934
Office-Officer Index	35	41	57	52	53

According to these figures, the number of offices held by the
average functionary would be:

1930	1931	1932	1933	1934
2.9	2.4	1.8	1.9	1.9

These data are not completely reliable, since only sample
lists of officials of somewhat uncertain representativeness were
available. Field observations seem to suggest that the above
figures underestimate the amount of plural office-holding,
thereby exaggerating the number of officials. This will tend to
counterbalance the probable error incurred by our failure to
include in our Refined Promotion Index the active party members who do not hold positions as functionaries or as writers,
speakers, or teachers.

Relying upon the above figures for plural office-holding, the
number of functionaries in the party may be computed for
each year:[2]

1930	1931	1932	1933	1934
300	391	878	748	1012

[2] These figures may appear contradictory to those above. Since
no party member may belong to more than one unit, there should be at
least as many officials in the district as a whole as there are representatives in the unit bureaus. In point of fact, however, many nuclei existed
only on paper. There is little doubt that the number of actual functionaries in the units was many times smaller than that indicated in the
previous table.

There are types of Communist propaganda activities, however, which are not necessarily carried on by party officers. Persons who are writers and editors, speakers, and teachers contribute directly to the volume of propaganda. Such persons usually operate through channels controlled by the party. For example, the teachers included in our calculations are those who have taught during the depression years at the Chicago Workers School. Editors and writers, similarly, were those who contributed to the publications of Communist controlled groups; while speakers and lecturers were those appearing at meetings of Communist or Communist affiliated organizations.

The number of persons engaged in these forms of propaganda activity were as follows:

	1930	1931	1932	1933	1934
Writers and Editors	50	46	55	78	51
Speakers	51	64	96	87	122
Teachers	5	8	22	24	29

Many of these persons, however, were functionaries of the Communist Party. In order to avoid duplication in arriving at the Refined Promotion Index, we eliminated the following numbers from the groups just indicated: [3]

	1930	1931	1932	1933	1934
Writers and Editors ...	18	12	18	24	20
Speakers	5	8	29	25	61
Teachers	5	1	7	6	9
TOTALS	28	21	54	55	90

When the remaining totals are added to our annual estimates of the number of Communist Party functionaries, we obtain what will be called the Refined Index of the total number of propagandists for each year. This constituted the base for our Refined Promotion Index:

[3] Particularly in later years, some of these were undoubtedly not party members.

	1930	1931	1932	1933	1934
Population (thousands) ...	3,376	3,458	3,523	3,491	3,530
Promoters	328	412	932	803	1,102
Refined Prom. Index	9.7	11.9	26.5	23.0	31.2

(expressed in thousandths of one per cent)

These figures are the most accurate that can be obtained on the basis of existing data.

Promotion Hour Index

More closely correlated to the volume of Communist propaganda than the Promotion Index is the Promotion Hour Index. This index is computed by comparing the number of hours spent in the preparation and dissemination of propaganda with the total number of waking hours available in the community.

In compiling such an index, we find ourselves on even more tenuous grounds than in the computation of a Promotion Index. Records of time spent in party activities are practically nonexistent, and there is no way of accurately estimating the time required in the preparation of propaganda and its dissemination through the many channels used by the party.

It is possible, however, on the basis of available data on party structure and membership, to arrive at figures indicating a maximum amount of time spent annually by party propagandists which was certainly not transcended, and most probably not reached in reality. Such maxima will be designated as values of the *Promotion Hour Index*. They serve to depict the relatively limited extent of Communist promotion activity in Chicago:

	1930	1931	1932	1933	1934
Promotion Hour Index .	1.32	1.94	3.71	3.07	4.09

(expressed in thousandths of one per cent)

In estimating the hours available for propaganda activities in the party, promoters were classified as paid functionaries, unpaid functionaries, and other party members. Speakers, writers, editors, and teachers, although independently considered in compiling the Refined Promotion Index, were for present purposes included in one or the other of these three groups.[4]

Only a small proportion of the functionaries of the party were obligated to give full time to their party work. On the basis of data available for three out of the five years, it has been determined that the following number of persons were on the pay-roll of the party. Figures for 1930 and 1932 were esti-

1930	1931	1932	1933	1934
3	4	6	6	6

mated. The small number of paid functionaries in the party was due to the limited finances of the organization. A liberal estimate of the amount of time spent by these leaders in propaganda activities (excluding organizational work) is 20 hours per week, or 1,040 hours per year.

In the case of other officers, the time was less, as there were few Communists who had independent incomes which enabled them to devote full time to party work. During the depression, however, the fact that a large percentage of the party membership was unemployed tended to increase substantially the amount of time that active party members devoted to the cause. For example, national Communist Party records show that in 1933 and 1934 there were respectively 9 and 10 full-time members in the Chicago District who were not on the pay-roll. These members may not, in fact, have devoted full time to the party throughout the entire year. However, their number, and the number of other officers who were able to give more time because of unemployment, increased the average amount of time devoted to propaganda work by the unpaid functionaries.

Taking these facts into consideration, together with estimates from field investigation, it is safe to say that the average unpaid functionary in the party devoted not more than 12

---

[4] Such persons who were not party members were disregarded inasmuch as their number was small and the amount of time they spent negligible in comparison with that of party groups.

hours a week to propaganda activities. This would amount to an average of 624 promotion hours a year.

Communist Party members (non-functionaries) devoted far less time on the average. As has already been explained, a large percentage of the party was inactive. Although a small proportion of unemployed, non-functionary members devoted much of their time to the spreading of Communist symbols, it is safe to conclude that the average member devoted no more than 3 hours per week, or 156 hours a year, to propaganda.

On the basis of these time estimates, we may compute the maximum promotion hours for each depression year:

	1930	1931	1932	1933	1934
Paid func. (at 20 hrs.)	60	80	120	120	120
Unpaid func. (at 12 hrs.)	3,564	4,644	10,464	8,904	12,144
Other mem. (at 3 hrs.)	1,383	2,895	4,113	3,024	4,107
Total hours per week	5,007	7,619	14,697	12,048	16,271
Total hours per year	260,364	396,188	764,244	626,496	846,092

The Promotion Hour Index represents the number of promotion hours in proportion to the total number of waking hours lived by the community. Figuring on the basis of a 16-hour day, the following indices were obtained:

	1930	1931	1932	1933	1934
Population (in thousands)	3,376	3,458	3,523	3,491	3,530
Total waking hrs. per yr. (in millions)	19,715	20,195	20,574	20,387	20,615
Promotion hours per year	260,364	396,188	764,244	626,496	846,092
Promotion Hour Index	1.32	1.95	3.71	3.07	4.10

(expressed in thousandths of one per cent)

The above Promotion Hour Indices show the same general characteristics as the Promotion Indices which have already been presented. They show the greatest increase during 1932, and the greatest magnitudes in 1934.

It must be pointed out, however, that since an absence of data made it impossible to vary basic time estimates from year to year, no reflection is found in the indices of the fact that the general level of activity of the party in 1932 far exceeded that of 1934. Partially because of the demands made upon the party for leadership during this outstanding year of unrest, it is probable that the actual time spent in promotion activities more nearly approached our maximum estimates in 1932 than in any other year. Thus it may well be that 1932 saw the absolute as well as the relative peak of promotion activity for the depression period.

In the present chapter we have given approximate answers to the questions of *how many people* spent *how much time* in the spreading of Communist symbols. It will be our next task to evaluate the amount of attention given to the symbols thus circulated.

CHAPTER XII

Volume of Propaganda: Attention

THE PROMOTION INDEX and the Promotion Hour Index, though important indicators of the volume of propaganda, illuminate only half of the total picture. The spotlight must be shifted from those who act to those who are acted upon — from the party promoters to those who pay attention to Communist symbols.

In order to appraise fluctuations in the amount of attention, we have constructed two indices comparable to those used to describe promotion. The *Attention Index* represents the number of persons, in proportion to the total population, who focus upon a given set of symbols. The *Attention Hour Index* compares the total number of hours bestowed upon such symbols with the number of waking hours lived by the entire population of the community.

The compilation of these indices is naturally an extremely hazardous task. It is virtually impossible to obtain quantitative information concerning the number of people affected by the many Communist channels, and the amount of attention which they devote to symbols circulated through these channels. Even in the case of such tangible media as publications, the difficulties inherent in such a task are insurmountable. Communist publications are notorious for the irregularity of their appearance, and it is impossible to determine the number of copies of each issue of the many Communist daily, weekly, half-monthly, or monthly newspapers, magazines, shop papers, and pamphlets which were circulated annually in Chicago. Nor would our difficulties end were such circulation figures available. For in order to construct the complete Attention and Attention Hour Indices, it would be necessary to know the average number of readers per copy of issues of publications, and the average amount of time spent by readers per copy.

Although it was impossible to construct satisfactory Attention and Attention Hour Indices for all channels of Communist propaganda, we have been able to construct, with a certain degree of accuracy, the indices for one important channel, the mass demonstration.[1] As defined in the previous section, the term "mass demonstration" includes four sub-channels: outdoor demonstrations, indoor meetings, parades, and " socials." Throughout the depression, these forms were consistently and effectively used.

Attention Index

The Attention Index is defined as the number of persons, in proportion to the total population, who during a given period of time focus their attention upon symbols of specified kinds for at least a certain (small) amount of time. In the case of the demonstration channel, such an index refers to the relationship between the net number of persons attending one or more Communist demonstrations during a given year, and the population estimates of that year. The following numbers indicate the annual variations in the Attention Index:

	1930	1931	1932	1933	1934
Attention Index	.76	1.00	1.69	1.39	1.50

The outstanding difficulty encountered in the construction of this index was in obtaining sufficiently approximate estimates of the number of persons present at Communist dem-

[1] For detailed data on demonstrations, see the Appendix.

onstrations. There were a number of sources where attendance estimates were available. Such figures were frequently given in the Chicago press and in the local and national Communist organs. Attendance was also recorded in the official records of the police for those demonstrations at which they were present. These sources were supplemented by the reports of our own field investigators.

The above sources frequently differed widely in their estimates of attendance. For example, on March 6, 1930 an outdoor demonstration was held at the corner of Halsted and Lake Streets. The *Chicago Tribune* in publishing the news story stated that 1,200 persons were present. The *Chicago Daily News* estimated 1,500. The following day, however, the *Daily Worker,* official organ of the Communist Party, appeared with the story that 50,000 demonstrators had been on the scene. Police records indicated that 550 persons were in attendance. At the March 6 demonstration no field investigator was present to offer a fifth estimate.

Although the wide discrepancy frequently found in comparing the *Daily Worker's* with other estimates was due to the fact that its figures were often published for propaganda rather than informative purposes, the variations between other sources reflects the difficulty of arriving at accurate estimates of the numerical strength of crowds. The crowd situation is apt to distort the judgment of the inexperienced observer.

The most realistic estimates were made by the police for their own use. Police officials in Chicago have had years of experience in judging the size of mass demonstrations. In addition, they took great care to obtain accurate estimates. In the case of parades, for example, observers stationed at vantage points recorded the number of marching columns. From these figures the total number of participants could easily be inferred, and such calculations were checked by the police against the amount of time required for the parade to pass. Thus, even when an actual count of marchers was not taken, police were able to make accurate estimates of the number of paraders.

Whenever the official attendance records compiled by the police were available, these were accepted for our purposes. Estimates of attendance from other sources proved so unreliable that it was found necessary to restrict quantitative analysis to these official figures. On the basis of police records, average attendance was computed for each type of mass demonstration, and these averages were applied to the 2,088 demonstrations held between 1930 and 1934. Average attendance at each type of demonstration was as follows:

	1930	1931	1932	1933	1934
Indoor Meetings	222	139	167	224	313
Outdoor Demonstrations	371	334	336	336	457
Parades	438	495	722	422	484
" Socials "	307	349	451	564	671

By multiplying the above averages with the corresponding annual total of each type of demonstration, it was possible to calculate the total annual attendance at each of these four forms of Communist functions:

	1930	1931	1932	1933	1934
Indoor Meetings	39,738	26,966	39,579	46,816	59,470
Outdoor Demonstrations .	18,550	44,756	57,456	48,048	53,926
Parades	4,818	10,395	28,880	18,146	15,488
" Socials "	13,815	20,591	53,218	27,636	30,195

Adding these figures, we obtain the total attendance at all types of Communist demonstrations for each of the five years:[2]

	1930	1931	1932	1933	1934
Total Attendance ...	76,921	102,708	179,133	140,646	159,079

These figures are as accurate as can be obtained. It must be remembered, however, that they rest upon estimates of at-

[2] Although not pertinent to the present discussion, it is interesting to compare annual variations in the average attendance at Communist meetings, irrespective of type:

	1930	1931	1932	1933	1934
Av. Attendance	270	252	316	317	413

tendance only at demonstrations attended by police. Since the police tended to appear only at the better-attended occasions, the final figures tend to be above the actual totals. However, to some extent this was counterbalanced by the fact that estimates of the Chicago police were generally conservative — a fact often protested by the Communists, who claimed that the police misrepresented the effectiveness of their propaganda. Another factor which tends to compensate for any exaggeration in the above data is the fact that police estimates only included active participants. In the case of outdoor meetings and parades, however, Communist symbols came to the attention of many additional thousands of persons who thronged the line of march or craned their necks from office buildings for a glimpse of the demonstrators.[8]

Accepting these data, however, as sufficiently accurate totals of the number of people in attendance at Communist demonstrations, it must be remembered that these figures represent the *total* attendance, whereas our index calls for the *net number* of persons attending one or more Communist meetings in a given year. We must therefore estimate the average number of demonstrations attended yearly by participants.

A small group of persons strongly identified with the Communist cause found most of their social as well as their political life in Communist functions. A high proportion of the total attendance figures was accounted for by this comparatively small group, a fact substantiated by any observer acquainted with the movement. However, the balance was largely composed of persons on the fringe of the movement. The composition of this group was in continuous flux; that is, the net number of individuals composing it was great. Few of these persons attended more than one or two demonstrations.

[8] The two factors just mentioned may also compensate at least partially for a duplication in our counts: we have not taken account of the fact that the demonstrating crowds contained persons who have been classified as " Promoters " in the Crude as well as the Refined sense and whose demonstration activities have already been explicitly referred to in our two Promotion Indices.

Taking these two components into account, we have conservatively estimated that a demonstrator participated on the average in approximately three mass demonstrations per year. On the basis of this estimate, the net number of persons attending Communist demonstrations annually was as follows:

1930	1931	1932	1933	1934
25,640	34,236	59,711	48,549	53,026

The probability of these results may be enhanced by comparing them with the attendance figures for the largest demonstration of each year. In 1934, for example, there were 14,000 persons participating in a parade on September 28. In view of this, it is not excessive to assume that the net number of participants for the entire year was somewhat less than four times as large.

Calculating the Attention Index on the basis of the net totals given above, we arrived at the following figures:

	1930	1931	1932	1933	1934
Attention Index	.76%	.99%	1.69%	1.39%	1.50%

Despite the fact that we have kept our estimate of the average number of demonstrations attended by participants per year constant, 1932 stands out clearly as the year of maximum participation. The prominence of this year would be even more evident if we had been able to vary this figure. As field investigations revealed, 1932 saw a maximum rate of turnover within the party itself as well as on the fringe of the movement. This makes it probable that the average number of demonstrations attended by participants declined substantially in this year; that is, that the net number of persons exposed to propaganda circulated through the demonstration channel increased correspondingly.

Attention Hour Index

The Attention Hour Index represents the relation between the total number of hours of exposure to symbols, and the number of waking hours lived by the community. In the case of mass demonstrations, this may be determined by computing the total time spent at Communist outdoor demonstrations, indoor meetings, parades, and "socials," and weighting this figure with the number of waking hours in the Chicago community, calculated on the basis of a 16-hour day. The index computed in this manner showed the following magnitudes:

	1930	1931	1932	1933	1934
Attention Hour Index	1.14	1.29	2.22	1.82	2.08

(stated in thousandths of one per cent)

Since the average time consumed by different types of demonstrations varied greatly, it was necessary to consider these forms separately. We have already computed the total number of persons in attendance at each type of Communist demonstration:

	1930	1931	1932	1933	1934
Indoor Meetings	39,738	26,966	39,579	46,816	59,470
Outdoor Demonstrations .	18,550	44,756	57,456	48,048	53,926
Parades	4,818	10,395	28,880	18,146	15,488
"Socials"	13,815	20,591	53,218	27,636	30,195

Earlier in this chapter we were interested in inferring from these figures the *net number of different persons* referred to in them. Now, however, we must use these figures in finding the *total number of hours* spent, irrespective of the number of people involved. To this end, it will be our task to estimate the average time spent at each of these types of meetings.

In written reports of Communist events the police invariably stated the time when each meeting was opened and when adjournment took place. This information was part of the regular report prepared by the police for their own use and was consequently available for all meetings which they attended.

On the basis of this information, as well as from field observation, we obtained figures as to the time consumed by each of a large number of outdoor demonstrations, indoor meetings, parades, and "socials." These figures were averaged, and, allowing a margin for error, maximum estimates were obtained of the average duration of each type of meeting. Differences between the various years were not sufficient to warrant consideration.

Type of Demonstration	Av. Time
Indoor meetings	3 ½ hours
Outdoor demonstrations	2 hours
Parades	1 ½ hours
" Socials "	3 hours

It is possible, then, by multiplying the attendance for each year by these time averages, to compute the number of attention hours devoted to each type of demonstration:

	1930	1931	1932	1933	1934
Indoor Meetings	139,084	94,381	138,526	163,856	208,145
Outdoor Demonstrations	37,100	89,512	114,912	96,096	107,852
Parades	7,227	15,592	43,320	27,219	23,232
" Socials "	41,445	61,773	159,654	82,908	90,585

Summing these up, the number of attention hours bestowed upon Communist demonstrations as a whole was as follows:

	1930	1931	1932	1933	1934
Attention Hours ...	224,855	261,258	456,412	370,079	429,814

As in the case of the Promotion Hour Index, we must find the proportion of waking hours lived in the community which these totals represent:

	1930	1931	1932	1933	1934
Population Est. (thousands)	3,376	3,458	3,523	3,491	3,530
Hours Lived (millions)	19,715	20,195	20,574	20,387	20,615
Tot. Att. Hrs.	224,855	261,258	456,412	370,079	429,814
Attention Hour Index	1.14	1.29	2.22	1.82	2.08

(stated in thousandths of one per cent)

In 1932 both the relative increase over the previous year and the absolute value of the index was greatest, despite the fact that the average monthly membership in the Communist Party was smaller then than in 1934. Inasmuch as demonstrations formed the central channel of Communist propaganda, it is probable that the volume of all propaganda was greatest in 1932.

A complete Attention Index would show the intensity of attention given to symbols by persons exposed to them. The indices used in this chapter might be rechristened the *Exposure Index* and the *Exposure Hour Index,* and two new indices constructed to correlate with intensity of attention (these might be named *Concentration Index* and *Concentration Hour Index*). Together the two groups of indices would constitute the Attention Index. Some investigators will no doubt prefer to use the Concentration Indices to measure magnitudes of propaganda *result* rather than magnitudes of propaganda. We prefer to regard them as indices of volume rather than result, assigning to result the acts of persons after their attention has been concentrated to a certain degree.

CHAPTER XIII

Volume of Propaganda: Expenditures

AMONG the indicators of the volume of propaganda, an important place is occupied by the amount of money spent for propaganda purposes. With regular and adequate resources, an organization can attract maximum attention with minimum promotion investment and hence attain a high degree of effectiveness.

In view of the numerous and persistent tales of "Moscow gold," it was of particular interest in this study to evaluate the amount of money expended in the Chicago area by the Communist Party for propaganda purposes. Our estimates are as follows:

	1930	1931	1932	1933	1934
Total Exp.	$15,500	27,200	57,300	23,900	64,200

In compiling these figures, the assumption has been made that annual income and propaganda expenditures were equal. Practically all money collected by the District, excluding such specified proportions as were forwarded to the Central Committee of the C.P.U.S.A., and including such subsidies as were handed down to the District from the center, were quickly spent. An examination of several financial statements of the Chicago District and of the Central Committee showed that only a small balance was carried forward from year to year. Most of the expenditure may be presumed to have been made for propaganda purposes, directly or indirectly. The maintenance of " centers " (including rent, telephone, etc.) and the payment of salaries of promoters are of course necessary for an efficient propaganda machine. Such small expenditures, which were not, directly or indirectly, related to propaganda, have not been deducted from our totals. Besides their relative smallness, a justification for this procedure is that we may presume the existence of funds not accounted for, so that our figures probably remain somewhat below the actual amount spent.

The party income was derived mainly from three sources: dues, receipts from admission to meetings and " socials," and donations (acquired by collections or in other ways). Although of minor importance, subsidies from the Central Committee have been analyzed as well.

Dues

Party dues are collected in the units, and it is the responsibility of the financial secretary to make such collections and to report the members who fall behind in payments. Dues are paid weekly, and in accordance with the amount of wages received by the member. According to the Constitution of the party, the scale of dues payments was as follows:

Weekly wage of member	*Weekly dues*
Unemployed	$ .02
Under $15 (and housewives)	.10
$15 to $25	.25
$25 to $30	.50
$30 to $40	.75
$40 to $50	1.00
Over $50	1.00 plus

50¢ for each $5.00 or fraction thereof

The 1935 Handbook of the party stated that only 40 per cent of the amount of money collected in the units in the form of dues was retained by those groups. The remaining amount was passed up through the party hierarchy: 15 per cent was retained in the section, 15 per cent in the district, and the remaining 30 per cent forwarded to the Central Committee.

According to the Financial Reports of the Central Committee of the Communist Party, the following amount represented the center's share of dues payments in 1931, 1932, and 1933:

1931	1932	1933
$39,744.55	33,267.34	25,234.77

Calculating on the basis of the percentage of the national membership found in the Chicago District during these years, we have computed the amount retained for propaganda work in the Chicago District. Totals for 1930 and 1934 have been estimated: [1]

1930	1931	1932	1933	1934
$10,000	13,500	12,000	5,400	14,000

In addition to membership dues, occasional assessments were made. Such extra assessments could only be levied with the permission of the Central Committee, however, and were usually used for national purposes. As a result, we have made no estimates of this form of collection.

Subsidies

It was the policy of the Central Committee to extend subsidies to the districts for propaganda purposes. Such subsidies varied greatly according to the district. In general, the policy was to grant the largest subsidies to those districts which were in the

[1] The figures for 1930 and 1934 are generous. They are large with respect to the other totals, however, inasmuch as during these two years the percentage of members in the party who were employed was greater. It was the large influx of unemployed members that caused the drop in dues receipts in 1932, despite a total increase in membership. The large decrease in membership in 1933, coupled with continuing unemployment of party groups, produced the low figure for this year. However, in 1934 the party made a determined effort to attract employed (and, particularly, skilled) workers. A new high in membership was reached. These factors resulted in the unusually high dues receipts for that year.

process of development. Thus Chicago, as one of the older and better-established districts, was practically independent.

It is interesting to investigate, however, the extent to which this was the case. Financial documents of the Central Committee give us the total subsidies made to districts for the years 1931, 1932, and 1933:

1931	1932	1933
$8,181	12,889	12,613

The total for 1931 was not itemized as to districts, but exact figures of the amount granted to the Chicago District were available for the other two years. The percentage of the total that the 1933 subsidy represented was extended to 1931. The subsidy for 1932 was excessively high owing to the election campaign carried on in all large cities by the party at that time.

The figures listed for 1930 and 1934 are merely averages of the amounts for 1931 and 1933. No attempt at exactness was made in the case of these figures. The amounts may have been as much as $100 to $200 off, but inasmuch as the income from subsidies represents such a minute proportion of the total income of the Chicago District, the error thus incurred is not significant. The following results were obtained:

1930	1931	1932	1933	1934
$25	20	452	30	25

Admission Receipts

Admission was almost invariably charged at the many Communist indoor meetings and "socials." As has been pointed out in an earlier chapter, "socials" were particularly useful as fund-raising occasions. Considering the fact that unemployed were frequently allowed reduced admission at such gatherings, we may estimate ten cents as the average admission fee at "socials" and indoor meetings. This figure was partially based on admission charges cited in police records, and on the reports of field investigators.

On the basis of this estimate and the total annual attendance figures for " socials " and indoor meetings,[2] the income from this source was calculated:

1930	1931	1932	1933	1934
$1,900	3,100	8,200	4,600	4,600

It must be pointed out that, particularly in the case of indoor meetings, most if not all of the money collected at the door was used to cover expenses incurred in arranging, publicizing, and staging the meeting.

Donations

Donations comprised the main source of party funds in Chicago. Included in this category were the funds taken up in collections at public meetings and " socials," as well as contributions of sympathetic individuals and organizations. The language organizations in Chicago were particularly important contributors to the Communist cause.

It is obvious that the amount collected in this manner is extremely difficult to estimate. No data exist on the total amount of donations made to the party in the Chicago District. Figures are available, however, for the amount received by the Central Committee for the years 1931, 1932, and 1933:

1931	1932	1933
34,335	87,261	56,767

The proportion of the residual income of the center which these sums represent was extended to the Chicago District. This proportion was as follows:

1930	1931	1932	1933	1934
23	39	64	58	71

Figures for 1930 and 1934 were estimated.[3]

[2] For figures on attendance at different types of demonstrations, see Chapter XII.

[3] The indices for these years were estimated in the following manner: The variations between indices for 1931, 1932, and 1933 were closely

Applying this index to the total income from sources previously discussed, we have computed figures as to the annual income from donations in the Chicago area:

1930	1931	1932	1933	1934
$3,560	10,625	36,665	13,850	45,600

The total was particularly high for 1932, as compared to 1931 and 1933, because of the extensive contributions from local sources made in connection with the election campaign, and because of the disproportionately large number of sympathizers who contributed to the Communist cause during that year of unrest.

Other Sources of Income

We have by now given estimates for the three major sources of income in the District. Numerous other methods of collecting funds were employed by the Communist Party, however. For example, sale of buttons, pamphlets, and sustaining publications all netted an income which, though it rarely covered the cost of the item, should be included as propaganda expenditure.

In addition, the expenditure of national funds for propaganda circulated at large throughout the country was not included. This includes funds utilized in the national election campaign of 1932, in the campaign against the Scottsboro verdict, and in other national issues sponsored by special committees with headquarters in New York City.

The total amount of money expended for propaganda in Chicago from these miscellaneous sources is not great, however, when compared with the amounts collected and expended in the District. It was ignored in compiling the present data because of the lack of adequate information.

---

correlated with simultaneous variations in total membership in the Chicago party. That is, the ratio of the index to party membership was approximately constant. This ratio was extrapolated to 1930 and 1934, and the indices for those years derived from it and from membership figures.

Summary

Following are the estimates for the four sources discussed above:

	1930	1931	1932	1933	1934
Dues	$10,000	$13,500	$12,000	$5,400	$14,000
Sub.	25	20	425	30	25
Adm.	1,900	3,100	8,200	4,600	4,600
Don.	3,560	10,625	36,665	13,850	45,600

Summing up these items, the total income, and hence the total expenditure for each of the five years, was obtained:

1930	1931	1932	1933	1934
$15,485	27,245	57,285	23,880	64,225

Expressed in per-capita terms (dollars per member):

1930	1931	1932	1933	1934
$20.36	20.05	25.47	13.60	26.96

The Communist Party has been greatly restricted in its activities by lack of sufficient funds. For the period of study the amount of money expended for Communist propaganda was highest in 1934, but at no time was it large enough to enable the party to disseminate its propaganda effectively through an area as large as the Chicago District.

Furthermore, it must be emphasized that this amount was not available in a lump sum for planning a campaign for any given year. It was collected and spent in driblets by many units, sections, and the District, and as a result much of its potential effectiveness was lost.

PART FIVE

THE INFLUENCE OF PROPAGANDA

CHAPTER XIV

Skillfulness

THE SUCCESS of propaganda depends upon the exercise of skill under favorable circumstances. Skillfulness is not enough. Able propaganda offensives have failed from lack of resources, and clumsy campaigns have succeeded through propitious circumstances. In this examination of Communist propaganda our task is to untangle the effect of skillfulness from the effect of other factors which determine receptivity or restriction.

Was Communist propaganda successful in Chicago? Since several goals were sought, the answer is not simple. As far as membership is concerned, Communist propaganda was by no means successful. In 1933 members were actually lost. If loss is attributed to housecleaning after rapid expansion, this implies a criticism of the recruitment policy of the expansion period.

The impression of comparative failure is deepened when it is remembered that Communist propaganda was less interfered with in Chicago by duly constituted authorities than it was in many other places in the United States (and in the world at large). Communists had a relatively clear field. There was something like free trade in propaganda during the Great Depression. Yet Communism failed to win in open competition with rival political parties.

In a sense our report is a study of how Communist propaganda failed. The mere fact of comparative failure is less important for us, as political scientists, than the discovery of the factors which contributed to this result.

Must we attribute lack of success to deficient tactical skill?

Or was there tactical skill but deficient strategical skill?

Or did skillfulness fail because of the strength of factors making for restriction over factors favoring acceptance?

By skillfulness is meant economy in reaching ends in view, and skillfulness in propaganda is the economical manipulation of symbols to control attitudes on controversial issues. Detailed procedures are matters of tactics; the general orientation of the operation is strategy.

Tactical skillfulness in managing symbols implies both " distinctiveness " and " adaptiveness." Some symbols must be chosen as key symbols. They must be somewhat distinctive in meaning and style; otherwise the propagandist will not be able to keep control of the attitudes which he fosters.

Key symbols need to be reinforced by appearing in contexts which carry the meanings which it is desired to organize with reference to them. The choice of key symbols and of supporting context needs to be adjusted to the possibilities of the setting in which the propaganda operates.

Distinctiveness also calls for the association of distinctive symbols promoted by a certain organization either with its distinctive (positive) symbols of identification or with its distinctive practices. " Communism," is a distinctive symbol with reference to " republicanism," " monarchism," " liberalism." But once the C.P.U.S.A. has succeeded in implanting positive attitudes toward " Communism," it is important to connect this symbol as immediately as possible with distinctive symbols and/or practices. Practices include: signing application blanks for membership in the Communist Party; subscribing to Communist Party literature; meeting Communist Party workers. Unless the distinctive symbols are intimately bound up with the distinctive term of identification of the party or/and with its distinctive practices, rival élites may appropriate the symbol and get the benefit of whatever favorable attitudes result from the propaganda. An "American Communist" or a "National Communist" party might be launched to control favorable responses toward the symbol "Communist."

Adaptiveness involves the choice of already existing practices (as well as symbols) appropriate to the end in view. For one, this refers to the channels of propaganda. When the members of a given community are to be reached by propaganda, it is sound tactics to make use of the established practices of focusing attention. If the community is accustomed to read newspapers, it is evident that this practice may be turned to the ends of propaganda by circulating appropriate symbols through the already existing newspapers, or by starting rival newspapers. If the community is accustomed to gather in conversational groups in public parks on Sunday afternoons, this practice may be captured for propaganda purposes by disseminating symbols among these groups. Such practices determine the focus of attention within the community, and the focus of attention is of crucial significance for attitude manipulation.

Adaptiveness refers not only to channels, but also to symbols of propaganda. It implies — and this refers to channels as well as to symbols — a quick adoption of apparently successful devices of rivals, and a quick defense against adverse symbols (by diversion of attention or by nullification). It equally implies quick discarding of devices which are apparently unsuccessful. This is implied in the use through time of only such patterns as are appropriate to the ends in view.

Where direct data concerning the skillfulness of propaganda devices are not available, one may arrive at presumptions about it from the observation of "indicators" like the adoption by rivals after initial surprise about their use.

Any objective examiner of Communist propaganda in Chicago during the Great Depression will certify to its distinctiveness. Key symbols were circulated which were neglected or attacked by rivals. Words like "Communist," "Communism," "U.S.S.R.," "Workers' International" were distinctive positive symbols of identification. References to the coming revolution of the proletariat in America were symbols of fact (symbols of expectation) which were less distinctive, since they were shared with the Socialists. But emphasis upon "the coming revolution" was much greater than in Socialist propaganda, and by association with "Communism" became a distinctive symbol. Some demands, though not exclusively used by Communist propaganda, were nevertheless so emphatically and so frequently invoked that they became highly distinctive. The demand for the recognition of the Soviet Union is representative of this list of prominent though shared symbols.

Our analysis of slogan styles confirmed the general impression that a small number of forms were constantly adhered to by the Communists, so that they themselves became distinctive of Communist propaganda. The basic characteristics of Communist slogans were sufficiently constant to become distinguishing marks of Communist propaganda. Socialist organizations oscillated greatly in the choice of slogan patterns and arrived at no stable style during the period studied. The Socialist committees tried out many more slogan forms than the Communist councils. Thus they made more experiments with "questions" than the Communists. Here are representative examples:

YES, WHAT HAS ONE YEAR OF THE NEW DEAL GIVEN YOU? RELIEF STATIONS? NEW RELIEF POLICY? NRA JOBS AND PAY RAISES? HIGHER STANDARDS OF LIVING? THEN, WHAT ARE YOU WAITING FOR?
(*Workers' Committee, 1717 N. Fairfield Avenue*)

ARE YOU HAPPY? THE H . . . L YOU ARE!
(*Spring 1934; Workers' Committee, Local 19, 1507 E. 55th Street*)

IS THERE A SANTA CLAUS FOR THE UNEMPLOYED?
(*December 1933 to March 1934*)

The combined "statement" and "question" forms were used in certain slogans:

HUNGER AND WANT ARE STARING HALF A MILLION PEOPLE
IN CHICAGO DIRECTLY IN THE FACE AND YET THERE IS PLENTY
FOR ALL!! THIS IS INHUMAN AND INEXCUSABLE. WHAT ARE
WE GOING TO DO ABOUT IT?
(April 18, 1932; Workers' Committee, Calumet District, Local 24)

There were some experiments with irony; statements were
made which were intended to be understood in an opposite
sense. Such slogan forms as the following were not paralleled
by the Communists:

PLAN TO TRY " FORCED LABOR " NEXT
(March 31, 1934)

DISCRIMINATION — INSULTS AND ABUSE FOR THE UNEMPLOYED
(March 31, 1934)

Communist propaganda concentrated so much on the imperative style that slogans which began with " Hands Off "
or " Down With " were generally understood to be Communist.

The Communists made deliberate efforts to point all slogans
toward action, and if possible toward distinctive action in the
name of the key symbols of the propaganda. Some symbols
demanded immediate response: words like " attend," " vote,"
" march " were pointed toward prompt action under the guidance of the Communist Party élite. The relationship of other
symbols to action was established not so much by their " manifest content " as by the circumstances under which they were
used. The Communists tried to arrange their symbols in contexts which clearly pointed to the immediate action desired.
Leaflets and posters were not distributed promiscuously, but
were concentrated along a line of march or within an assembly
hall where opportunities for immediate participation were
plainly visible.

Several dangers are connected with distinctiveness, especially when the key symbols are unavoidably associated with
" foreignness." The Third International was undeniably

" alien "; it was a world-wide, centrally disciplined organization, and its headquarters were Moscow. " Subversive foreign influences " were already viewed with suspicion in the United States, and the key symbols of Communist propaganda were thus predestined to carry heavy burdens of negative sentiment. The long-run objectives of the Third International involved the use of certain symbols which were charged with negative sentiment in the lives of most Americans. There was the demand, not only for " revolution," but for " world revolution." There was the denial of optimistic expectations about the future of American institutions, and the assertion of their inevitable and catastrophic disappearance. Thus the nucleus of Communist propaganda was composed of symbols which were counter-mores in America.

The perils of distinctiveness could be circumvented to some extent by adaptiveness. The " irreducible minimum " of world revolutionary radical symbols could be chosen for key symbols, but these could be associated with other key and accessory symbols which were less loaded with negative sentiment. An examination of the slogans used in Communist Party propaganda shows some striking examples of adaptiveness of this kind. " Bosses " were often assailed in the place of " capitalists." Yet our study of slogans showed that the slogans put out by the party itself made tenacious use of " alien " symbols. We found that 40 per cent of the symbols utilized in slogans on leaflets signed by the party were " alien " (measured by the frequency of use). " Foreign " terms were, however, " diluted " by the groups which supplemented the party. The slogans circulated by the " cover" organizations were far less given to the repetition of these terms. The effect of expanding the number and activities of " cover " organizations was to reduce the relative prominence of " alien " symbols in the whole symbol output of the Communist-controlled associations. Hence we are justified in saying that Communist propaganda became less and less distinctive as the depression advanced.

Declining emphasis upon certain distinctive symbols implied a certain degree of adaptiveness of Communist propaganda. Another index of adaptiveness was the prompt inclusion of the grievances of special groups. We have already compiled a list of the groups which were singled out for specific and positive mention in Communist slogans. The range, it will be recalled, was wide and embraced the following:

Unemployed	National Guardsmen and
Relief Clients and Workers	R.O.T.C
Small Taxpayers	Athletes
Small Depositors	Families
Small Property-Owners	Single Persons
Small Home-Owners	Children, Pupils, Parents
Farmers	Youth and Students
Teachers and School-Board	Women
Employees	Negroes
Ex-Servicemen	Jews
	Foreign-Born
	Neighborhoods

Another indication of the promptness with which special grievances were incorporated in Communist propaganda is given by the nature of the issues which were featured in demonstrations at different phases of the depression.

The demonstrations may be tabulated in ten groups according to their principal issues. In 1930 "labor demands" accounted for 22 per cent of the total number of demonstrations, which was the maximum figure for this group during the period in question. This seems to correspond to a similar predominance of such grievances within the total system of grievances of the wage-earners, since in 1930 the main deprivational aspects of the depression for the wage-earners were the lengthening of hours, cutting of wages, and deterioration of " working conditions " rather than unemployment. The NRA and the business revival increased the importance of problems of labor organization during 1933 and 1934 as against the two preceding years, and a glance at the record shows that " labor demands " reached a second high point, accounting for 17 and 16 per cent of the total number of demonstrations in these two years.

1930 was the first year when unemployment was making itself sharply felt and when protests against unemployment would be expected. This is indeed the case: 12.5 per cent of the demonstrations were arranged as protests against unemployment; it was the peak year of this category of demonstration. Later the general protest against the plight of unemployment gave way to the concentration of attention on grievances arising from the relationship of the unemployed to relief administration. In 1934, when the relief issues fell into the background, simple protests against unemployment again played a more prominent role, rising to 8 per cent of the total number of demonstrations.

" Special Days " would be expected to show much stability in relative frequency over short periods of time. This expectation is borne out by the facts (they vary between 4 and 7.5 per cent of the demonstrations). Since the role of ceremony may be presumed to be greater in " Special Days " demonstrations than in any other of the ten groups, it might be expected that their relative frequency would vary inversely to the insecurity level. This seems to be confirmed by the circumstance that " Special Days " were most frequent in 1930 and were least frequent in 1931 and 1932. Thus the relative stability as well as the character of the fluctuations of this group of demonstrations may be accounted for by properties of acts of ceremony; they are collectively internalized acts and go forward at customary times with a minimum of short-run responsiveness to changes in reactivity or environment.

1931 was the year which marked the high point of protest against evictions (6 per cent of demonstrations), and earlier data have shown that the incidence of evictions rose most rapidly in 1930 and 1931.

A great many demonstrations demanded freedom of action for protesting groups. Into this category came complaints against interference with freedom of speech, press, association, or assembly, complaints against violence by police and employers, and against "class justice" and similar issues. The following are representative demonstrations:

Demonstration to demand release of Harry Eisman, Young Pioneer (fifteen-year-old boy Communist in New York), in front of Board of Education, 460 S. State Street, April 12, 1930.

Mass meeting against the killing of Solomon Brooks (unemployed Negro), Odd Fellows' Hall, 3335 S. State Street, June 26, 1930.

Mass meeting to protest against the threatened imprisonment of seven Gastonia defendants (textile strikers in North Carolina), Temple Hall, Marshfield Avenue and Van Buren Street, April 13, 1930.

Demonstration against the refusal of a permit for the use of Union Park, American Theater, Madison Street and Ashland Boulevard, July 4, 1930.

Demonstration against the deportation of Mr. Serio, Jefferson Park, Polk and Lytle Streets, September 19, 1930.

Mass meeting demanding release of Tom Mooney and defense of Communist prisoners, Peoples' Auditorium, 2457 West Chicago Avenue, September 23, 1931.

Mass meeting to pledge support for the campaign fighting for the repeal of the Criminal Syndicalism Law, Polish Falcons Hall, Ashland Avenue and Division Street, December 28, 1931.

Mass meeting to demand release of the Scottsboro boys, repeal of the Criminal Syndicalist Law, abolition of the Red Squad, Pythian Temple, 3737 S. State Street, January 10, 1932.

Mass meeting to protest slaying of workers at the Ford plant in Detroit, Coliseum, 15th Street and Wabash Avenue, April 18, 1932.

Mass meeting against Melrose Park Massacre and to protest against police violence, Coliseum, May 13, 1932.

Mass meeting to defend the workers' press and to demand the release of the editors of the Lithuanian daily *Vilnis,* Lithuanian Auditorium, 3133 S. Halsted Street, December 19, 1932.

Mass meeting, a "Public Inquest: Was Art Anderson murdered?" (unemployed worker), 923 E. 75th Street, October 17, 1933.

Demonstration against arrest and trial of workers charged with violation of injunction issued to break the strike at the Kimball Piano Company, Judge Friend's Court, County Building, March 22, 1934.

Mass meeting to demand freedom for Andrew Guerriero: " Food for his family. He stabbed a case worker because his family had been let to starve. Who is guilty? " 1323 Blue Island Avenue, May 18, 1934.

Mass meeting to fight for free speech, St. Louis Avenue and Roosevelt Road, August 25, 1934.

From the outset of the depression clashes with the police rose in frequency until 1933. The relative frequency of demonstrations for " Freedom of Action " is positively and significantly related to these changes in the environment. The years 1930, 1931, and 1932 showed a steady rise: 10, 13, 14.5 per cent. The two remaining years witnessed a substantial drop: 9 per cent in 1933, 7 per cent in 1934.

Under " Party Activities " have been listed the conventions, conferences, and similar meetings of the party. They would be expected to be relatively more frequent in the presidential-election year 1932, and lowest in 1933, when no major elections were held. Intermediate magnitudes would be expected in 1931 (a mayoralty-election year) and in 1930 and 1934 (congressional-election years). These hypotheses are confirmed by the facts: 1932 is the banner year (22 per cent), and 1933 is the low year (7 per cent). 1931 is 18, 1930 is 17, and 1934 is 11 per cent.

Protests about the administration of relief are separately listed. Since relief administration was not functioning on a large scale in 1930, we would expect that protests would be much lower in 1930 than in the years 1931 through 1933. 1933 would be an important year of protest against relief administration because of the technical difficulties introduced by the transfer of clients to work relief. By 1934, routines were established. The figures confirm these expectations: 1930 and 1934 were the low years of protest (7.5 and 13 per cent respectively).

The other years run: 19.5 per cent in 1931, 20 per cent in 1932, 29 per cent in 1933.

Demonstrations against war and Fascism or in favor of the Soviet Union are all grouped together among those relating to "Major Political Symbols." In view of the emphasis in the Communist Party (as a *world* party) on world issues, it could be expected that considerable attention would be continuously directed toward such symbols, and that the triumph of National Socialism in Germany would precipitate strong protests among Communists everywhere. Demonstrations concerned with "Major Political Symbols" remained stable (fluctuating between 11 and 13 per cent) until 1934, when they comprised 27 per cent of the total. Anti-Nazi protests were the most frequent.

There were some demonstrations which demanded protection of the consumer, but such demands were too sporadic to present a significant relationship to changing circumstances.

The foregoing analysis of issues at demonstrations has shown the high degree of adaptiveness of Communist propaganda. This analysis has proceeded in terms of the symbols utilized to enunciate specific demands. It is possible to corroborate the general result by examining some formal attributes of the symbols invoked.

Symbols which pointed sharply toward action used the imperative form of the verb. The year 1931 was the year of maximum deprivation during the Great Depression in Chicago, and it was also the peak year for the imperative form of the verb in Communist propaganda slogans. 1933 was the year which saw the most indulgences, and 1933 was the year which registered the low point in the use of imperative verb forms. The year 1931 was the highest for the symbols of most circumscribed reference, and the lowest for the least circumscribed references.

By studying separately each quarter of the Great Depression, these results may be scrutinized in greater detail. The quarters have been classified in Chapter II as quarters with a predominance of indulgence or deprivation, or as quarters in which there was a balance of the two (with or without considerable changes in both directions). Demand slogans may be classified according to their directness in respect of action. " Simple " slogans — that is, slogans composed of one or two symbols — may be said to show a high degree of such directness. Examples:

>Against War! (one unit)
>Demonstrate against War! (two units)

The table which follows shows that quarters which were deprivation quarters or balanced quarters showed a higher frequency of simple slogans than indulgence quarters. The sign (plus or minus) means that the proportion of simple slogans to all slogans increased or diminished over the preceding quarter. The figure shows the percentage of change. The quarter is given by year (1930–) and order within the year (1, 2, 3, 4).

Deprivation Quarters	Balanced Quarters [1]	Indulgence Quarters
− 60 (1931–2)		− 85 (1931–4)
− 45 (1933–2)		− 50 (1932–4)
		−100 (1933–3)
+100 (1930–3)	+782 (1931–1)	+ 61 (1930–4)
+226 (1931–3)	+ 50 (1932–3)	+ 13 (1934–2)
+200 (1932–1)	+249 (1933–1)	+ 24 (1934–4)
+ 1 (1932–2)	+100 (1933–4)	
+ 12 (1934–1)		

Thus variations in the intensity of the stress toward action, which presumably varies inversely as the net balance of indulgences and deprivations,[2] was met by adaptive changes in the styles of the Communist slogans.

[1] The " inactivity " quarter (1934–3) is not included.
[2] At least as long as this balance does not fall below a considerable negative magnitude, where " passivity of destitution " may set in.

The adaptiveness of Communist propaganda is evinced with reference to practices as well as symbols. It is easier to demonstrate the degree to which the Communists furnished a model for their rivals in respect of practices than of symbols.

The Communists were foremost in expanding available channels of mass contact during the Great Depression. No doubt the two most potent means of reaching the focus of mass attention were the demonstration and the cover organization. These practices were not invented by the Communists. But they were promptly appropriated and elaborated from the usages of the American environment and the Russian model. Novelty consisted in fusing separate manifestations into a comprehensive enterprise which embraced everything from local protests against eviction to nation-wide hunger marches and election rallies.

As a reminder that the Communist Party did not invent the mass demonstration in 1930, it may be pertinent to recall that the Proletarian Party (one of the Communist fractions of 1919) established a Chicago section in 1921 and became the chief instigator of street meetings. In the autumn of 1923 from 15 to 20 street meetings were being held each week, and in the following year the party organ could truthfully declare: " More street meetings are held by our organization than by all other working class political groups combined " (*The Proletarian,* November 1924). In the Great Depression the Workers' Committees failed to copy the demonstration practice, and the Workers' League (organ of the Proletarian Party) was too weak to cut any figure. The Unemployed Councils practically pre-empted this channel for the duration of the crisis.

It has long been a common procedure for organizations of all kinds to control as much of the lives of their members as possible by means of youth's, women's, and other auxiliary subdivisions within the organization. When the organization in question was a propaganda organization, some of these sub-associations were able to proselyte by providing social or serious occasions for contact with unbelievers. The Communists, however, were the first protest organization to work out to their fullest extent the possibilities of the cover organization. So effective were some of these special-purpose associations that the rivals of the party copied the pattern as elaborated by the Communists. The Socialists and liberals, for example, copied the special organizations of the unemployed in 1931. The Unemployed Councils (Communist), however, remained the most numerous, having over 80 locals at their peak. The Workers' Committees (Socialist) had no more than 70, the Workers' League (Proletarian) had about 10, and other groups about 15. The 175 locals had a constantly changing member-ship, with reference to composition as well as to numbers. On the average, they may have numbered about 10 each, so that the total would have been 1,750 during the active years. By examining the number of complaints concerning individual cases presented by these groups it is possible to estimate the number of certain kinds of contacts made with the rank and file of the unemployed; it appears that in their heyday these organizations were reaching, in the special way just indicated, about five or six thousand relief applicants (which was about five per cent of the total population on relief).

The Communists took the lead in the use of English rather than foreign languages in propaganda periodicals: 41 per cent of the Communist periodicals edited in Chicago between 1919 and 1924 were published in some other language than English, but during the same period 70 per cent of the Socialist and 78 per cent of the syndicalist (I.W.W.) periodicals appeared in a foreign language. In the years 1930 through 1934 the Com-munists reduced their foreign periodicals to 10 per cent, the Socialists to 54 per cent, and the syndicalists to 50 per cent. The details are given in Table I (see next page).

The Communists also took the lead in publishing local and functional periodicals in Chicago. During the first third of the post-war period (1919–24) the Communists published no local periodicals, and the Socialists and syndicalists had but one each. Between 1924 and 1929 the Communists put out

TABLE I

*Revolutionary Periodicals in English and in Foreign
Languages*

	Communist		Socialist		I.W.W.	
	Number	Per Cent	Number	Per Cent	Number	Per Cent
1919–24:						
Foreign	11	41	14	70	18	78
English	16	59	6	30	5	22
1925–9:						
Foreign	9	38	11	73	2	40
English	15	62	4	27	3	60
1930–4:						
Foreign	5	10	7	54	2	50
English	44	90	6	46	2	50

41 local papers, which was 84 per cent of their output in
Chicago. The Socialists, meanwhile, rose to 38 per cent (5 of
their 13 publications). Most of the Communist rise is to be
attributed to the shop paper (a "functional" periodical),
which they sought to develop as a means of reaching the
worker in the factories. For the details see Table II.

The Communists were not only the leaders in the publication of native, local, and functional periodicals: they cheapened and popularized all forms of printed matter. The Communists applied cheap methods of printing to cheap paper,
and other groups followed in line. A striking example of this
is the shop paper, which as a rule was mimeographed. The
Communist pamphlets exercised a decisive influence on the
pamphlets of all rival parties. As the Communist pamphlets
became less long and formal, all pamphlets became more
brief and popular. Leaflets showed the same trend.

The Communists were less original in relation to some of
the channels of subordinate importance. They copied well-

TABLE II

Local and National Periodicals Published by
Revolutionary Groups in Chicago

	Communist		Socialist		I.W.W.	
	Number	*Per Cent*	*Number*	*Per Cent*	*Number*	*Per Cent*
1919–24:						
Local	0	0	1	5	1	5
National ..	27	100	19	95	22	95
1925–9:						
Local	6	25	0	0	0	0
National ..	18	75	15	100	5	100
1930–4:						
Local	41	84	5	38	0	0
National ..	8	16	8	62	4	100

known models, and they were less originally elaborative than in the field of demonstration, cover organization, and periodical. The forum was one of the less distinctively used channels in Communist hands.

In 1930 there is a record of four forums under the auspices of the Proletarian Party, which was the most active " Leftist " party in the forum field at the time, and of but two forums controlled by the Communist Party. In 1931 the Communists increased their proportion of " Left " forums from the 20 per cent of the previous year to 43 per cent. 1933 was the biggest forum year, which suggests that when demonstrations were banned at relief stations, energy went into indoor activities. " Left " forums in Chicago (see next page).

Study classes were well-established practices among protest parties in Chicago. The Proletarian Party, for example, was holding four classes weekly in different parts of Chicago in 1922. Three of these classes were for new members and

	Communist-Con-trolled Forums		Other " Leftist " Forums	
	Number	Per Cent	Number	Per Cent
1930	2	20	8	80
1931	5	43	7	57
1932	3	30	7	70
1933	8	48	9	52
1934	6	67	3	33
1935	2	50	2	50

(Compiled from the notices appearing in the " Leftist " press and in the leaflet collection)

one was for all comers. The *Proletarian* announced an average attendance of 30 (October 1922) and spoke of plans for expansion.

Participation in election campaigns is another standard practice even of parties which entertain no hope of immediate success, but seize the opportunity for propaganda during these formalized crises. Many minor practices (like the use of buttons) come from the patterns usually associated with electoral activity.

In some cases the party failed to discard practices which had very little success. Tag days, for example, yielded very little financial return and had no demonstrable effect on recruiting.

The foregoing examination of skillfulness in distinctiveness and adaptiveness has convincingly shown the tactical brilliance of Communist propaganda in relation to its revolutionary rivals. The failures of Communist propaganda were not tactical; we must search elsewhere for an explanation of the comparative unsuccess of this propaganda in Chicago.

Strategy, as already defined, is not a matter of procedural details but of general orientation. The canons of strategy may be subsumed under two principles: the principles of *combination* and *precaution*. The object of strategy is the predominance necessary to the goal pursued, and the probability of its attainment is enhanced (1) by certain combinations of favorable influences (principle of combination) and (2) by the prevention of certain combinations of opposing influences (principle of precaution).

Communist propaganda, a world revolutionary radical propaganda directed from the center of the most recent world revolution, seeks the following goals: (1) the consolidation of the influence of the revolutionary élite within the Soviet Union; (2) the addition of new members to the Soviet Union. In a state beyond the Union, like the United States, the special strategical goals may be stated as follows: (1) the defense of the Soviet Union; (2) the preparation of the masses for revolutionary action under the guidance of the Communist International; (3) the preparation of the American party (a local élite) for revolutionary leadership.

The data which have been assembled in this investigation are more relevant to (2) and (3) than to (1). The recognition which was given to the Soviet Union under the Roosevelt régime was a goal for which the Communists had been working, but this does not necessarily imply that their propaganda aided the result. Special study would be necessary to discover the degree to which the advocacy of recognition by the Communists delayed it by associating it in the minds of influential Americans with an alien and subversive policy.

Adverse criticism can be directed against Communist strategy in Chicago on the score of a violation of the principle of combination by giving too much attention to the unemployed at the expense of the employed. The point of this criticism is not that the Communists would have been justified in ignoring the plight of the unemployed. Manifestly one of the tasks of a world revolutionary radical propaganda is to direct insecurities, however caused, against the established order and toward the desired order. The negative judgment emphasizes only the disproportionate amount of energy which was expended upon the unemployed. Results appeared very easy to get, but these results were in many ways unstable. The " housecleaning " of 1933, in which members were extensively dropped, was a strong indication of the failure to direct recruiting campaigns toward potentially reliable persons. The recognition of this mistake became a commonplace among Communist leaders (but this subjective consensus on the part of the leadership does not, of course, establish the fact).[3]

A perhaps still more serious criticism of Communist strategy alleges that the principle of precaution was neglected. This principle demands the prevention of an overwhelming concentration of enemy influences. Ever since the dramatic success of National Socialism in Germany in 1933, there has been general agreement upon the suicidal character of a " Leftist " strategy of disunion. The Socialists and the Communists in Germany fought with one another until their enemies grew powerful enough to annihilate them. Broadly speaking, the middle-class groups occupy the balance-of-power position in states like Germany and the United States. For historical reasons connected with the early phases of growth of proletarian Socialism, the " petty bourgeoisie " has been a target of abuse and the " proletariat " an object of love and esteem. However, proletarianism has often been used to appeal to middle-class formations (in addition to skilled workers), and the analysis of the social composition of most " proletarian " parties has shown that they draw heavily on middle-class support. The attitude cleavages which are fostered by the exclusive glorification of the " proletariat " and the adverse references to the " petty bourgeoisie " are a danger to unified " Leftist " activity. Apart from the symbols used in radical revolutionary propaganda, these attitude cleavages are of course sustained by the differences in relationships to the processes of production which separate the agricultural laborer, the unskilled factory worker, the skilled factory worker, the clerk, the small merchant, banker, and manufacturer, and the low- and middle-income professional groups from one another.

At the 1928 Congress of the Communist International the party issued a declaration of war against the Socialist parties of the world, bracketing them with " Fascist " elements. This

[3] See Appendix.

World Congress announced that a " third period " had arrived in the development of capitalism since the Russian revolution. This period, beginning, it was said, in 1928, was alleged to be distinguished by the cementing of the alliance of Social Democracy with world capitalism and by the assumption of a Fascist character by the Social Democrats. The new tactical line called for sharp denunciation and exposure of the " Social Fascists." A few months before this Congress (late in 1927) the authorities in the Soviet Union had announced a vast program for the industrialization of Russia, the Five-Year Plan, scheduled to start in 1928.

It was obvious that the opportunity to " build Socialism in one country " depended upon freedom from outside intervention in the affairs of the Soviet Union. This, indeed, was constantly emphasized by the Communists. What policy would diminish the probability of wars by foreign states against the Soviet Union? The sound answer is a policy which would preserve friendly attitudes on the part of middle-class and working groups toward the Soviet Union. This would have meant free and frank co-operation with most of the existing Leftist and liberal elements in the politics of Germany and every other significant state, including the United States. The alternative policy (directing fire against the Socialist and liberal elements) could only be successful in the case that revolutionary crises should occur in the great powers (and even then the foreign affiliation of the Communist Party might strengthen restrictive factors and weaken diffusion factors so as to prevent the actual control of the revolutionary development).

As it was, the leaders of the Soviet Union turned their attention to internal affairs and adopted a policy of deliberate provocation in foreign affairs. By labeling the Socialist and liberal elements " Social Fascist," they dug their own grave in Germany and laid the foundations of a similar development in the United States.

The bitterness which the Communists engendered among Socialist and liberal elements during the Great Depression in Chicago will be abundantly evident in the details to be discussed in the chapters which deal with the restriction of Communist propaganda. In this place we will present some data concerning the growth of the more extreme forms of anti-Communist associations, the as yet feeble and fumbling possible precursors of developments parallel to the national revolutionary radical propagandas which cut short the life of the German Republic (and even earlier, the Italian parliamentary democracy).

A census of the smaller organizations which recruited membership among the unemployed reveals a number of relatively nationalistic and conservative societies such as the American Citizen's Loyalty Association, the All Nations League of America, which considered itself a " patriotic " organization, the North Side Community Bureau, organized by a number of lawyers with the support of an alderman, the Off-the-Street Club, an organization underwritten by the Chicago Association of Commerce and several wealthy business men and manufacturers, the People's League of America, which claimed that it was " organized for the protection of independent merchants and for better conditions of the relief rolls," the Protectors, an organization which considered its purpose as one of " protecting the family and the home and the constitution," the United Workers on Unemployment, a conservative split-off from a Workers' Committee local, and the Melting Pot League of America. A great many of these organizations were underwritten by local business men, especially in the residential districts near the " country towns " within Cook County and just beyond the city limits of Chicago. Many acknowledged as their intention competition with radical organizations such as the Unemployed Councils in order to remove these " Communistic blots " from their communities. Sometimes the organizing personnel came from disaffected officers or members of other relief organizations more to the " Left." There are indications, though the evidence is sporadic, that such conservative organizations were becoming more numerous as the depression proceeded until the crisis was passed.

Of special interest as a nationalistic and counter-revolutionary organization is the Progressive American Club. This organization explicitly stated in its constitution that among its purposes was the spreading of counter-propaganda against the Communist Party and all other revolutionary groups (a purpose which may be taken as typical for the kind of organization here in question).

" Whereas good results are obtainable only by organized preparatory education and whereas we American Citizens believe the government of the United States to be a sound and just government which gives every person under its protection an equal opportunity and provides constitutional guarantees to all persons alike, and knowing that certain elements are working against the best interests of this government, we hereby declare it to be the purpose of this organization to unite action to protect the government of the United States against all enemies."

The constitution states further on:

" Every person who applies to become a member of this club shall first be investigated and if it is found that he belongs to the Communist Party, or any one of its branches, he is automatically barred from membership."

These organizations, though few in numbers, without mass following, and un-co-ordinated among themselves, were of significance as possible precursors of more vehement and widespread and co-ordinated nationalistic and counter-revolutionary action which might have ensued if the crisis had been more protracted.

Our analysis thus far has led to the provisional conclusion that Communist strategy, not Communist tactics, was at fault in the failure of the Communists to make more successful use of the opportunities which were given to them in Chicago by the Great Depression. This provisional finding, however, cannot be conclusive until we have examined the circumstances which were operating in the Chicago situation to favor or to block world revolutionary radical propaganda.

CHAPTER XV

Facilitation

COMMUNIST propaganda in Chicago was in competition and conflict with several revolutionary propagandas which were appealing for the loyalty of the masses. The old I.W.W. (Industrial Workers of the World) was not entirely extinct. Its orators proclaimed the unity of the workers of the world, predicted the inevitable success of the proletariat, and demanded the unification of the workers in " one big union " capable of revolution and reconstruction. The Proletarian Party claimed to be a Communist Party and possessed a tiny nucleus. The Socialist Party carried on, though a shadow of its pre-war self.

Communist propaganda fought with all the propagandas of the established order as well as with rival revolutionary programs. The machines of the Democratic and Republican Parties stood in firm possession of traditional loyalty and available patronage.

To what extent was the acceptance of revolutionary symbols favored by certain factors in the Chicago situation which were beyond the control of the propagandist? To what extent did the propaganda of Communism get the benefit of facilitating circumstances?

In this chapter we disregard what the propagandist contributes to success and explore what the situation contributes to it.

The factors which facilitate revolutionary propaganda are certain changes in the environment which impinge upon certain predispositions. Together they constitute the matrix within which the propagandist may carry on his work of particularizing and intensifying attitudes.

It is not difficult to offer a general statement about the nature of the environmental changes which foster the rejection of established symbols and the acceptance of new ones. Deprivational changes favor revolution.

The analysis of predisposition is somewhat more involved. The predispositional factors relevant here are (1) pre-organized attitudes, and (2) levels of reactivity. Pre-organized attitudes are defined as attitudes which are organized with reference to the symbols which figure in the propagandas which are being studied. Attitudes which are not specifically related to such symbols contribute to the level of reactivity. The difference may be exemplified by saying that some persons were definitely committed to "Communism" before 1930 (pre-organized attitude); others were discontented with themselves, but referred their discontent to no political symbol (their discontent contributed to the level of reactivity).

We are now in a position to indicate the kinds of predisposition which facilitate the spread of revolutionary propaganda: (1) pre-organized attitudes which are positive with reference to the positive symbols of the propaganda; (2) pre-organized attitudes which are negative with reference to the negative symbols of the propaganda; (3) a high level of insecurity. Insecurity is characterized by dysphoria (uneasiness or discomfort, for example, rather than joy or comfort, which are among the euphoric states).[1]

[1] A more exact conception of the insecurity level may be stated in these terms: "anxiety" may be defined to refer to subjective events which show (1) acute dysphoria, and (2) stress toward action. This definition is made with special reference to the intensive observational standpoint of psychoanalysis, but it may be used, although with different definitions of the terms of which it is composed, to refer to phenomena observed from less intensive — more extensive — standpoints. Anxiety events arise in the course of conflicting tendencies to act, and neurotic symptoms are modes of resolving conflict which mitigate (with-

That acceptance of revolutionary radical propaganda is facilitated by deprivational changes in the environment is confirmed by the march of events in Chicago during the Great Depression. Communist attitudes spread most rapidly at the beginning of the depression, which was when deprivations increased most rapidly. Later on, as the environment became more indulgent, the spread of Communism was retarded or curtailed. Communism was the chief revolutionary propaganda of the depression period, and the broad curve of its diffusion is representative of the fate of revolutionary propaganda as a whole.

The variations of balance of local indulgence and deprivation have been indicated, in the second chapter of this report, for the five years which succeeded 1929. 1930, 1931, and 1932 were years of greater deprivation than 1933 and 1934. The volume analysis of Communist propaganda in Chicago, given in the third section of this report, showed that Communist propaganda reached its peak in 1932. 1933 was a year of severe setback, and 1934 was not as full of propaganda activity as 1932 had been.

More detailed inspection of developments quarter by quarter does not disconfirm the general proposition that there is a close positive connection between deprivation and the ac-

---

out abolishing) anxiety. Neurotic symptoms include hysterical distractibility, bodily disabilities of a functional nature, obsession, compulsion, and kindred phenomena. For details, consult any standard treatise on psychiatry, such as William A. White: *Outlines of Psychiatry*. Attention may be called to the treatise by Harry Stack Sullivan which is appearing serially in *Psychiatry; Journal of the Biology and Pathology of Interpersonal Relations,* under the title " Psychiatry: Introduction to the Study of Interpersonal Relations."

In a collective (distributive) sense we may speak of the level of insecurity. The term refers to the frequency of the events of anxiety which occur in a given interval of time in a specified group. For a discussion of certain political problems from this point of view, see Harold D. Lasswell: *World Politics and Personal Insecurity* (New York, 1935). The terms "euphoria" and "dysphoria" have been used by Radcliffe-Brown in approximately similar senses to those given here.

ceptance of revolutionary symbols. Yet during the shorter periods the results become more difficult of interpretation. In part the difficulty comes from the crudity of the data, and in part from the disturbing effect of processes which are running to completion through different intervals of time.

Can we establish invariant quantitative relationships between changes in deprivation and changes in pro-revolutionary response? Are there discoverable relations between the amount and rate of deprivation and the amount and rate of revolutionary activity? Will it be possible to predict the magnitude of revolutionary effort which follows a specified magnitude of change in the environment? Can we at least determine the general structure of the relationship between these factors; for example, is it a linear or a more complicated function?

The chief technical problem is to discover indices which are both satisfactory and available substitutes for the terms which are used in stating the general propositions. It is easy to utter the proposition that revolutionary activity varies directly with deprivation, and that the form of the relationship is linear. But the distance between statement and confirmation (or disconfirmation) is much farther than we are at present able to go.

However, some promising regularities of relation have appeared in certain bodies of data. The census of 1930 divided Chicago into census tracts and reported the rental value of residential property in five categories. We undertook to compare demonstrations in census tracts which differed according to the rental value of property within the tracts. The same number of tracts (20) was chosen in which most of the property rented below $20 a month (tracts A), between $20 and $44.99 (tracts B), and between $50 and $99.99 (tracts C). It may be noted that there were no tracts in the city in which property predominated whose rental was in excess of $100. The census of unemployment made it possible to compute the average rates of unemployment for the three sets of tracts. The lowest-rent tracts had the highest rate of unemployment

(5.7 per cent), but tracts C had a higher rate than tracts B (4.8 as against 3.7 per cent).

All demonstrations held in these census tracts were tabulated for the years 1930 through 1932. It was found that there were 26 demonstrations in tracts A, 15 in B, and none in C. The rates per 10,000 population were .10 for tracts A, .06 for B, and .00 for C.

An indicator of the intensity of collective reaction is the number of persons arrested by the police in connection with demonstrations. If police policy toward demonstrators is assumed to remain constant, the number of arrests may be expected to vary as the provocativeness (the intensity) of the demonstrators. In recording arrests the persons were classified according to their home address, not according to the place where the demonstration was held and the arrest made. The results conform closely to the demonstration data: there were 51 arrests made affecting tracts A, 26 affecting B, and 3 affecting C. The rates per 10,000 population were 2.9 for A, 1.4 for B, and .2 for C.

These figures imply a very close connection between the magnitude of unemployment in tracts B and A, and the response. The amount of unemployment which struck those living in B was 65 per cent of the amount which affected those in A. The amount of response of those in B was 60 per cent of the magnitude of the response of those in A, in terms of demonstrations. It was about 50 per cent of the response of A, by the number of arrests. The residents of C were far less active. They experienced 85 per cent of the unemployment of those in A and showed little protest of the kind here recorded.

Sharper differences between A and B might have been predicted on the following grounds: the extent to which unemployment is a deprivation depends upon the extent to which the loss of income involved impairs the material position of the individual. Individual A may have no reserves (indeed, he may have negative reserves, in the sense that his debts exceed his assets) when he is thrown out of a job. Individual B may have reserves large enough to maintain his usual standard of expenditure for several years. Individual C may lose a job, but his truck garden may leave him more self-sufficient than his neighbor D. The size of reserves is positively correlated with the size of income and so is the amount of rent. Presumably those in rental tracts B have more reserves than the residents of tracts A. Hence they might be expected to suffer less deprivation when unemployed than the latter, and therefore to show relatively less revolutionary protest than the inhabitants of A. Yet the figures given above indicate that the B group responded about as sharply as the A group.

From another point of view this proportionality may be somewhat surprising. Predispositional factors might be expected to militate against a counter-mores response among the residents of the B tracts. Those who belong to middle-income brackets may be expected to be more tightly bound to the established standards of conventionality than the lower-income groups. After all, it was not considered good form for " respectable " people to march in demonstrations or to get entangled in violent encounters with officers of the law. The rental bracket between $20 and $50 included a sizable proportion of the middle-income groups of the city of Chicago. The activism of the tract B residents may thus lead to the presumption that the " proletarianization " of the people of Chicago had gone much farther prior to the depression than is generally believed.

There is no conclusive body of data now at hand to describe the attitudes which prevailed among different income groups in Chicago at the outset of the depression. We wish we had the results of a survey of the attitudes of members of different income groups toward different forms of mass action. Perhaps we should have found that the persons in the B tracts exhibited the same attitudes as those in the A tracts.

Since such explicit studies of attitudes were not made in Chicago, propositions about predisposing attitudes must rest upon much less satisfactory data. Our own studies did not begin until after the onset of the Great Depression, and as far as earlier data were concerned, we were as dependent as any historian upon the accidental residues of the past. (The most satisfactory methods of studying attitudes involve the contemporaneous observation of events.)

Our data from the census tracts seem to warrant the following statement: at the outset of the depression in Chicago, persons paying less than $50 per month rent responded to unemployment with the same degree of collective revolutionary protest. Those paying above $50 per month rent responded with less collective revolutionary protest. Data are inconclusive with respect to the relative importance of financial reserves and of predisposing attitude differences.

Given the limits of our research, the best available method of studying predisposition toward revolutionary activity was to examine the differential characteristics of those who accepted Communist symbols and practices, as against those who accepted the Socialist (and liberal) ones. For this purpose comparisons were instituted between the leadership and the membership of the organizations of the unemployed which were under Communist and Socialist control. The Socialist- (and liberal-) controlled organizations (Workers' Committees) offered demands for less radical and revolutionary action to the unemployed than the Communist-led Unemployed Councils. Both organizations were revolutionary, predicting and demanding all power for the proletariat. The Workers' Committees, however, expressed revolutionary aims as remote aspirations rather than as uncompromising immediate demands and laid less emphasis than the spokesmen of the Councils on the probability or necessity of violent revolution. The Workers' Committees were more chary in referring to the world-wide character of their demands than the Councils, which were constantly demonstrating on behalf of revolutionary action abroad. The Councils demanded and employed more drastic means of advancing toward the classless society than the Committees. (Drastic means have been defined as means which were regarded as permissible by the community, if at all, only under conditions of great provocation.)

The Communist Party undertook to record significant characteristics of all persons who became connected with them. It was hoped that the records would be a dependable source of information about the composition of the party and its affiliated organizations. But the party information was highly unreliable. Often the material was collected in the most casual way, and after checking upon representative reports, we decided to disregard this apparently promising lead. Far more dependable knowledge could be obtained from the case histories prepared by the agencies of public and private relief. Hence it was decided to select samples of Council and Committee leadership and membership for comparative analysis. Data were assembled on 100 leaders of the Committees and 100 leaders of the Councils, and on 100 members of the Committees and 100 members of the Councils. The same criteria of selection were employed in both cases in the interest of comparability. The leaders were chosen from those who had attained city-wide prominence in the work of the unemployed organizations. The members of both organizations were chosen at random.

The case histories contained records of contact between the relief agencies and their clients. Life-history material had been collected by interviewing the client and acquaintances of the client. Some documentary details were at hand, such as the transcript of records made during pre-depression contact with employers and with relief agencies.

As was stated above, factors of predisposition facilitating the acceptance of revolutionary propaganda are:

> Positive attitudes toward positive
> symbols of revolutionary propaganda;
> Negative attitudes toward negative symbols
> of revolutionary propaganda;
> Insecurity Reactions.

As an index of positive attitudes we have taken previous affiliation with radical, revolutionary symbols. Negative attitudes are indexed by anti-authoritarian conduct. Negative attitudes may be indicated [2] by traits or relationships which occupy low deference positions in the community. Insecurity reactions may be shown by emotional instability.

The case-history data show that the Communist-led organizations of the unemployed were recruited in greater degree than the Socialist-led organizations from persons who had been affiliated with radical organizations before the depression. In Table I we find that 23 per cent of the leaders and

TABLE I

Previous Radical and Revolutionary Affiliations

Type of Organization	U.C. Leaders	U.C. Members	U.C. Combined	W.C. Leaders	W.C. Members	W.C. Combined
Less Radical ...	5%	2%	3.5%	9%	0%	4.5%
More Radical ...	23%	4%	22%	5%	2%	1.5%

4 per cent of the members of the Communist-controlled organizations had previously been affiliated with radical political organizations (like the I.W.W., the American Workers' Party, the Communist Party). The corresponding figure for the Socialist and liberal Committees were 5 and 2 per cent.

An unfavorable attitude toward authority is to be expected from those who have broken with the legal and mores stand-

[2] The term " indicator " is used in place of " index " when the data referred to are not referred to in the definition of the attitude in question. An " index " of attitude is an act like signing an application card for party membership. An " indicator," for example, of negative attitude toward established symbols and practices is belonging to the Negro race — a trait which is believed to expose the individual to social stigma and to arouse some degree of answering resentment against the established order. Strictly speaking, the assertion that a certain phenomenon is an " indicator " for an attitude is equivalent to the prediction that, were the proper studies made, the " indicator " data would be shown to be positively correlated with " index " data.

ards of the community. Or, phrasing the expectation more exactly, those who have deviated from conventional norms in the past are more disposed to deviate again than those who have not so deviated.

It may be noted, however, that previous violations have led in many cases to the suffering of deprivation at the hands of duly constituted authority (arrest, punishment). The fact of suffering may imply that the violation was a failure and not a success, and we may predict that responses which fail are less likely to be repeated than responses which succeed. Against these considerations we set the following: those who come into conflict with the law often suffer some permanent stigma on the part of non-revolutionary elements in the community (their deference position is thus permanently impaired). We also know that arrest and punishment may increase the deference received from non-élite groups: we have seen how much is made of persons who can show certain kinds of prison records. Hence it is justifiable to use the fact of past offense as an index of predisposition against authoritative symbols.

TABLE II

Offense Against Law and Mores

	U.C. Leaders	U.C. Members	U.C. Combined	W.C. Leaders	W.C. Members	W.C. Combined
Arrests	33%	17%	25%	10%	11%	10.5%

Another index of anti-authoritarian attitudes is non-attendance at church. Table III shows that the councils recruited more heavily than the Committees from those who did not attend church.

TABLE III

Non-Attendance at Church

U.C. Leaders	U.C. Members	U.C. Combined	W.C. Leaders	W.C. Members	W.C. Combined
49%	19%	34%	24%	11%	17.5%

Foreign birth or Negro birth imply some divergence from the most "valued" antecedents in the United States. Table IV shows the nativity of the Council and the Committee groups:

TABLE IV

Nativity

	U.C. Leaders	U.C. Members	U.C. Combined	W.C. Leaders	W.C. Members	W.C. Combined
2nd Generation Native-Born and over	26%	17%	21.5%	41%	31%	36%
1st Generation Native-Born ..	23%	17%	20%	22%	25%	23.5%
European Foreign-Born	30%	41%	35.5%	28%	32%	30%
Negro	21%	25%	23%	6%	5%	5.5%
Mexican	0%	0%	0%	3%	7%	5%

Only 26 per cent of the leaders and 17 per cent of the members of the Communist-controlled organizations were second-generation native-born or over, as contrasted with 41 per cent of the leaders and 31 per cent of the members of Socialist-controlled organizations. Second-generation native-born or over would possess a heritage which would render an individual relatively "indigenous" with respect to attitudes toward "American" institutions. First-generation native-born we find approximately equally distributed. We find, however, slightly more individuals among those recruited to Communist symbols who were European foreign-born.

Of the Unemployed Councils and affiliated organizations 21 per cent of the leaders and 25 per cent of the members were Negroes; 6 and 5 per cent were the corresponding figures for the Committees. (The Negroes are known to be among the non-élite of deference in Chicago.)

Table V supplies data which confirm the differences just

established. We have recorded here the affiliations before the
depression with non-American cultural societies and with
American societies. (Clubs and fraternal orders are included.) Of Communist-controlled organizations 10 and 16
per cent of the leaders and members respectively had previously belonged to their race or nationality organizations, as
compared with 6 and 3 per cent of the leaders and members
of Socialist-directed organizations. Of the leaders and members of the Socialist-controlled organizations 20 and 13 per cent
respectively were affiliated with organizations bearing American names (Elks, Moose, Masons) as compared with 14 and 4
per cent of the leaders and members respectively of the Communist-controlled organizations.

TABLE V

Prior Affiliations with Clubs, Societies, Fraternities

Type of Society	U.C. Leaders	U.C. Members	U.C. Combined	W.C. Leaders	W.C. Members	W.C. Combined
" Non-American "	10%	16%	13%	6%	3%	4.5%
" American "	14%	4%	9%	20%	13%	16.5%

By examining the nature of offenses against the law we
may discover something about the personality structure and
the anxiety level of those who affiliate with revolutionary
radical patterns. Hence we may establish presumptions about
which " personality groups " are predisposed in this direction.
Table VI distinguishes between the kinds of crimes for which
individuals were responsible. The large proportion of political offenses committed by the leaders and members of
the Communist-controlled unemployed organizations is to be
attributed to the fact that in their previous protest affiliations
they belonged to the most radical and revolutionary, and thus
would both level the most severe attacks against the established order and suffer the most deprivation at its hands.
One of the most significant differences appears in the entries

for " petty personal offenses " and " premeditated crimes." A large proportion of the offenses previously committed by members of the Communist-controlled organizations were committed in anger or other emotional excitement, while a similarly large proportion of the offenses of the leaders and members of the Socialist- and liberal-led organizations were crimes committed after calculation (thefts, forgeries, for example). We have already noticed that those recruited to the most radical symbols and practices were distinguishable from the " established " racial, national, and cultural characteristics, and hence were peculiarly exposed to suffer deprivations at the hands of the established order. Such persons would presumably resort to counter-attacks which on some occasions would take the form of violent acts committed in anger (or other state of excitement). Those recruited to the Socialist and liberal organizations were less distinguishable from the established patterns, and hence less exposed to certain deprivations. It is reasonable to anticipate that their offenses would more often be of a calculating kind. The differential here in question may be related not only to the environmental differences just discussed, but to personality structure.[3]

TABLE VI

Type of Offense	U.C. Leaders	U.C. Members	U.C. Combined	W.C. Leaders	W.C. Members	W.C. Combined
Petty personal offenses	18%	9%	13.5%	2%	2%	2%
Premeditated crimes	3%	2%	2.5%	6%	8%	7%
Political crimes	12%	6%	9%	2%	1%	1.5%

[3] As stated later on, extremist reactions are probably connected with the personality group called " externalized rage types."

As a means of illuminating the figures which have been set forth in the tables, we have selected the following series of ten leaders of councils of the unemployed. All the data are from case-history records. The leaders range all the way from persons who had been professional Communist functionaries before the depression to individuals who had little previous history of organized anti-authoritarian action. Some of the leaders were predisposed toward organized, revolutionary, and radical action by virtue of many social and personal characteristics; others were so predisposed merely by virtue of transitory situational factors, and thus had less permanent attachment to general symbols of protest against capitalistic society. The data are summarized as of 1934.[4]

Leader #1 has been an active member of the Communist Party for ten years. He was born in a New England city in 1904, coming to Chicago in 1925. There is no record of offenses against the law save those connected with Communist activities. He broke from his church long before his membership in the Communist Party. He is an American Negro, married to a native-born white woman. This marriage, however, took place within the past two years — that is to say, long after his Communist affiliation. There is no record of conflicts with employers or of offense against the mores.

Since arriving in Chicago leader #2 has been employed by the Communists or by Communist sympathizers. He was first employed by a Communist press as a printer, and for a short time as a cobbler and a bootblack. Through his connection with the party he has occasionally earned small sums. Just before his marriage he applied for and received aid from the Clearing House for Men; later, when married, he was transferred to the Cook County Bureau of Public Welfare. In August 1933 he was transferred to the Unemployment Relief Service. In his first position he earned $18 a week; in his second, $12. He owned no real property, and his debt was small, $30. He suffers from ulcers of the stomach, and claims always to have been of delicate constitution; but he refused to attend clinics as suggested by his case workers. He has been

---

[4] Details are interchanged, but the individual pattern remains consistent.

officially active in agitprop work for the party in District #8, has organized for the Trade Union Unity League, and has spoken very frequently at meetings of the League of Struggle for Negro Rights.

He completed high school, did two years of post-graduate high-school work, and took three years of university extension work. He was much interested in electrical engineering and studied it to some extent. His wife is a member of the Communist Party, and his life has centered wholly in Communist activity.

Leader #2 headed one of the most militant councils in Chicago. He was a Communist candidate for a state office. About 1927 he became very active in the Socialist Party, and since 1929 in the Communist Party. He is a member of the American Legion and also of the Workers' Ex-Service Men's League (a Communist affiliate). He has been active in trade unions, having previously been a member of the Sheet Metal Workers' Union, and since joining the Communists he became a leading spirit in the Industrial Building Laborers' League, competing with the A. F. of L. union in the same trade.

Leader #1 was born in Chicago in 1890 and has resided in his present neighborhood for twenty years. Between 1911 and 1931 he was employed as a sheet metal worker, earning incomes ranging from $48 to $66 a week. He owns his own home and has incurred a debt of $900. He is a grammar-school graduate. He is a native-born American of Protestant tradition, married to another native-born American of similar tradition. He has not attended church since he was nineteen years of age. There is a record of previous contact with the Juvenile Protective Association because of marital discord and the abuse of his children. He is a chronic drunkard and frequently beats his wife. He has received help (for the first time) from the Rural Service of the Cook County Bureau of Public Welfare since January 1931.

In this case the person was active in revolutionary radicalism before the depression, and simply continued his association with it. He has a long record of organized protest activity, and some indications of difficulties in his intimate adjustments.

Leader #3 had formerly been a member of the Proletarian Party. He was also one of the founders of the Workers' League of

America, and a member of the Cab Drivers' Union. There is no record of earlier contact with penal welfare agencies, nor of any previous offenses against law. He is a native-born American, married to a foreign-born German; both come from Protestant backgrounds. He was born in a small town in a Middle Western state in 1895, came to Chicago in 1916, and has resided in his neighborhood for the last seven years.

Leader #3 finished the second year of high school. He was employed as a government meat-inspector, foreman in a packing plant, chauffeur in a large cab company, and small construction contractor. From 1916 to 1917 he earned $35 a week. From 1918 to 1919 he earned $40 a week. From 1919 to 1926 he earned $35 a week; from 1926 to 1929 he earned $50 a week. He owns his home and also a number of vacant lots. He owes a debt of $500.

Leader #3 was known to many of the workers and supervisors in his relief district as an unusually aggressive person. He had made successful contacts with higher administrative officers in the relief service, and frequently went over the heads of the local officials in order to get results. This "cocksureness," coupled with skill in manipulating persons, caused much resentment among the local administrators. He promoted a number of large-scale plans for coping with the unemployment problem, and higher officials gave them sympathetic consideration. He was given a scholarship to the Wellesley Institute for Social Progress, and an observer wrote of him: "In sessions where relief was featured he had a great deal to contribute and felt enough at home the second week to suggest a special meeting on certain phases of relief. He organized the meeting, planned who should join in the discussion, and it went off very well." In 1927 he had a quarrel with his employer and was discharged. It is worth noting that although there is a record of three shifts in occupation, two of them improved his earning power.

Leader #4, unlike the men just cited, was not fully connected with revolutionary parties before the depression, but he had been active in labor unions, some of which were intimately associated with the Communist Party. During the depression he became a minor figure in the party. His union experience included the machinists', the cabinet-makers', the textile workers', and the chauffeurs' unions. There is no record of previous contact with penal welfare agencies or of offenses against law or mores. As a result of his Communist and Unemployed Council activity he has been arrested several times at his district relief station and at demonstrations. He is a native-born American of German extraction married to a native-born American. He belongs to a religious sect, the Truth Center, having broken away from a large Protestant denomination.

Leader #4 was born in a small town in the East Central states in 1892, and has resided in Chicago since 1923. He is a high-school graduate and has taken several extension courses at a Middle Western university. He had a long career as a foreman and superintendent in textile mills, and has written some pamphlets on technical subjects. He has earned incomes ranging from $600 to $300 per month. He owns no real property and has a debt of $600. Medical examination shows that he suffers from arthritis of the spine. He sustained an accident to the cartilage in his knee which has stiffened the knee to such an extent that he is no longer employable. This accident occurred through the hands of a certain alderman during a raid by the police at a park laborers' meeting which #4 attended in the role of an observer. The alderman pushed him as he was entering the police car.

Several case workers found him extremely aggressive in personal dealing. One wrote: " #4 is an unadjusted person of a choleric and vehement temperament. He is a professional disturber and tells proudly of the various troubles he has made as a member of the Unemployed Council." Another one described an incident at the district office: " #4 was shouting, gesticulating and making a general disturbance in the waiting room. The gist of his remarks was that if the clients stood together they could succeed in wresting their rights from welfare agencies, but unless they united they would lose everything."

Leader #5 had also been on the fringe of Communist activity before the depression, and was drawn into more direct association through the Unemployed Councils. He had previously been a member of the West Side Forum Council, a Communist-directed organization. He had also been an active member of the International Union of Bakery and Confectionary Workers. There is no further record of organizational experience, save his army service in France during the World War. There is no record of contact with penal welfare agencies, and his sole offense against law was committed when, as the leader of his local branch of the Councils, he was arrested in his relief district office for " causing a disturbance." He was charged with " disorderly conduct" and was freed on bail. He is an American Negro, married to an American Negro, both of Protestant tradition (he no longer attends church). There is no record of conflict with employers or offenses against the mores.

Leader #5 was born in a small Southern town in 1889, coming to Chicago in 1917 and remaining there except for his service in the infantry during the war. He had a grammar-school education, and earned his living as a cook for hotels and railroads. His income was around $100 a month, which is below the average of the leaders investigated. His rental was relatively low and his debts small, only $20. His first contact with welfare agencies took place in June 1926, when for a short time, owing to unemployment, he applied for and received aid from the United Charities. In 1927 and 1928 there are records of registration with the United Charities and the Cook County Bureau of Public Welfare, again owing to layoffs.

Leader #5 lacks many of the predisposing experiences which are found in many of the other leaders. To some extent his experience in the war, his residence in a Northern industrial community, and his opportunities for travel in connection with his work would undermine the submissiveness which may be expected after rather long subjection to peonage in his Southern environment. Such sophisticating experiences were utilized by the Communists in their forum agitation, and in the crisis of unemployment the Communists gave positions of leadership to members of the Negro race as a tactical device. He was handicapped by his rather low literacy and rather mediocre intelligence.

In the case worker's report we find the following information: Leader #5 boasted to his case worker of being the Communist organizer in the relief district. He claimed that his followers were two thousand strong, and that they were planning to stage a hunger march to arouse Governor Horner.

On one occasion he explained to his case worker " that he is a communist, and that he had respect for all women. But as far as men are concerned, he could knock the hell out of all those of the capitalistic or bourgeois class."

Quotation from a letter to Governor Horner:

"Mrs. S. in the County Commission Office advises our committee she thought this way of having the Randolph Street Office would be more better satisfaction to the Unemployed Councils than the Relief Station. But this is proven unsatisfaction. It takes too longer of hours to get immediately relief for starving families.

"We are sending our committee from all our Unemployed Councils to your relief station — both families very badly in need of immediately attention. Should our committee continue to be disregarded we will then appeal to the mayor."

Quotation from a case worker's report:

" #5 has a peculiarity in that he requested that the word ' relief ' be used in place of ' we ' when worker speaks of this organization. The latter word, according to #5, causes a peculiar unexplained reaction upon him.

" #5 impressed workers from the office as being of low intelligence and of a highly emotional and excitable nature.

"The Unemployment Relief Service referred him for a psychiatric interview. #5 refused to keep his appointment."

Leader #6 had no organizational connection with revolutionary radicalism or with affiliated organizations before the failure of his business in 1929 and the loss of the job which he immediately took. He organized two Negro locals of the Unemployed Councils, using his home as the meeting-place.

Leader #6 is an American Negro, married to an American Negro. He was a relatively large-scale farmer in a Southern State where he was born in 1885. He came to Chicago in 1916 and has resided in his present neighborhood since 1917. After coming north he became an excavating contractor and was successful until 1929. For a short time he was employed as a varnisher, earning $35 a week. He joined the painters' union. In January 1931 he applied to and received relief from the United Charities. In September 1932 he was transferred to the Unemployment Relief Service. The report of an interview by a case worker:

" #6 and his wife were at home. #6 had been called to the attention of the Unemployment Relief Service because of his connections with the Unemployed Councils, whose activities have placed him in disrepute with U.R.S. #6 accounted willingly for the development of his attitude in this organization.

"He was a farmer, owning his own property and doing successful business. He came to Chicago, took up excavating, and acquired four teams. He was so successful that he began buying himself a home in a very nice district. In 1920 he sold his farm and put his money into his new venture, but in 1929 his business went down. He attributes his failure to the general tendency of competitive business. A large scale excavator put six teams in his district and worked for half price. He crippled #6's business. During the next six months a mortgage on his home was foreclosed. He states that it had been hard to see the fruits of all his years of labor snatched away, and to find himself a victim of an evil of business organization.

"Last year #6 and his wife went out of the state to pick cherries and #6 said he was appalled at the waste, on the farms throughout the country. He says the government should have devised some plan to utilize this food for the hungry people.

"#6 stated that since he himself has been a sufferer he has great sympathy with anyone else who is traveling the same path. He stated that the Unemployed Council intended to co-operate with the relief organizations, and that even in its inception it did not advocate any idea of violence to obtain relief for the families it undertook to 'investigate' and represent to the relief organization. He insists that there is a serious lack in a government which permits its business to get to a place where a few citizens can tie up the country's resources.

#6 has a good business mind. He seems at present to be in a state of indecision, and confusion as to how to remedy the situation. He is not really converted to revolutionary ideas, but could easily be made an agitator."

Leader #7 had no record of direct or indirect contact with revolutionary radicalism before the depression. He was in the National Guard in 1905 and served in the army in 1918. He formerly belonged to the American Legion. After January 1934 he was active in Unemployed Councils, often speaking in connection with demonstrations. He gave up a part-time job selling in order to devote all his time to organizational work.

Leader #7 was born in a city in a Western plains state in 1889, came to Chicago in 1919, and has resided on the south side since 1929. He is a native-born American married to a native-born American, traditionally Protestant, but inactive. He graduated from high school and had two years of business college. From 1919 to 1928 he was employed as a valuation expert at $44 a week. Between 1929 and 1931 he was employed as an appraiser at $275 a month. During 1933 he was employed as a salesman on commission for a cash-register company. He previously had invested $2,000 in stocks and bonds which are now valueless. He owns property by inheritance and has an income of $20 a month from this property. He has incurred a debt of $350, has received relief from the Unemployment Relief since 1933, and gradually became interested in the work of the Councils and of the Communists.

Leader #8 had no record of contact with revolutionary radicalism before the depression and never became intimately attached to the work of the Councils or of the Communist Party. For a time he came into local prominence as chairman of the grievance committee of an active local. Before the depression he was an active member of the bakers' union. He is of English origin, and was born in a small Middle Western city in 1889. He is married to a native of similar origin, and also of Protestant traditions. He has not attended church for a decade. He came to Chicago in 1928. He is a grammar-school graduate and spent a year in business college. Since coming to Chicago he was a chief baker, earning from $45 to $50 a week. In September 1931 he sought and received aid from the United Charities. Two months later he was transferred to the Unemployment Relief Service. Physical examination showed that he suffered from " latent syphilis." One of his letters to a supervisor read:

"I am an American and it is strange that I have not the right to live as an American. I would not even listen to a radical speaker until a little over a year ago. I was 100% American (K.K.K.), but today I have learned the difference why conditions are so. My wife and children don't see red, but if you want them to think like me and turn radical, then don't pay the rent. My wife still believes in her religion and church and the children go also, but when people find their rights suppressed and taken away and evicted, when there is hundreds of thousands of too many houses and too much of everything, then the people see the trickery of religion."

Then, from a letter to the supervisor a week later:

" In writing this I will try and be more calm in my ideas, as I was very blue and discouraged when I wrote that last letter. It is hard to go on in this manner much longer. . . .

" I expect to be helping to get Alderman X re-elected soon now, and have given up any Unemployed Council long ago. I turned against their idea of fighting for relief for the people. I wasn't even with them that time I was asked on that committee of four in the relief station, only the police told them to get a committee of four and they could not get any others quick and asked me. I went with the four and Mrs. C. told us to wait until Mr. M. came and I did not wait and no one did wait, I heard; I wasn't interested with it, but I came there for my own case and I did not act on my own case all that day.

" My wife quarrels with me when we have not things to live decently any more with, and I have no job and it makes life not worth while, and if things don't change soon I guess I will leave home and travel and try that way, too."

Leader #9 served for a time as an agitator and as chairman of the grievance committee of an active council. She was drawn into this as a result of the following incident, described by a case worker: " #9 apparently was not an agitator until a man was injured by a policeman at a demonstration near the relief station. #9 was near the scene of the trouble and brought a doctor to attend the victim. For this activity #9 was arrested and remained in jail overnight. From that time she has been very active in the work of the Councils."

Leader #9 was a native-born American Protestant whose German ancestors came to America after 1848. She was raised on a farm in the Northwest, and graduated from high school. When employed as a housemaid in a hotel she met her future husband, who was an Italian Catholic recently emigrated from Naples. She told the case worker that she believed she became interested in him because forbidden by the hotel manager. Her husband was the houseman and employees were not supposed to keep company with one another. He had a grammar-school education. He was arrested twice, once for larceny and once for disorderly conduct. He was occasionally unemployed and #9 was compelled to work. They were constantly under pressure because of insufficient and somewhat uncertain income. The husband was formerly a member of the pressers' union and was a member of a Workers' Committee for a time.

Leader #10 was chairman of the grievance committee of an active local of the Unemployed Councils. He served in the American army in the war and also in Honolulu in 1924 and 1925. The case worker reports: " In 1915 he ran away from home, and finally got down to Texas. For excitement he crossed the border into Mexico and joined the Second Cavalry at Vera Cruz. One of his fellow soldiers dared him to shoot an officer. He shot him. He was imprisoned for nine months, at the end of which period he was given the choice of going to jail or receiving a dishonorable discharge. He chose the latter."

Leader #10 was born in a small Middle Western city and came to Chicago in 1926. He is American, native-born, married to an American native-born. Both have Protestant traditions, but he does not attend church. Between 1920 and 1924 he was employed as a foreman for a construction company at $45 a week. In 1924 and 1925 he was employed as a truck-driver by the post office at 65 cents an hour. Between 1925 and 1930 he was employed as a truck-driver for a furniture company at $36 a week. He applied to and received aid from the United Charities in 1930 and 1931, and was transferred in 1932 to the Veterans' Service of the Cook County Bureau of Public Welfare, and in the same year to the Unemployment Relief Service. He is characterized as a chronic drinker and described by his case worker as being inclined to occasional fits of violence. He has stated to his case worker that he thinks he is going crazy and has asked her to be referred to the Psychopathic Hospital.

This summary of personalities receptive to organized, revolutionary, radical propaganda during times of general deprivation has emphasized the importance of position within the value pyramid of the community. Practically all of the individuals involved came from those occupying middle or lower positions in the hierarchy of income and deference.

Exposed to the added blow of the depression, they dealt with their insecurities by associating themselves with demands for fundamental change by radical methods in the established order in which they had previously held a modest position. Many of them, however, were so deeply identified with this order that their share in organized protest was dependent upon small, "chance" incidents. Thus leader #9 became active in the Councils as a result of the "accident" of being held by the police in connection with a demonstration in which she was merely a spectator.

Many persons, essentially bound to the established order, joined protest organizations for what they could get out of them in the redress of their individual deprivations, and ceased to be interested in them when more profitable avenues seemed to appear. Leader #8, for instance, had shifted from the Councils by 1934 and busied himself with "respectable" party activity on behalf of an alderman.

At the other extreme were persons who had already before the depression acquired a vested interest in the Communist Party as professional agitators or organizers. Leader #1 had been identified with the party from his youth, and depended upon it entirely for his livelihood. Leader #4 had been long connected with organizations which were closely associated with the party, and consolidated his position during the depression.

Within these limits fall certain marginal cases which have much theoretical importance. In addition to their disadvantaged position in the value pattern of the community, they are disposed to anti-authoritarian activity by reason of deep personal insecurities. Before the depression their connection with organized protest groups may have been limited. But their previous life showed many evidences of profound inner conflict. Often they had abstained from participating in democratically organized associations, or had but brief contact with them. Characteristically they had clashed with specific individuals in authority or had broken authoritative rules of law or custom. They had much in common with individuals who remained aloof from organized protest during the depression itself, and engaged in hyper-assertive acts against individuals in authority (like relief administrators). Often, too, they left organized protest after a brief period of bitter agitation, vehement organization, or violence. Leader #10 is by no means among the most extreme examples of this type of history. He had recurring factional difficulties with his colleagues and passed in and out of organized activity. Many personalities like him were found among those who organized or agitated for rival groups to the Councils.[5]

[5] These personalities were not studied by methods as intensive as psychoanalysis. But the case histories were built up by interviews and direct observation over several months, and are far from casual and irresponsible observation. The case workers were given as much training and supervision as the emergency nature of the relief administration permitted.

It may be remarked that there is a continuous gradation of observational standpoints which may be taken up with reference to the persons who compose a given community. An example of the " intensive " standpoint of observation is that of the psychoanalytical interviewer in relation to his subject. The psychoanalyst focuses his attention for a long time upon the career line of a specific person, and uses a special procedure (the technique of free association) to disclose the finer structure of the personality. In a shorter interview the interviewer may use no complex method of observation. The case summaries just given were accumulated in " extensive " rather than " intensive " observational standpoints.

Since it is usually impracticable to psychoanalyze everybody (or even representative persons) within a given group, it is necessary to consider the relationship of the intensive and the extensive standpoints to one another. When we give psychoanalytical " interpretations " of the data collected by extensive, not intensive, procedures, we are predicting that proper investigations would demonstrate certain relationships between psychoanalytic data and extensively collected data. An advancing social and psychological science will move toward the " calibration " of the different standpoints with one another. Thus it will be possible to say, with a degree of confirmation already established, that if a certain timespace region is described as C' from the observational standpoint I, it would be described as C'' from the standpoint II.

The study of those who exhibit particularly high anxiety levels is relevant for political science in so far as it enables us to state some of the conditions of political extremism. Students of politics are especially concerned with extreme instances of political activism. Within a given context of relationships, we know that there are zones of special sensitivity to changes in the context. In other words, there are zones of persons who are predisposed toward assertiveness in the name of collective symbols; and within such zones there are sub-zones of persons predisposed toward assertiveness on behalf of collective protest symbols. Persons who take the initiative to modify or to defend the existing distribution of values (and the correlated practices) may be called the "hyperreactives." Some of the hyperreactives — persons who advocate drastic methods on behalf of fundamental change — are "radicals." (On the other hand, some but not all "radicals" are "hyperreactives.") The hyperreactives are those who take the initiative, whether for radical or moderate methods, and whether for (counter-) revolutionary or (counter-) reformist goals.

The composition of protest movements (like that of any other political movement) is constantly changing as the zone of hyperreactivity varies in extent, intensity, and direction.

The hyperreactives, as we have said, are defined as the ensemble of persons in whom are focused the opposing tendencies of the context. Our study of the Chicago cases has confirmed the general proposition that personalities whose anxiety level is high are predisposed toward political activism. Leaders like #10 fall in this category, and since persons of this kind have been intensively explored by psychoanalysis, data of the kind reported above may be set against this deeper perspective.

Leader #10 is one variant of the general pattern of political personality. The fully developed political personality dis-

---

The present interpretations of such data as those given about #10 are to be understood in the sense just stated. Their confirmation depends upon the future of scientific investigation.

places private motives upon public objects in the name of collective values. The distinguishing mark of the political personality is emphatic demand for deference; this must be coupled with skill in manipulating the environment and with timely circumstances, for an effective politician to appear.

What are the predisposing factors toward strong demands for deference? A necessary, though not a sufficient, factor is the failure of early adjustments to the intimate environment. Another factor is that such failures are met by continued action upon the environment rather than by complete recession into the self. When failures occur — that is, when libidinal impulses are denied completion — such ego reactions as persistence or rage reactions occur. If the reaction employed removes the obstacle which has been in the way of completing the act, it is likely to be relied upon in the future when deprivations occur, and hence to become a basic feature of the personality structure.

If the environment is cowed into submission by means of rage reactions, the personality may develop into an " externalized rage type." [6] Such types respond with ungovernable outbursts against deprivation. In the extreme instances they are so domineering that they are regarded as intolerable. In our civilization they may be kept on the move, passing from one environment and from one altercation to the next. They struggle against their own tendencies to submit and to give up the rage reaction; and they struggle against their own deep craving to give and to receive affection. They react against their submissive tendencies by exaggerated truculence toward the environment,[7] and they center their affections, not upon external objects, but upon themselves.

It is obvious that the possibility of co-operating with others

[6] The basic distinctions are found in H. D. Lasswell: *Psychopathology and Politics* (Chicago, 1930); *Politics: Who Gets What, When, How* (New York, 1936).

[7] For illuminating case material, see August Aichorn: *Wayward Youth* (New York, 1935).

depends upon directing assertive impulses against acceptable goals, and turning love toward common symbols and practices. This involves some relinquishment of rage reactions in primary relationships, and some limitations of secondary narcissism.

During periods with high insecurity level the personalities who conform to the type just described are given favorable opportunities for managing a transition from isolation to participation in organized activity. During crisis their fellows become very indulgent toward anyone who takes the lead in expressing and directing destructive impulses toward the symbol of the enemy. When the rage types possess skill in words, they may win the admiration of their contemporaries; and admiration is a form of affection which can be more readily accepted by these types than simple affection. If their skill is not in words, but violence, they may spring to head crowd action. In any case their social role is to intensify collective reactions through extreme statement and impetuous action.

Such types are so dependent upon huge and instantaneous supplies of deference that they cannot endure lack of appreciation or criticism. Thus when the organization meets with rebuff, their impulses recoil against the primary self and revert to older channels of expression. Hostile tendencies may be turned away from successful opponents to the other leaders or to the members of the organization itself, thus heightening factional conflict. In disgust they may "throw the whole thing overboard" and retire altogether from collective protest, perhaps working off their assertive impulses in individual attacks upon such authority objects as the administrators of public relief.[8] If they have an admiring circle, they may secede and launch a rival organization, resolving their emotional crisis by the multiplication of groups.

[8] For the client-administrator relationship, consult Gabriel Almond and H. D. Lasswell: "Aggressive Behavior by Clients toward Public Relief Administrators: A Configurative Analysis," *American Political Science Review*, XXVIII (1934), 643–55.

Even in their withdrawal phase, these rage types continue to perform their social function of intensifying the current collective tendencies. When protest is blocked and energies are turned back against the primary and secondary self, the rage types respond in ways which further weaken protest organizations (through withdrawal, factionalism, secession). Such personalities are constantly poised on the edge of proud isolation and of spectacular participation in mass action. Although they are peculiarly susceptible to propaganda for organized radical and revolutionary movements during crises, they heighten the internal conflicts within these movements whenever difficulties arise.

By examining the part which such hyperreactives play, we learn something of the psychological structure of movements of political protest, and especially of the difficulties which arise from the fact that revolutionary strategists are dealing to a considerable extent with people suffering great emotional stress. Opposing tendencies within a situation, all of the latent bipolarities, focus in personalities of the rage type; and the requirements of their inner life are such that revolutionary as well as counter-revolutionary functions are performed with impunity.[9]

The analysis which has just been made of factors affecting the acceptance of revolutionary radical propaganda has dealt with certain features of environment and of predisposition. The acceptance of revolutionary radical propaganda has been related to deprivational changes in the environment and to certain pre-organized attitudes and to certain levels of initial insecurity. The most intensively predisposing attitudes were those which were favorable to the pattern of revolutionary

[9] Notice Ernst Kretschmer's discussion of sensitive reactions in *A Textbook of Medical Psychology* (London, 1934), Chapter XIV, and in *The Psychology of Men of Genius* (London, 1931). Many forms of personality are not discussed here. For two important case histories of Negro Communists in Chicago, see Harold F. Gosnell: *Negro Politicians* (Chicago, 1935) Chapter XV. The interviewer was Dorothy Blumenstock.

radicalism and unfavorable to prevailing symbols and practices. Such attitudes were indexed by previous affiliation with revolutionary radical organizations or symbols, and by acts in violation of law and mores. They were indicated by alien and stigmatized affiliations, and by low income; in general, then, by non-élite position in the value pyramids.

The level of initial insecurities was studied for certain personalities, especially for some active leaders of Communist-led organizations of the unemployed. Attention was concentrated upon a type which was hyperreactive at the peak of crisis, followed by withdrawal, factionalism, and secession when difficulties arose as crisis died down. Such " hyperreactives " (not necessarily, be it repeated, "radicals") are very important in the political process, since they concentrate in their own personalities the opposing tendencies within any given context. They are the active points within certain zones of potential action; they actualize all the potential directions at all levels of intensity.

We may sum up the meaning of this investigation of revolutionary radical propaganda for the general theory of propaganda. The probability of the acceptance (A) of any pattern of propaganda (p^1) over alternative patterns (p^2 . . .) varies directly with the proportion of positive over negative relationships to the context in contrast with alternatives. These relationships depend in their turn on the structure of the environment (E) and the state of initial reactivity, or predisposition (P). The acceptance of Communism took place most often in the early days of the depression, when the symbols and practices of the established order were most often associated with deprivational features, and positive references to Communism were high. Acceptance declined as symbols and practices of the established order (alternatives to Communism) became more often associated with indulgences (relief granted through government channels, expressions of concern for the welfare of the unemployed). The comparative failure of revolutionary radical propaganda was to be pre-

dicted from the magnitude of the positive features connected
with the established symbols and practices of America prior
to the onset of the depression. As between the two chief rivals
for response (Communism and Socialism) in the name of
revolutionary radicalism, the data are too scanty to admit of
satisfactory characterization. Certain factors can be demonstrated to have worked in favor of the Communist propaganda,
but it is not possible to state their relative significance in the
whole context.

This survey of factors facilitating acceptance in Chicago
during the Great Depression contributed certain data which
bear upon our appraisal of the strategy of Communist propaganda. We have seen that Communist propaganda was able
to draw successfully upon the unemployed, but we have seen
that the very factors which fostered immediate success worked
for eventual difficulty. Besides this, by appealing to the personalities with the deepest anxieties, Communist propaganda
recruited unstable human material. Concentration upon the
unemployed has been criticized as a strategical error because
of the comparative neglect of the employed and of some other
layers in society. It may also be criticized for recruiting a disproportionate number of persons of a type predisposed to play
disruptive roles in organized political activity.

CHAPTER XVI

Restriction by Nationalism

COMMUNIST propaganda was in conflict with many of the established symbols and practices of American life. It exalted loyalty to the world destiny of a class above loyalty to the American nation; it substituted the prophecy of revolutionary collapse and rebirth for the " manifest destiny " of traditional Americanism; it demanded the sacrifice of the self to the discipline of an army of professional revolutionists. American nationalism and American individualism were both flouted by the Communists.

Communist propaganda had two choices when confronted by the difficulties presented by such an environment as the American. The propaganda might (1) continue to exhibit a high degree of distinctiveness at the expense of adaptiveness, or (2) increase adaptiveness at the expense of distinctiveness.

The first alternative would mean emphasizing the class character of the movement, stressing the inevitability of incorporating the world in the Soviet Union, emphasizing the Union as the true homeland of every worker, demanding constant preparation for the seizure of power in a future crisis. These are distinctive symbols; there are also distinctive practices. The revolutionary party could be recruited from persons who were put through very exacting tests and subjected to uncompromising discipline. The goal would be to build up a " monolithic " revolutionary nucleus fanatically loyal to the central symbols of the Third International and professionally devoted to their propagation.

The second alternative would mean de-emphasizing class and alien loyalties and connections, and stressing symbols peculiar to American tradition. These are modifications in respect of symbol; there might be modifications in respect of practice. Greater leniency could be shown in admitting members and in administering party discipline.[1] Such adaptations need not be deliberate; they may even be denied with sincerity.

Immediately after the appearance of the new world revolutionary pattern in Russia, rather rapid processes of diffusion and restriction began to take place. The symbols of the new pattern explicitly rejected many of the symbols in the name of which élites in other states justified their authority, and affirmed symbols in the name of which the authority of these élites was attacked within their native states. The emergence of the world revolutionary élite was a threat to practically every established élite in the world, and the resulting adjustments were the processes of diffusion or restriction of the revolutionary pattern.

Total diffusion involves the incorporation of the whole world revolutionary pattern, including the symbol of identification of its center (the Soviet Union) and the practice of affiliating with the Union. Partial diffusion involves the incorporation of some (not all) of the symbols and practices of the revolutionary pattern. Thus the symbol "proletarian" may be more frequently used in a positive sense, and a practice (like strict party discipline) may be paralleled.

Restriction (total or partial) may involve the intensification of old patterns. In our western European civilization parochialism is an established pattern (the sentimentalizing of symbols of identification which refer to areas smaller than the world). When to a local symbol is associated the demand to

---

[1] There might be: (1) symbol modification without practice modification; (2) symbol modification with practice modification; (3) practice modification without symbol modification.

become (or to remain) a state, the pattern is called nationalism. When to the local identifying symbol is associated the demand to preserve (or to extend) the influence of the state which is associated to this local symbol in a "nationalistic" symbol pattern, the pattern is called "patriotism." (There is, thus, no "patriotism" without "nationalism"; but there may be "nationalism" without "patriotism.") In the United States nationalism and patriotism were both intense; and they were intensified by many groups in the face of the anti-nationalism and anti-American patriotism of the Communists. Restriction of the scope of the revolutionary élite by the intensification of parochialism ("geographical restriction") is one of the most widespread responses to such threats. Its negative symbolic aspect consists in denying the claim of the new world revolutionary élite to "represent" persons and groups beyond the new world revolutionary center. Thus after 1789 élites beyond France denied the claims of the French revolutionaries to speak for all mankind everywhere; they spoke of the "*French* revolution" rather than the "revolution for human rights." The revolutionaries in Russia were confronted by the same counter-affirmations: the revolution was a "*Russian* revolution."

The restrictive processes may be two-sided: they may be acts of those who are unaffiliated with the revolutionary center, or acts of those who are affiliated with it. In the former case, we have "restriction by others"; in the latter, "restriction by self." If the Communists increase their invocation of the "Russian" or any other national symbols, they are intensifying one of the basic patterns which they rejected *in toto* in the original symbol pattern of the new world revolutionary wave. The "pure" world revolutionary pattern kept nationalistic symbols at a minimum. Yet they did not wholly disappear; and this facilitated the later intensification of their use by an élite which continues to claim descent from the original world revolutionary élite. Thus the fact that even during 1917–21 it was legitimate for Russian Communists to use

"Russian" in some combinations made it easier at a later time to sanction phrases which were proscribed in the "heroic period" of the revolution.

Hence if the Communists in America intensify their use of the traditional symbols of Americanism, they exhibit "restriction by self" through partial incorporation of an established pattern (which may be called a "counter-revolutionary pattern").

We know that at the peak of the period of prosperity the Third International stigmatized the Social Democrats as "Social Fascists" and thus maximized its distinctiveness. The World Congress of 1928 practically forbade friendly co-operation with the leaders of trade unions not affiliated with the "Profintern" or national Communist parties; or Socialist and liberal organizations. The slogan of the "United Front" — with the addition of the qualifying terms "from below" — was restricted to the rank and file and the lower levels of the officials of rival mass organizations. The higher officials of these organizations were vilified with an absence of restraint which was unprecedented in the history of the Third International.

If Chicago Communists followed the directives of the World Congress of 1928, they were bound to maximize distinctiveness at the expense of adaptiveness. Did the Chicago Communists hew to the party line or did they diverge from it? It will be recalled that the World Congress of 1935 marked a drastic shift in the line of the Third International. This Congress practically eliminated the insulting epithets of 1928 and called for unity against Fascism. Do we find such tendencies in the Communist movement in Chicago before they were explicitly expressed in the central agencies? On an international scale such tendencies first became visible in 1934. Could we, by studying the dynamic processes of the Chicago party, discern evidences of the shift before 1934?

The data show that the Communist Party in Chicago

manifested opposite tendencies in respect of the party line of 1928: (1) the leaflets which were circulated by the party in its own name emphasized the symbols of world revolutionary radicalism (maximizing distinctiveness in conformity with the " general line "); (2) there was more and more reliance upon cover organizations which used symbols and practices closer to the traditional American pattern (augmenting adaptiveness and deviation from the " general line "); (3) some of the cover organizations failed to expand because of internal opposition to the Communist fractions which sought complete control and invoked distinctively Communist symbols (emphasis on distinctiveness in conformity with the " general line ").

The data about (1) have been detailed in Chapter X, and the data about (2) have been given in Chapter V. What is meant by (3) is shown in the story of a north-shore branch of the International Labor Defense. This document is quoted at length in this chapter. The account was written by a liberal lawyer who played a leading part in the affair, and relates his experience without animus and with regret that the enterprise failed. The narrative indicates how the Communist leadership procured the support of Socialist and liberal elements at the beginning and then lost this support by seeking to exercise exclusive control and to invoke distinctively Communist symbols. This report is reproduced in some detail because it is by an uncommonly able professional man. It shows most vividly what was involved in a distinctive Communist line, and it is representative of many similar situations.

The History of a North-Shore Branch of the International
Labor Defense. Why the " United Front " Failed
(By a liberal lawyer and leader)

When in August 1932 Comrade A, a member of the Communist Party, approached a group of radical intellectuals in the conservative suburb on the North Shore with the suggestion that they form an ILD branch, his suggestion was favorably received.

Some members of the group had had a little experience with the weaknesses of the ILD and set up the goal of building a better branch, with carefully planned meetings and a program working toward gradual development of radical thinking among the members, who, it was hoped, would be representative of all social and economic groups.

Most of the original members realized immediately that Comrade A knew very little about the realities of American life. His approach was certainly not suited to Americans, for he failed to take into consideration the revolutionary backwardness of the American masses.

The group realized that the usual type of Communist slogans and the waving of the " red flag " would gain them few converts, but would rather alienate those whom they wished to reach. They felt that a program of gradual " radicalization " would be far more effective. Comrade A agreed to be guided by the decision of the majority.

Organization of a Local Branch

At the first meeting, at which there were about 75 present, the District Secretary of the ILD was the main speaker, pointing out what the organization stands for, inviting Republicans, Democrats, Socialists, members of all creeds, colors, and political beliefs to join. He stressed the fact that the ILD is not a Communist organization, but that it protects victims of the class struggle, and endorses the Communist Party because the fundamental principle is the class struggle and improvement of conditions for workers. The audience was stirred and won over, until Comrade B, as chairman, another member of the Communist Party, blatantly burst forth in a tirade against capitalist governments, run by millionaires, oppressing the workingmen. He called upon the audience to unite with other members of the proletariat to overthrow the ruling classes, using language that jarred and startled the unprepared audience. The District Secretary of the ILD had succeeded in evoking a sympathetic response. This response was vitiated by the blunders of the chairman. A post mortem was held by the original committee, and the chairman was frankly criticized. He agreed thereafter to follow instructions.

The Scottsboro Campaign

Two months thereafter a Scottsboro Protest Meeting took place. The meeting was held in a Negro Y.M.C.A. and was aimed to draw in Negro and white workers who had never been reached by the radical movement. Committees made door-to-door canvasses of the working sections of the suburb giving detailed descriptions of the Scottsboro case, and how the efforts of the ILD saved the victims. Many of the workers had never heard of the case. Literature was distributed freely and the response was gratifying. The details of the meeting were minutely planned. Emphasis was to be on the Scottsboro case, as one manifestation of race prejudice, and stress was to be laid on discrimination against the Negro in every field of activity, social, political, and economic. Dignified informative leaflets were distributed.

Three hundred Negroes attended the meeting, all middle class. They showed deep interest as members of the committee went among them before the meeting explaining further about the Scottsboro case and the efforts of the ILD to save the boys. And here again the discipline of the committee was destroyed and their plans ignored. Comrade B, infuriated by the statements of the Secretary of the Y.M.C.A. that the directors had asked that no more " red " meetings be permitted on the premises, lost all sense of discretion. The Scottsboro boys were consigned to the background and again followed a tirade against capitalism and talks of police terrorism. The audience trickled somewhat fearfully out.

A definite split occurred within the branch. All had worked earnestly for the success of this meeting, and most felt the meeting was a failure because of the blundersome tactics of the " party fraction," that failed to recognize the psychology of the community and of the audience. Comrades A and B were again severely criticized, and again promised to abide by majority opinion.

The Story of the Tableaux

Then a dance was given. A series of tableaux representing the worker in 1933 were staged, from his discharge from his job through the various stages of deterioration. These tableaux were portrayed in a satiric fashion. One of the members, a skillful writer, wrote the script, other members played the roles. It was a powerful presentation of the problems, graphic and stirring. The group felt the program should be repeated, this time for money-raising as well as propagandistic purposes, before a bourgeois group, under an assumed sponsorship. A and B objected. They felt that only before ILD groups should these tableaux be presented — a fallacy, since ILD members need the propaganda least.

Again the District Secretary of the ILD was called in, this time in a private home, to discuss with the Executive Committee the problems that threatened destruction to the branch. Secretary repeated that the ILD is an auxiliary organization and that its approach must be different from that of the Communist Party. A contended that the approach of the group was wrong, that it was not communistic but socialistic, that it stressed evolution rather than revolution and was opportunistic. The District Secretary confirmed the view of the majority that enlightenment should be gradual, that the psychology of a particular community should not be overlooked, but he did not convince A and B.

Hunger March

Shortly thereafter many of the members attended the United Front Hunger March meeting at the Congregational Church in Chicago, at which Communists, Socialists, labor organizations, unemployed groups, American Federation of Labor, and Trade Union Unity League groups, among others, were represented. The hall was in an uproar most of the time, with booing, hissing, and heckling. The United Front meeting concentrated not on United Front plans or on attacking causes responsible for the depression. Instead, the members of the Communist Party and auxiliary organizations burst forth in name calling — " Misleaders — traitors — betrayers " — not against the common enemy, the employing class, but against the leaders of other groups represented. The resentful rank and filers of the other groups backed their leaders and the United Front meeting was threatened with disintegration, when Comrade M, the leading defense attorney of the ILD, arose and in epic language presented the view that he refused to call the leaders of the other groups traitors until they had proved themselves traitors. In his gentle convincing manner, he stressed his feeling that in a courtroom all workers are equally persecuted when they are arrested in a labor cause, no matter what their political or economic creed. He pleaded that the United Front be not destroyed, that efforts be concentrated against the real enemy and not against other workers. He won by this time the recalcitrant groups, and all voted to continue in the United Front. These unifying efforts were almost vitiated when prominent Communist Party leaders arose and repeated again the epithets and accusations against the leaders of other groups participating. This time several members of the Executive Committee of the previously described ILD branch, Communist sympathizers, booed the Communist speakers, while A and B looked resentfully on.

Some time later the little suburb was stirred by attempts of an Anti-Communist Crusader, Paul Revere organizer, who with the American Legion had been trying to keep the North Shore safe for the ideals of the D.A.R., to break up a Socialist, pacifist meeting held in a church.

Meeting on the Soviet Union

The following week the ILD branch advertised a talk by a Negro woman on " Minorities in the Soviet Union." The crusaders announced in the newspapers their intention of breaking up the meeting, which " plans to preach violent overthrow of the U. S. government." The speaker was poor. The audience of 350, the largest the group had ever drawn, was restless. Many of the American Legionnaires were on the verge of breaking up the meeting, harmless though it seemed. An emergency call was made for Comrade M to supplement. He drew a beautiful picture of the Soviet Union, pleaded for tolerance and fair play for new ideas, and completely carried his audience. When the crusaders threatened a disturbance, they were forced by the police to leave the meeting-hall, and on the outside held a militant indignation meeting, ending with the singing of the " Star Spangled Banner." The sincerity and logic of Comrade M, plus the unintelligent opposition tactics, made many gains for the ILD cause.

Expulsion

In June 1933, Comrade M was expelled for his views on the United Front and for his criticism of the Communist Party. Comrade M had stressed united front with the leaders, if necessary, in a common cause. He felt it was poor political strategy for the Communist Party to call the rank and file of all workers' organizations together in a united front, agreeing with the leaders not to preach any particular creed, then disregarding the agreement, present the Communist platform and denounce other leaders. A case in point, he felt, was the United Front meeting previously described, when the rank and file of all organizations, growing more militant because of proximity to the Unemployed Councils and Communist Party, swung to the right again when their leaders were attacked. He felt that American views on sportsmanship could not be ignored.

Another element of disagreement was Comrade M's insistence upon his right to criticize tactics and policies of the Party. He felt the very wholesome attribute of self-criticism was being used on the less important aspects of party activity, while major policies were decided and passed upon by a mere handful in a dictatorial fashion. He denied that party practices were democratic, and challenged the very foundation of the party, for the implications to be drawn were that political thinking was not being developed, but that a group of political nincompoops were developing in no way differing from the Nazis with their blind faith.

Flagging Interest

Comrade M's expulsion was arresting. The members of the above mentioned branch of the ILD were startled and almost overwhelmed by the loss to the movement of such a capable individual. Frequent discussions regarding the controversial points took place within the branch, discussions which were wholesome and politically developing. Before long word reached the branch that derogatory remarks were being made by the District Secretary (a new one) to the effect that the branch, which had been previously hailed for its achievements, was becoming a forum, a debating society. Then Comrade M was removed as attorney for the ILD staff. This, too, was a shock. And what was even more disturbing was the statement in the *Daily Worker* that he had hindered rather than helped the workers' cause.

A committee was appointed to discuss the matter with the District Secretary. This committee was received very coolly, even superciliously. The members were told that they must have faith in their leaders — this from the party that boasts of self-criticism.

Many felt like resigning. However, their interest in the class struggle was uppermost, and they did not resign. Without doubt, their ardor was somewhat lessened.

Is the Communist Party applying and carrying out Lenin's teachings about what its role is to be, viz.: to gather around it not only all the workers, but also the small bourgeoisie, and to be political strategists, taking advantage of every weakness and every split in the bourgeois ranks, and thus building a strong Party?

From its record in the United States so far, it would seem that it is failing miserably in its efforts to become a factor in American life, and it can blame itself for its lack of growth and effectiveness.

The same sequence of initial success and subsequent failure had been lived through by the Communists in connection with their earlier efforts to make effective use of cover organizations in Chicago. Communist organizations in the United States were driven underground in 1919 and did not reappear until the emergence of the "Workers' Party" at the end of 1921. The Trade Union Educational League, founded by William Z. Foster in 1920, was the first striking American example of the deliberate use of a special-purpose organization as a means of "boring from within" and fighting for the control of existing mass organizations.

This particular agency was not set up at the instigation of the Communists, but was founded by Foster himself and brought by him to the door of the Communist International when he visited Moscow in the summer of 1921. The year 1921 was the year when the authorities in the Soviet Union altered their expectation that the world revolution was expanding and gravitated toward the view that the crest of the post-war revolutionary wave had passed.[2] This was the year when a "united front" tactic was announced, and when the Red International of Trade Unions was established as a means to the end. It was not desired to build rival unions, but rather to mobilize effective action among the members of mass or-

[2] See Arthur Rosenberg: *A History of Bolshevism from Marx to the First Five Years' Plan* (London, 1934), Chapter VIII.

ganizations for the purpose of instigating a pro-Communist change in leadership.

The Denver convention of the A. F. of L. met in June 1921. For the first time in fifteen years Samuel Gompers had a rival for the presidency, John L. Lewis of the United Mine Workers, who polled one-third of the votes. Discontent was running high, and by 1922 the TUEL were organizing " cells " in the most susceptible unions. Headway was made in the United Mine Workers, the International Association of Machinists, the Fur Workers, the International Ladies' Garment Workers' Union, and elsewhere. Several unions which had radical traditions were attached to the Gompers machine only by considerations of expediency, and in a general scramble might be pushed loose from their awkward moorings. The Brewery Workers' Association, for example, was traditionally socialistic, and went over to Gompers because he was able to extend their jurisdiction to include yeast, cereal, and flour mills, thus enabling the union to make up for losses suffered in the alcohol industry as a result of prohibition. The needle-trades unions needed the support of the union leaders and their political connections in the small towns where clothing-manufacturers were trying to operate small shops. The anti-union bread trust forced the radical Bakery Workers to look to the support of conservative trade unions for the sake of strengthening the market for union-label bread.[3]

The TUEL attacked with great vigor, the campaign against craft lines took the form of demanding " amalgamation " along industrial lines. Foster concentrated his fire, not on the most recalcitrant members of the Gompers machine, but on many of the leaders who were in actual opposition to the rule of Gompers and many of the traditional practices of the A. F. of L. William Johnston of the Machinists, John Fitzpatrick of the Chicago Federation of Labor, and John Brophy of the United Mine Workers were bitterly assailed as reactionaries.

[3] J. B. S. Hardman, in *American Labor Dynamics in the Light of Post-War Developments* (New York, 1928), Chapter I.

Socialists, many of whom had for many years sought to un-
seat the Gompers machine, were attacked with the utmost
bitterness.

At the close of the war the Chicago Federation of Labor was
a gathering-point of movements hostile to many of the dominant policies of the A. F. of L. As early as 1919 the Chicago
Federation had endorsed a Labor Party. Although the Labor
Party polled fewer votes than the Socialist Party in the presidential election of 1920 (265,411 to 919,799), the Chicago Federation of Labor adhered to the idea of a separate party. In
1922 the Chicago Federation endorsed the principle of industrial unionism, unquestionably in part an outcome of the work
of William Z. Foster. The state convention of the Illinois
Federation turned down the proposal; Gompers and Woll
actively campaigned against it.

When the Communist Party emerged as the Workers' Party
it sought to instigate new parties and to capture control of
already existing ones in the name of farmers and of labor. In
1923 the Chicago Federation of Labor and the Farmer-Labor
Party issued a call for a national meeting of progressives in
July. At this meeting persons known to be attached to the
Workers' Party, and thus in bad repute as " Communists,"
took over the convention. The farmer and the non-Communist labor groups walked out. This episode was joyfully interpreted by A. F. of L. propagandists and others as showing
that nothing but total surrender to the Communists was possible if one worked with them. The conspicuousness of the
connection between the TUEL and the Communists was such
that the label " un-American " could be effectively pinned on
the doctrines of the League and on the League itself. Trade-
union and Socialist organizations, emulating the ruthlessness
of the Communists, began a witch hunt against Communists
in their ranks. At the national convention of the A. F. of L.
in 1923, William F. Dunne, although an accredited delegate,
was unseated, and in general Communist members and sympathizers were given summary treatment.

Representative of the struggle was the course of events in Illinois. A bitter fight at the 1923 convention of the State Federation led to the defeat of a resolution in favor of industrial unionism. The "radicalism" issue was a decisive club (the vote was 313 to 80). The state convention also opposed independent political action, repudiating a policy which had been adopted in 1919 at the instigation of the Chicago Federation of Labor. "Radicalism" was again the issue.

Communist-supported candidates in such unions as the machinists' and the mine workers' occasionally won; but in every important instance the candidate promptly turned against his allies and repudiated their support, endeavoring to dissociate himself from the "red" label. When the Communists captured power, as they did in the International Ladies' Garment Workers' Union in New York (an organization 35,000 strong), they were discredited and defeated within a year (1925-6). As time passed, the strength of the Communists in the unions had tended toward the vanishing-point. The years between 1922 and 1924 were the years of vigorous action and some success; they left the old leadership of the A. F. of L. entrenched in control, swathed more than ever in the American flag, and fearful of visible concessions to the program of industrialization, unionization of the unskilled, and independent political action.

As we have seen, the Chicago Federation of Labor, buoyed up by the labor assertiveness of the war period, carried over into the depression of 1920 its demands for a change of line on the part of the A. F. of L. Rebuffed by the State Federation in 1923, defeat became complete when the electorate failed to respond to the La Follette campaign of 1924. The Chicago leadership relaxed their crusading efforts, and when the depression of 1930 arrived, it took no risks. "Radicalism" spelled defeat. Assertiveness during the period of deprivation, which followed the indulgences of war-times, had resulted in failure. Thus when the indulgences of the twenties were followed by the deprivations of the Great Depression, the symbols and practices associated with former failures were not invoked.

The first period of vigorous " united front " action in the trade unions had labeled the Communists as wreckers and destroyers. Socialists and orthodox leaders of mass organizations were indignant and resentful of the behavior of Communist leaders. The period closed with the TUEL reduced to impotence. By fighting everybody at once, the League had provoked a combination of all the elements strong enough to work its destruction. Here was a campaign vitiated by a major strategical blunder. The problem of the Communist, like any propaganda, is to move toward what it wants by methods which prevent rather than provoke such enemy combinations.

Such strategical mistakes greatly strengthened the tendencies to restrict the spread of the latest world revolutionary initiative by means of geographical (parochial) symbols. Communists stood out as " Russian," " foreign," and " un-American." At the same time the scope of the Third International was restricted by the partial incorporation of some of the practices of the new pattern. Socialist and trade-union leaders, threatened by the Communists, became more alert and ruthless in suppressing opposition from within.

With the defeat of the attempt to penetrate the trade unions and to capture or create mass parties, assertive impulses of party members were turned back against the party itself. A bitter factional struggle broke out between the Foster and the Ruthenberg-Lovestone groups. In 1928-9 in connection with the Sixth World Congress of the Third International came the climax of Communist isolationism; the TUEL, having failed to bore from within, became a dual union organization, the Trade Union Unity League, seeking to organize the mass-production industries and redoubling assaults upon the existing leadership of existing mass organizations. Results in the Chicago area were inconsequential.

Some increase in skillfulness had occurred, however, in the handling of Communist " fractions " within mass organizations. It was perceived that the TUEL defeated its usefulness as a cover organization by circulating slogans which were identical with those currently promoted by the party. One main issue of the early years was the demand for immediate recognition of the Soviet Union, which was so far afield from the focus of attention of the ordinary wage-earner that the new union movement was easily stigmatized as " foreign " and " Russian."

In the technique of controlling the organizational work within the TUEL unions the party again fell short: organizers devoted themselves almost completely to trade-union work or else, doing practically no trade-union work, concentrated wholly on the party.[4] Thus, if the propaganda too closely resembled that of the Communist Party to serve union purposes, the organizational structure, on the other hand, was not sufficiently controlled to yield adequate results to the party.

Throughout the 1920's the number of affiliated organizations grew, chiefly through the subdivision of the Trade Union Unity League, into formally independent union groups. Such organizations continued to be, for the most part, " fronts " for the party, the leadership and the rank and file being the same. It was not before 1930 that the Communist Party began to grasp the potential importance of mass organizations as agencies for reaching sympathizers who could be approached by way of a wide variety of interests. The issue was raised early during 1930 in the Draft Theses for the Seventh Convention adopted by the Central Committee Plenum of the CP, USA, on April 3. The draft stressed the need for organizing the " United Front from Below " and the danger of waiting for spontaneous response from the " unorganized masses." Only casual attention was given to the problem of building new and controlling already existing mass organizations to serve these " unorganized masses "; thus discussion was limited to Communist-controlled organizations already in existence at the

[4] W. Z. Foster: " Party Trade Union Work during Ten Years," *The Communist*, VIII, No. 9 (September 1930), 488–93.

time. The resolution adopted by the Twelfth Plenum of the Central Committee on November 24 of the same year laid considerably more stress upon this issue. It stated that the party recognized its principal weakness to be that it had not understood " how to mobilize the masses for struggles for their immediate demands and especially for the economic demands." Despite recognition of this inadequacy, it failed to anticipate the important role which the affiliated agency would play during the depression. As a result, instead of controlling the " mass organizations " which it had created, the party found itself, in the crisis years 1931–2, frequently swept along in a tide of activity which originated from these organizations.

The number of Communist affiliated organizations has shown an unmistakable tendency to increase from year to year. By 1935 there were more such organizations in operation than at any other time in the history of the party. Party documents show that the leadership became increasingly aware of the usefulness of " mass organizations." Already in the summer of 1930 the *Party Organizer,* the organ of the party devoted to current organization problems, contained an article on this subject, stressing the need for changes in party tactics and underlining the necessity for co-operation between cover organizations. At that time the traditional theory of " fraction work " (the control of organizations by a majority of leadership) was emphasized. It was asserted that without " fraction work " the influence of the party remained ineffective. The idea that " mass organizations " could operate satisfactorily without " fraction work " was called " naive self-consolation."

The position of the party in relation to cover organizations modified steadily after 1930. The policy of 1928 was, however, still binding. In the Congress of the Communist International of 1935 a much freer hand was given to associated organizations of the party than ever before. The new formulations about this question represented in part an official policy; in another sense it represented an official acceptance of a state of affairs which already existed prior to that time. The depression gave a basis for party activity among groups which it had previously been unable to touch. But long years of stubborn bucking from the Left had dimmed the perception of the leadership past any point where it could take substantial advantage of the situation. The party created more " mass organizations," but its efforts went into " fractional control"; nevertheless some of the organizations, quickly growing many times the size of the party, achieved a certain degree of self-determination and even influenced the party. In 1931 and 1932 in Chicago certain cover organizations, notably the Unemployed Councils, grew in membership and number beyond the point where they could be completely controlled by the party. Although the " mother organization " continued to assume responsibility for their militant activities, these activities to an increasing extent developed quite spontaneously within the organization and often culminated in acts which were definitely counter to party policies.

With increasing favorableness of the indulgence-deprivation balance after 1932, membership fell off in the cover organizations. The central committee of the party in the open letter of July 1933 recognized the party's relative failure to capitalize on the strength of the mass organizations. In the period of its decline in 1933, the party showed a tendency to concentrate on its own organization, thereby leaving more latitude to affiliated associations.

Thus before the change of line signalized by the World Congress of 1935, we see halting and oscillating tendencies at work in Chicago with reference to an " American Front " as a means of survival and growth. Two predictions might reasonably have been made on the basis of observations confined to the years 1930–4:

1. As the Communist Party in Chicago is diminishing distinctiveness, a purge is pending;

2. Diminishing distinctiveness will be endorsed by larger units of the party.

In 1934 there was a severe local crisis of the type that is periodically necessary when the party line is highly distinctive. In 1935 the World Congress altered the party line to legitimize large-scale sacrifices of distinctiveness. This was tantamount to restriction of the world revolutionary pattern by those associated with it through the partial incorporation of established symbols of the various parochial (national) symbols.

The picture, then, is of the Chicago party struggling to maintain the line of distinctiveness (the line of sectarianism) in the face of much defeat (deprivation). The strength of the patterns of Americanism was so great that success (in terms of membership) seemed to depend upon more adaptiveness. Under such circumstances tendencies toward partial incorporation of American symbols and practices were plainly visible. Such sacrifices of distinctiveness were instances of " restriction by self " of the world revolutionary pattern. The increasingly flagrant deviations from the line of 1928 which were implied in the tendencies referred to precipitated purges by revolutionary fundamentalists in the national and international party. A withdrawal to maximum distinctiveness sharpened the conflict with the American environment because of the strength of Americanism. Its symbols could always be invoked by the leaders of rival protest organizations (as well as by Rightist organizations) to attack the Communists. The party was condemned to perpetual internal strife by the line of 1928; the conflict could be reduced for a time, at least, by the line of 1935.

CHAPTER XVII

Restriction by Individualism

THE INDIVIDUALISTIC pattern of American life glorifies the individual and cultivates private initiative in personal affairs. The international leaders of Communism thought of themselves as the generals of an army of trained and disciplined professional revolutionists. They sought to control as much as possible of the time and energy of party members and to exact military discipline from them.

There is in present-day America nothing unheard of about this voluntary absorption of the individual in the service of rather inclusive secondary symbols (witness the devoted service of God in the sects and denominations of the country). However, very few religious organizations demand a preponderant quota of the time left over from work and sleep from their members; but this was done by the "secular religion" of Communism. It was safe to predict that the practice of extensive work for, and of rigorous obedience to, the party would clash with the established ways of life in the nation and precipitate chronic difficulties.

The responsible leaders of the party were dissatisfied with its membership achievements and sought many explanations of this comparative failure. They complained of the high turnover rate of the party in Chicago. Despite the care which was supposed to be exercised in the selection of personnel, the turnover was between 40 and 50 per cent during the years when relatively adequate records were available.

Our previous analysis has already indicated that the Communists pursued methods which resulted in recruitment for instability. Disproportionate energy went into work among the unemployed. Emphasis upon meetings and demonstrations as recruitment occasions implied giving great importance to the impetuosity of crowd states, which induced the most suggestible (the least stable) personalties to sign application blanks.

When they looked back upon their work, the central leadership of the party was well aware of former mistakes. But in the thick of the depression rush, they kept small technical considerations in the foreground to the exclusion of fundamental criticism.

Party officials often insisted that the delicate period of transition from without to within the party should be handled by tactful methods. In 1930 the agitprop department of District 8 issued a bulletin, *How to Train and Keep New Members.* The unit was said to be responsible for training new comrades by these methods: (1) by assigning an experienced comrade to take charge of each new member, talking to him about the party, visiting him in his home, taking him to meetings; and (2) by informal discussions, an hour before regular meetings of the units, for the benefit of new members. The agitprop issued a list of *Questions for New Members,* which included such questions as: What is the difference between capitalists, petty bourgeoisie, farmers, and workers? What is the purpose of the fake relief and charity measures of the bosses? What is an imperialist country? What is the difference between the Communist's conception of the election campaign and the Socialist's conception?

During the period under survey the membership was already too driven by other tasks to put these ameliorative suggestions into practice.

The truth of the matter is that officials talked about the problem without stating or dealing with the major difficulty: the pursuit of too many goals by too elaborate methods resulting in too heavy demands on party members.

The world revolutionary party ceaselessly exercised tremendous pressure from the top down. This pressure from the top is an integral part of what the party calls " democratic centralism."

In accordance with the Communist theory of " democratic centralism," all lower party organizations are subordinated to the higher bodies. The decisions of the World Congress of the Communist International and of its subsidiary committees must be carried out by all parties belonging to the Third International. The National Convention and the Central Committee, the next in rank of authority, make decisions which must be carried out by the district bodies.

The District Convention and Committee make decisions which must be carried out by the sections; the Section Conventions and Committees make decisions which must be carried out in the party units or cells. The essential feature of this form of organization is that the decisions of a body are binding on all lower bodies. The Communist International, the seat of highest authority, makes decisions, however, generally regarding only the broad lines of policy. (There are exceptions, like the famous demand made on the French Socialist Party Congress at Tours in 1920 — which had just decided in favor of affiliation with the CI — to exclude from the party certain Socialist leaders who were designated by name.) It is the duty of the National Convention and the Central Committee to make more specific the tasks of the party laid down by the Congress. The decisions of the national bodies are invariably published in the national organ, the *Daily Worker,* and also in booklet form. It becomes the task of the next lower level of organization, the district, to translate the decisions of the higher centers into terms specifically applicable to its own territory. This task is carried out in the District Convention and District Committee, the decisions of which are once more passed down to the Section Convention and Section Committee, whose decisions are binding on the shop, street, and town units in each section.

The officers of the executive committee of the Communist International bring pressure to bear on the executive officers of the national central committee, who are responsible for preserving the vitality of their national committee; the executives of the national committee bear down on the district organizer, who prods his own district committee as well as the section organizers; the section organizer stimulates his committee and works on the unit organizer, who in turn operates on the committee of the unit, and members of the unit. Printed "theses and resolutions," mimeographed instructions, letters, visits, conventions, and conferences (to say nothing of general party publications) descend in unceasing profusion upon the tiers beneath.

A frequent theme of complaint is the lack of effective initiative in the lower ranks. A representative example of such "self-criticism from above" is the following portion of a "resolution on organization" adopted by the plenum of District 8 in November 1929:

"It is of tremendous significance that during the latest attack upon the Party, with the leading comrades in jail, not a single Section Executive Committee, not to speak of the units, issued a statement or literature of any kind to the workers in the shop or territory of the section about this attack.

"This fact is a clear indication that the units are not yet established as political organs and leaders in the section. This has been due very largely to the shortcomings of the leading District Committees. The tendency has been to do too much from the center and over the head of the section and unit buros.

"Instead of instituting centralization by means of close supervision and direction of the leading committees, the tendency has been to take over and centralize all the activities in the hands of the District Office and its full time functionaries.

"At the same time there has been a tendency to direct units and sections too much by means of circulars and written instructions. The result has been that the directions from the center are not properly coordinated with the regular activities and tasks of the units and the carrying out of the tasks tends to become mechanical.

" The DEC (District Executive Committee) must plan its campaigns so that these should be carried out through the sections and in turn by the units. The DEC must hold the SEC's (Section Executive Committees) strictly responsible for the utilization of all political and economic issues as arise in the territory of the section. This principle must, in turn, be extended to the units. In this connection section two (old Plan) failed to give direction in the Pullman plant when an important Negro issue developed and when, because of this, the Party missed an excellent opportunity to put forward its position and give leadership.

" Section five failed to take advantage of the feeder bus issue which assumed large proportions and was utilized by local bourgeois politicians. On the other hand, sections two, three, and five all developed local issues in the Negro territories, in connection with Jim-Crow practices and developed many other local issues. These instances, however, are yet only exceptions instead of being the rule."

The difficulties which were the subject of the foregoing remarks were connected with the problem of arriving at a favorable proportion between *centralization* and *decentralization*. Another set of problems crops up at each of the upper levels in connection with the " departments," which are authorized to handle special fields of activity (like agitprop). The " resolution on organization " quoted above goes on to reveal some of the problems connected with the balancing of *concentration* and *deconcentration:*

" What has been said of the concentration of work is true particularly in connection with the departments. The Pol-Buro (Political Bureau) and the Secretariat have assumed and dealt with too many problems which correctly should have been handled through the respective departments. The departments, in turn, do not sufficiently give direction to the functionaries under the category of the given department. The departments do not develop and utilize the apparatus which is necessary to carry out their decisions and put them into effect in the lower units.

"The Pol-Buro must review the composition of each department with a view to drawing in new proletarian elements into leading work. This task must be extended to the Section and units so that immediately a new cadre of comrades can be drawn into work, releasing former functionaries for other activities.

"The departments must institute continuity of work. Until the present time no department has kept a record of its activities. No systematic record has been made or kept. The org department functions without accurate information and statistics as to the industries, the number and categories of workers in the industries, the number and character of mass organizations, etc."

The failure of the elaborate party apparatus to produce satisfactory results, despite all the pressure from above, is reflected in the failure or very partial success of many campaigns. An example of ineffective operation was the membership campaign which was prescribed by District 8 in 1931. On the 25th of September the organization department addressed all section committees and language bureaus, having laid down the goal of doubled membership by November 7:

"We print below a table which should startle every Section Committee into some serious thinking. In 11 weeks after accepting 458 new members (paid initiation, issued books, etc.) into the Party, we find *we have not made a single step forward*. The dues sales are exactly the same and that is the only real and acceptable yardstick we will use in gauging the increase in membership.

"If we were to judge superficially, then section two has already doubled its membership, but until the dues sales correspond to the membership figures, we will not believe that a single new member has been kept in the Party.

"Recruiting figures as such are absolutely unsatisfactory and at the *present tempo* we will not double the membership by November 7, *which is only six weeks off*. This decision was made in a very serious manner and if some Sections are incapable of doubling their membership it is not the fault of the workers, but of the Party in that Section.

" THE WORSE SECTIONS ARE:

Sect. 3, Chicago 7 members in 11 weeks
St. Louis   1   "   "   "   "
Rockford   1   "   "   "   "

" Other Sections such as Section 1, 5, Milwaukee, Calumet, Waukegan must overhaul their entire methods of recruiting.

" SECTIONS WHO HAVE DECLINED IN MEMBERSHIP:

Section 3 from 98 dues standing to 62
"   5 "   173 "   "   " 149
"   6 "   53 "   "   "   41
St. Louis "   64 "   "   "   53
Rock Island "   25 "   "   "   15

" This week we cite the following examples of how the Sections keep workers out of the Party (reprint in all Org Letters) and look up last week and see if you took care of them.

" *Example #4.* In June a woman worker filled out an application card for a second time and paid 50¢ initiation. It was given to Section three, but now is September and she hasn't heard a thing! What about it, Section three?

" *Example #5.* Another woman worker filled out an application card for a second time and paid 50¢ initiation. This comrade collected $15.00 for the *Daily Worker* this summer but we want to keep her out of the Party. Section five has a long way to go to double its membership but still they resist new workers. What about the worker on Warren Blvd. mentioned last week?

" *Example #6.* Last week we mentioned the organizer of Unit 106 who has no book. He still has no book. But we also found out this week that Organizer of Unit 105 also has no book. Section one must tighten up on things."

The problem of revolutionary parties is not only to recruit new members, but to avoid the recruitment of spies and agents. In August 1932 the Central Committee of the party (in New York) circulated this letter:

" Instructions in this letter being sent to all Districts must be followed out implicitly.

" After a painstaking survey made by direct sympathizers in high groups, it was decided that many districts have permitted spies and stool pigeons to creep within, until the situation has become serious.

"Information has reached Police, Private Detective Agencies, and the Capitalist Government Officials that in many sections has done injury to the Workers' Cause.

"The recent uncovering of the stool pigeon Arthur Zagaria in the Boston District, who wormed his way into the district bureau, is an example of the methods used against the workers.

"Other cases numbering at least 150 persons have come before us, but still the evil persists.

"Chicago, Los Angeles, Pittsburgh, Cleveland and Detroit are full of it. Here in New York we have overcome the situation but it will never do for the comrades to fall asleep.

"Upon receipt of this, call a special secret meeting of the District Committee and then take up the matter in a determined way. Check over every one, and if any are 'queer,' use your judgment in checking them up. Do not act hastily, but take up any suspected case with the CCC through this office.

"There is absolutely no let up on the previous instruction to have photographs of all functionaries, no matter what is the nature of the office. If they should prove traitors to the Workers cause, then the Bureau has photos to warn other groups.

"Comrades on the district Bureau must not underestimate these spies, some are really clever, have a fair understanding of the working class struggle.

"The one big mistake that most of them make is the asking of too many questions. Another method is the anxiety of some to get ahead quick in Party circles, to the holding of important places.

"Do not sleep on this, get busy quick and keep in touch with D . . . of the CCC, as well as Smith, on every suspected case."

In the period 1929–30 there were 20 members expelled from the American party as members of police departments or as agents in the employ of plants, which was 10 per cent of the persons expelled during that period (from the confidential report of the Seventh National Convention of the Communist Party, June 1930).

An insight into recruitment problems is afforded by the dis-

ciplinary action of the party. The following bulletin is typical
of reports on expulsions in the Eighth District:

" Below are decisions of the District Control Commission concerning members of our section who have gone up before the
District Control Commission on various charges. The number of
cases of drunkenness, stealing of money, brings up very sharply
our methods of recruitment. Although we should have a more
intensive recruitment, yet we should bring into the Party more militant and class conscious elements. This would give us a healthier
situation, and would actually turn the units from their present situation of inactivity and make them active political leaders in their
unit territory, leading the daily struggles in the shops, for relief,
for Negro Rights, etc.

" This would immediately show itself in an immediate decline of these cases and a weeding out of all unhealthy tendencies
and bringing in of better fighters into our ranks. Where cases do
again arise, of drunkenness, financial hooliganism, gossiping, etc.,
we must take immediate and drastic action to root these out.

" These many cases of drunkenness bring up the necessity of
changing the entire character of the house parties given by our
units, from drunken orgies into recreational and social gatherings
of workers, having a political content.

" Below are those expelled from the Party by the District Control Commission:

" *Case A:* Joined Party to win prestige amongst Negro people
in order to get them to vote for Democratic Party. Worked as a
judge for Democratic Party during elections and when approached
in a comradely manner to quit Democratic Party said, ' I don't
make a living from the Communist Party.'

" *Case B:* Utilized the prestige of being a Party member
amongst the masses to develop an individual racket and charges
workers $2.00 for turning on their lights.

" *Case C:* Withheld money from the Metal Workers' Union
and also from general ticket sales. Always tried to get a position
where he could get money. He is also a drunkard and thus became
a discredit to the Party. When union refused to elect him financial
secretary he refused to give up records of union and threatened to
report the Union and Party members to police. He should be ex-

posed to the workers as the last offense of being an informer is the worst treason to the working class.

"*Case D:* Expelled for financial hooliganism, stealing of money received for dues, tickets, etc., as well as never being willing to submit reports of money received, and other activities.

"*Case E:* Expelled for being an undesirable element. Is a general troublemaker and disrupter in the unit and elsewhere. Carries weapons even to unit meetings and broke up one meeting of unit 209 by his disturbing methods.

"*Case F:* Expelled for being an incessant talker and gossiper and betrays all kinds of Party information to everyone, including police."

Against incessant pressure from the top, those who stayed in the party developed several means of protecting themselves, means whose function, as a rule, was not candidly admitted nor consciously understood, but which worked in favor of the preservation of some degree of privacy and independence against the party's demands for sacrifice and discipline.

The means of self-protection may be classified into *evasions of responsibility* and acts of *disguised nonconformity*. One of the most persistent ways of evading responsibility was the substitution of talk for action. This has the advantage of giving to oneself and to others the impression of sincere interest in party life. Whatever stultification occurs seems the unintended by-product of an excess of zeal. Talk enables the individual to distinguish himself and provides an enjoyable social experience as an alternative to possible rebuff among enemies. Thus the reiteration of fundamentals and the elaboration of trivialities may easily proceed in protracted discussion until most of the available time and energy is consumed.

In one of the innumerable articles of instruction and criticism concerning organizational matters, the problem of the unit committee is presented in terms which reveal this form of sabotage, doubtless seldom premeditated, of unit officials, who merely discuss matters which they are supposed to decide. They are criticized for multiplying occasions for the lengthy consideration of details, not only among themselves, but among the members of the unit as a whole.

" The Unit Buros in a Bolshevik Party are actually the leading committees of the basic unit, and they make decisions within the scope of their activity that are binding on the unit members. . . .

" The unit membership meeting has the power to review, reverse, or approve the decisions of the unit buro.

" However, such actions do not take place under normal conditions unless the buro is composed of comrades who are incompetent or have serious political differences with the unit as a whole. . . .

" Our unit buro up to the present time met and discussed all the problems and formulated proposals for each of these problems which were brought into the unit and again discussed point by point and finally voted upon.

" The result was that the initiative and the authority of the unit buros was not developed and their effectiveness was destroyed.

" Today we still have the situation where the agenda of a unit meeting contains 10 to 15 points and the meeting lasts 3 to 4 hours most of which time is spent on details of relatively small importance, each of which should have been finally decided upon by the buro.

" Such matters as who shall sell the *Daily Worker* on Wednesday or who shall bring the platform to the street meeting, leaves of absence, transfers, disciplinary action and so on must be decided by the unit buro.

" The unit buro being composed of the most developed, active and reliable comrades is best fitted to take action on the detail routine problems of the unit as well as to outline the main political activities.

" This method of work leaves the unit meeting free from details and creates the possibility for a thorough discussion of the main problems."

Max Bedacht, speaking somewhat contemptuously of words without deeds, in the name of the Central Committee of the party, once said:

" Our Party members must stop embracing the whole working class and instead select an individual member of the working class for this embrace."

Many other ways of protecting the primary ego through the evasion of responsibility are disclosed in the party's comments upon itself. Such self-protection proceeded not only through the substitution, for little gratifying duties, of more gratifying actions in the name of the party; it proceeded also through the simple omission of duly assigned tasks. " Organizational looseness " was a frequent term of criticism from above, which usually alluded to this kind of evasion. The organization department of District 8 wrote to the units on May 15, 1931 as follows:

" Everywhere in the Party we meet the cry of too many meetings — *too much work loaded on a few comrades and not on others.* In the units, when it comes to assigning work, *excuses of every kind* are given, some bad. In order to overcome this, we are telling each unit and section, if any of their members have worked elsewhere, so that they will be able to check up."

A common complaint in periods of deepening crisis, and hence of increasing demands, was the phlegmatism of old party members. A district organizer, in a confidential memorandum about organizational looseness in District 8 (1930), wrote:

" Numerous examples can be given from our recent experiences, but we will only relate one. . . . A new member, who is a machinist, and who came to our Party as a result of the TUUL activities, was placed in charge of the Metal Trades fraction. He called in a meeting of our Metal Trades fraction, sent out 90 letters and only five showed up. This discouraged him a great deal and he actually told the comrades in charge of the TUUL that there is a great gap between what he heard about our Party before he joined, and what he finds now when there is little discipline, responsibility and desire for actual participation in the class struggle.

" While we must not start a campaign of eliminating old members, it should be remembered that in many instances the old members who cannot digest the new line — and especially carry it out in practice are a drag on the new members. For instance in Whiting, Indiana, it was absolutely necessary to eliminate the old members in order to retain the new members. We have now instances in the City of Chicago where old members sent in their resignation, some without excuses, others frankly stating that the greater demands of the Party, because of the sharpened struggles, make it impossible for them to remain in the party.

"We had recently a discussion in all the Party units on the TUUL. At one of the unit meetings one of the two petty bourgeois elements has resigned from the Party and some of the new members have joined the TUUL."

An organizational bulletin declared:

"Merciless self-criticism and the most energetic extension of inner Party democracy must be accompanied with drastic improvements in discipline and the eradication of petty bourgeois tendencies.

"Such acts as insubordination of comrades to organizational decisions of the Party as exemplified in the refusal of a comrade to take up duties as an organizer in a strike situation in Kansas City, as well as other instances of comrades showing hesitation to undertake direct Party activities, must be rooted out.

"The refusal of some of the members to place property at the disposal of the ILD must also be regarded as a tendency incompatible with membership in the Communist Party."

The protection of individuality from absorption by party life and the rigorous discipline of the party went further than evasiveness. There were frequent examples of nonconformity to the party line which again typically appeared to the self and others as actions evidencing high zeal in party service. The protracted discussion of generalities and trivialities immobilizes the party; " petty Leftism " was a positive rather than a negative danger. Instances of officially disapproved truculence, of incitement to violence, of flagrant sectarianism in dealing with potential party members, are cited from time to time in the course of this report.

We are now able to state the psychological function of one of the most prominent features of Communist Party practice, the incessant self-criticism, many instances of which have been cited in what has gone before. What is the significance of this extraordinary emphasis upon confession of error, re-affirmation of loyalty, and promise of improvement? Evidently we have to do with a symbolic reaction which eliminates some of the guilt arising from inaction and deviation by expiation and diffusion of responsibility. Verbal expiation is obvious enough; but it is worth observing that most of the self-criticism is couched in the language of " us " rather than " me," " we " rather than " I." Responsibility is shared by the primary self with the group in whose name the actions in question proceed. Displacement of party activity to more gratifying and less important kinds of behavior, slothfulness, and non-conformity are to be attributed to the severity of the requirements which are incessantly pressed from the top; the ritual of self-criticism liquidates some of the resulting psychological stresses by the use of speech only. Orgiastic self-criticism, then, is itself a symptom of the revolt of the primary ego against absorption by, and lack of independence in, activity in the name of inclusive secondary symbols.

That this self-criticism is poorly adjusted to reality is implied in the constant preoccupation of self-critics with the improvement of details where the situation clearly demanded a revision of basic practice. Higher party functionaries were constantly recommending all sorts of " technical " means for diminishing turnover rates; yet the inappropriateness of imposing tremendous burdens on members in situations which were admittedly non-revolutionary was not directly faced. Such an obstinate adherence to means which are flagrantly inappropriate for the achievement of the ends in view reminds one of the symptoms of a neurosis. Yet when discussing political movements, it is wise to be particularly chary of judgments of pathology. We must therefore examine afresh the Communist International for the sake of investigating whether anybody received substantial indulgences as the result of a party practice which as a matter of " principle " tries to drive full speed ahead with all brakes on.

There is nothing legendary about the pressure from the top, the control which is exercised from Moscow over the American Communist Party. At the time when the struggle between the Foster and the Ruthenberg-Lovestone factions broke out, Foster went into the convention of the American party with two-thirds of the delegates. When the delegate of the Communist International revealed that he had been instructed to support the Ruthenberg group, this group promptly took charge and won a majority at membership meetings of the party. In 1929 the Lovestone group had nine-tenths of the delegates and four-fifths of the popular vote; yet reluctance to yield to the demands of the Executive Committee of the Communist International led to expulsion from the party. Only a few hundred persons followed Lovestone; the membership soon lined up with the victorious faction. What is the basis of this submissiveness on the part of the American party as a whole?

A ruling factor is plainly the staff of officials who have been on the party pay-roll through several years, and who are dependent upon the Communist International for subventions. The turnover of the membership is not matched by the turnover of the organizers. Here we have a relatively permanent body of officials who veer to the right or to the left in accordance with the directives of the Third International.

It will be further noted that party conventions contain a large proportion of delegates who are financially dependent upon the central authorities in New York, and hence in Moscow.

As was said above, the organizational structure of the party is usually described by the party as conforming to the requirements of " democratic centralism." Thus far we have had occasion to stress the " centralism "; what of the " democratic " features of the system? The term "democratic" in "democratic centralism" emphasizes the arrangement by which the membership of the Communist parties as a whole is supposed to determine the policy of the Communist International. The primary units of the party send delegates to the section, the section sends delegates to the district, the district sends delegates to the national, and the national sends delegates to the World Congress of the Communist International, which is the highest agency in the system.

The organizational chart of the Communist International thus shows two " families " of lines of authority running in opposite directions: there are lines flowing upward from the units to the World Congress and down from the World Congress to the units. Debate and discussion are expected to occur before decisions are made, and to cease when they are made. A stream of suggestion and criticism is supposed to flow upward from the units, intimately connected with the masses, to the central organs of the International. From the International, in turn, comes a stream of directives mandatory upon the agencies beneath. Such is the blue-print of " democratic centralism."

Owing to the turnover of members among the primary units, Communist Party democracy was vitiated at the source. Under such conditions the overwhelming influence is exercised not by continuous initiatives from below, but by incessant pressure from above. The stream emanating from the hydrants at the top, shot at high pressure through the official pipe line, is matched by no ascending current; from the myriad of leaking, shifting local faucets there oozes but a feeble trickle.

The Americans have had negligible influence upon the policies of the Communist International as a whole. American syndicalists were somewhat disturbing elements at the " world congress " of trade unionists which was held in Moscow in July 1921. William D. Haywood and William Z. Foster were among the most prominent delegates from beyond the Soviet frontiers.[1] Only as exponents of " archaic " syndicalist heresies did the Americans ever exercise a significant effect upon general policy.

The passivity of the American party in the life of the International, reflecting the lack of vigor in basic units of the party, has also been fostered by the uncertainties which prevailed during the period about the structure of the primary units of party organization. The Communist Party inherited the territorial pattern from the Socialist Party, but strove to transform itself into a network of functional — that is, of working place — organizations. The transformation of the Communist International from a " street " to a " shop " basis was stressed in the World Congress of 1924. The problem was tackled with renewed energy in 1928, but in 1929 the Eighth District Plenum resolved as follows, giving clear evidence of the considerable difficulties of internal organizational integration under a " dualistic " system:

" The outstanding weakness of the Party apparatus is the failure to establish street and shop units as the basic political *leaders* within the specific shop or territory. Some successful steps can be recorded in this direction. Recently the territories of the sections and units have been readjusted on a more correct basis. Section boundaries have been changed with a view to the industrial struc-

---

[1] The American IWW demanded the formation of new trade unions and the smashing of the old ones. They also co-operated with the French syndicalists in a bitter attack upon the proposal to unite both trade-union and political organizations in one International. Syndicalist delegates were by definition hostile to the supremacy of political over union organizations, and they were greatly stirred by the shooting and jailing of anarchists and syndicalists in Russia. The Americans Emma Goldman and Alexander Berkman were by this time outspoken in their criticism of the Communist régime in Russia. As a concession to syndicalist sentiment a separate trade-union International (the RITU, the Red International of Trade Unions) was set up, but each International was to be organically connected with the other by being represented on the executive of the other.

ture of the given section as against the old boundaries which had been constituted entirely on the basis of electoral districts.

" In this readjustment or reorganization, members who for years had lived outside of their territories were properly assigned.

" The task of assigning territories and shops to the units for specific concentration was given over to the sections.

" The factories must form the center of activities for every street nucleus. These must seize hold of every issue in the factory, make leaflets or utilize the party press for stories on the shop, — and by all such methods secure connections and strive to organize shop nuclei. An excellent example in this connection can be cited in the Illinois Central Shops where response to the work of the Party has been clearly marked.

" In some instances, as for example the North Western Railroad Shops, a decline in shop activities must be noted. Shop bulletins generally do not come out regularly. Many comrades, especially language [foreign language] comrades, evidence complete underestimation of shop work. In some instances comrades have worked in a shop where a shop nucleus functions but have consciously avoided membership in the shop nucleus.

" In order to establish supervision over the work of shop nuclei and in order to help and stimulate the work of the units, leading comrades of the district and section committees shall be attached to shop nuclei. Comrades so attached must regard participation in and attendance of the meetings of their unit as a major responsibility."

All kinds of factors militated against the success of the struggle for " shop " nuclei. Relief, of course, was administered territorially, not by factory, and protests about relief and eviction fell readily into territorial districts. American election districts continued to be apportioned by population.

The party experimented with many different devices all through the period. One result was the internal consumption of party energy. Another result was the emasculation of democratic control at the base.[2]

[2] So important are the factors thus far discussed in contributing to the centralization, concentration, and de-democratization of the party

It has already been mentioned that, since several factors, among them pre-eminently rapid membership turnover, enfeebled the primary units of the Communist Party, the party officials at the center were thrust into extraordinary prominence. Hence the plausibility of the bitter complaints against "bureaucracy" which have figured so prominently in inner and outer criticism of the party. Anarchists and syndicalists were prepared from the outset to rebel against the strictness of the discipline and the influence of the officials in the Communist Party; and these groups have been joined by elements who received their practical and theoretical schooling in the party and were not hostile as a matter of principle to all hierarchical arrangements. Representative of these currents of adverse criticism is the comment of former party member Albert Weisbord on Communist officialdom (with special reference to the period since 1928): " Heavily subsidized as they were, and thus dependent for their livelihood, not upon the membership they could win in America but upon close adherence to the line of Stalin, the new bureaucracy outdid itself in multiplying its inherent opportunism with all the crimes of left Sectarianism." [3]

that other factors are rather cast in the shadow. No doubt the system of indirect rather than direct election of representatives to international and national congresses played into the hands of the élite in control of the party machine.

It is not possible, on the basis of existing material, to appraise the consequences of what may be called " nuclear " as distinguished from " enlarged " constituencies. By a nuclear constituency we mean a constituency composed of persons who are few in number and in intimate contact with one another; an enlarged constituency is numerically large and contacts are more formal than intimate. It seems reasonable to surmise that nuclear constituencies pass around the burden (or privilege) of representation among the individual members with a higher probability than " enlarged " constituencies. This implies, then, that assemblies or legislatures composed of representatives from nuclear constituencies are likely to show a higher turnover than when they are selected from enlarged constituencies.

[3] *The Conquest of Power* (New York, 1937), II, 1116.

Comments of this kind were constantly being made by ex-members of the Communist Party in Chicago. The accusations which are directed against the Communist Party (and the Soviet Union) of "bureaucratism" may be profoundly significant for the future trends of world politics. We have already outlined some of the processes by which the scope of the élite which seizes power at a new center of world revolution has been circumscribed in the past. We have spoken of restriction by parochial symbols (restriction by geographical differentiation). Thus American nationalism has restricted the diffusion of Communist symbols in America (as we recorded in the preceding chapter). This chapter has given in greater detail some aspects of the inner life of the party which thrust the alien control of the party into great prominence, emphasized the threat to American nationalism, and precipitated increase in the use and the sentimentalizing of the symbols of the American tradition. The present chapter shows how the conspicuous control over the party line by a small group of permanent officials has made "bureaucratism" as well as "foreignism" among the most prominent complaints against the Third International.

Objections to "bureaucratism" may mark the beginning of *restriction by functional differentiation*. It was a turning-point in the history of modern world politics when the "French" or "democratic" revolution was called the "bourgeois" revolution. Here the challenging counter-symbol was not parochial; "Prussia" was not opposed to "France." In both cases there is denial of the fundamental allegation of the carriers of the revolution that they represented, not merely "Frenchmen," but the rights of all men everywhere. But the second challenge was made in the name of a "functional," not a territorial group. Those who challenged the claim of the carriers of the revolution of 1789 to speak for "*humanité*" now invoked the name of the "proletariat." They charged that the main beneficiaries of the revolutionary surge of 1789 had been, not all mankind, but the "bourgeoisie." They confronted the "bourgeois" revolution with predictions of, and demands for, a "proletarian" revolution which would, in fact, benefit everyone.

The charges which are today directed against the élite in control of the Soviet Union and of the Third International are that they do not, in fact, represent the "proletariat." It is alleged that a social formation other than the proletariat has benefited most — namely, the "bureaucracy."

The state which has been set up in Russia has lodged "effective control" (as distinguished from "formal authority"), not in the manual workers, but in groups skilled in organization, propaganda, violence, and engineering. In place of the previous mixture of elements of "the landlord state," "the official bureaucratic state," and "the business state," we now have a "party bureaucratic state," in which control is exercised by the propagandists and organizers of the Communist Party. They command favorable income positions; and they enjoy maximum deference in governmental decisions in a pattern characterized by the governmentalization of social activity at large.

This means that possibly the Russian revolution will enter into history as the "second bourgeois revolution" in the same way in which a consensus about the characterization of 1789 as the "bourgeois" revolution has tended to establish itself. The implication is that the aristocracy and the plutocracy were liquidated for the benefit mainly of those who possess skills appropriate to an era of governmentalized social life.

During the period under survey the Communist Party in Chicago was condemned to chronic internal crisis by the rigid insistence of the central party leadership upon standards of party performance which clashed with the individualistic practices of American life. These burdens were imposed upon persons in a situation which was admittedly not in acute revolutionary crisis, and where the motives for extraordinary self-sacrifice were therefore largely absent. When the party lowered the standards of performance and discipline, the cen-

tral élites instigated the " purge "; when the local party leaders
adhered strenuously to the party line, they condemned themselves to a limited membership which, unconsciously for the
most part, sought to protect their primary ego by evasiveness
and by sabotage through seemingly conformist acts of indiscipline.

The restrictive effect of American individualism was expressed in several direct and indirect ways, but the common
net result was to accentuate the conflict between local and
central units of the Communist Party, and hence between
" American " and " foreign," " rank and file " and " bureaucracy."

CHAPTER XVIII

Restriction by Catharsis

DID Communist propaganda in Chicago during the Great Depression diminish the stability of the established order or did it have the "paradoxical" result of increasing its stability through the harmless dissipation of insecurities which were generated in the lives of those who suffered serious deprivation?

The results of any propaganda may be different magnitudes of catharsis, readjustment, or coercion. By "catharsis" is meant the dissipating of insecurities without significant change in established patterns. By "readjustment" is meant the modification of established symbols and practices. By "coercion" is meant the occurrence of coercive acts for or against the established order. (These acts may not deviate enough, as to frequency and intensity, from the frequencies and intensities referred to in the definition of established practice to constitute readjustments.)

If Communist propaganda absorbed the energies of many members of the community in propaganda, the effect may have been to alleviate the inner crises of these persons, without considerably modifying the established order; hence the role of Communist propaganda would have been to stabilize the status quo. Our present task is to explore the data in the light of this possibility.

Did Communist propaganda aid or impede the restitution

of income to the unemployed in the form of relief? This
bears on the question of the impact of Communist propaganda
upon the environment.

We know that the customary practice in coping with such
emergencies in America has been private relief, supplemented
by public relief. In the Great Depression there was an important change. The assumption of liability by local and state
government was relatively prompt, and the federal government was itself involved from a comparatively early date.

There is no question about the alertness and self-sacrifice of
Communists during the depression. Since they specialized in
the circulation of protest symbols long before the depression
began, they were able to respond quickly to the changes in the
environment, striving to leap to the forefront of mass protest
and to capture it for Communist slogans.

The initial prominence of Communist leadership and of
Communist slogans provoked anxiety, hatred, and stubborn
resistance on the part of many agencies of constituted authority and many sections of the community at large. To what
extent did the Communists, in contrast with their declared
purpose, diminish the prospects of relief by associating the
demand for relief with " alien " and " subversive " symbols?
The contribution of this factor to the total result has never
been appraised, and until this is done we cannot be certain of
the degree to which antagonism against the Communists nullified the effect of their activity among the masses.

The Unemployed Councils, chief agencies of Communist
activity among the unemployed, can be credited with getting
prompt results on several occasions when relief cuts were made
or threatened. In certain cases there was nothing more tangible than a rumor that relief cuts were imminent, and protest
demonstrations were organized at once.[1]

[1] From the standpoint of social psychology, such instances are particularly interesting, because the " milieu " changed without a change
in the " environment "; the expectations of a cut precipitated protests
which acted as a deterrent upon such changes in the environment.

However undecided we may be about the net effect of Communist propaganda on the position of the unemployed within the income pyramid, we may be sure that Communist propaganda increased self-deference among the unemployed, and deference toward the unemployed on the part of other elements in the community. Communist propaganda put the blame for economic distress on the " system " and not the "individual," thus rejecting an axiom of America's individualistic symbolism. The intensity of the personal crises which were precipitated by the deprivations of the depression were alleviated when the sufferers attributed responsibility to forces outside themselves (especially when they failed to recognize that such symbols were part of a counter-mores symbolism). Communist propaganda often utilized methods which brought the unemployed to the focus of public attention and increased the extent to which they were taken into consideration in public affairs. Communist propaganda contributed to the appearance of spokesmen of the unemployed as factors to be reckoned with by relief and other authorities. As before, we must set against this result the hostility which was directed against the unemployed because of their association with "radicalism."

The Communists performed an unintended but significant function early in the depression for the business men and politicians who tried to divert the blame for the depression away from themselves and to a "foreign " and " subversive" scapegoat, " the reds." But the anti-Communist campaigns of 1930 soon lost strength; it rapidly ceased to be plausible that a few " agitators " were to blame for the chaos of American economic life.

The traditional prestige of business in the United States suffered severe setbacks during the early years of the depression when eminent figures in the business world came toppling to the ground (epitomized for Chicago in the fall of Samuel Insull, the public utility magnate), and when private action among business leaders was not sufficient to restore prosperity or even to cope with collapse. Confronted with the growing militancy of the deprived, business leaders felt constrained to abdicate their leadership and to turn to the hierarchy of government as the only available source of prompt and effective large-scale action. First the state (at Springfield) and then the national government at Washington were appealed to for support to pay the relief bill of Chicago.

The declining deference to business men was accompanied by rising deference to government; but it could be foreseen that some business groups would revive and fight the expanded scope of party propagandists, party organizers, officials, and their advisers ("the Brain Trust"). This trend became visible immediately after the shock of the banking collapse of 1933 had begun to wear off; but it was not until 1934 that campaigns against the policies of the national government were launched on a grand scale. Some Chicago newspapers and business groups were particularly active in this regard. The attack on the expanded scope of the national government proceeded to some degree by glorifying self-government in units smaller than the nation ("states' rights"); but it was also often accompanied by demands to restrict the scope of government at every level. The Communist scapegoat again rose to some significance in 1934 when certain groups tried to pin the "red label" on the Roosevelt administration; but the elections showed that these campaigns were relatively ineffective. Meanwhile the wave of optimism induced by President Roosevelt, who presented himself so successfully over the radio and who sponsored many measures of aid to the distressed, contributed to the decline of the Communists. Early in 1933 the party was seriously demoralized in Chicago.

The relationship of revolutionary propaganda to the distribution of safety in the community has several interesting and difficult aspects. When unemployment first began to spread and the Communists tried to increase the frequency of acts of organized protest, the police "cracked down" on them with great vigor, interfering with indoor meetings as well as assemblies in the open air. As a means of diminishing the frequency of spontaneous outbursts over the city, the police eventually began to permit certain demonstrations. At the suggestion of the police, committees were appointed to negotiate details, and although the relations between the police and the demonstrators were often tense, the result of the accommodations made was to keep violence and even less severe forms of coercion at a minimum. (A factor which had contributed to police repression against the Communists at the start of the depression and presumably diminished in importance later by "abreaction" was the indignation of members of the police force against the interracial and anti-religious propaganda of the Communists.) The number of arrests made by the police in connection with demonstrations varied as follows (by quarters):

1930				1931				1932				1933				1934			
1	2	3	4	1	2	3	4	1	2	3	4	1	2	3	4	1	2	3	4
Records not centrally kept				89	48	201	120	270	125	181	126	312	133	165	39	100	119	128	77

The peak which occurred in the first quarter of 1933 came in connection with the rigorous enforcement of the new rule requiring complaints to be made at a central bureau rather than at local relief stations.

It seems probable that the Communist Party exercised an important influence in restricting the amount of violence against persons and property during the depression. As was already noted, at the very outset of the depression unorganized and law-breaking mass action often occurred in resisting evictions and in supporting complaints against administrators of relief. Such forms of expression were fostered by the fact that the police, by repressing indoor gatherings, closed down on those channels of protest which predominantly used symbols of wider reference than the primary ego and remained on the symbolic level; this at a time when deprivations were rising throughout the community. Under these conditions many of the most deprived became direct-actionist, and the Unemployed Councils were swept along into many " ultra-Leftist " violations of person and property. It became common for their leaders to preach direct action and thus to keep in step with the rising tension and affect of the masses. Illegal acts began to occur in more organized ways. When there were evictions, committees were sent to restore the furniture. Where gas or electricity was shut off, Unemployed Council electricians made the necessary connections, leaving their sign: " This light has been connected by the Unemployed Council."

As soon as the police gave wider latitude for demonstrations, however, the Communist Party leadership undertook to extirpate " petty Leftism " among its own members and the affiliated organizations in favor of concentration on disciplined and sustained action to " construct " a party capable of seizing power in a future crisis.

The foregoing review of the relationship of Communist propaganda to the distribution of income, deference, and safety in the Chicago area implies that the chief effect of Communist propaganda was the catharsis of insecurities rather than the readjustment of established patterns. Participation in propaganda, whether as producer or consumer, gave " harmless " issue to the energies of thousands of persons who were severely buffeted by the loss of income and deference. To some extent participation in Communist propaganda afforded an alternative for " private " violence against persons and property.

The tremendous amount of energy expended by those who were intimately connected with Communist promotion in Chicago has already been described in detail. We have seen how the " wheels within wheels " of the complicated machinery of the Communist Party consumed much of the energy of members in internal party work. At the peak of the opportunities provided by the Great Depression (1932), a communication from the Central Committee in New York to all dis-

tricts reminded the party again of the instructions of the 14th
Plenum Resolution, which read:

" The work of the lower Party organizations must be basically
changed. *Nine-tenths of all the work of the lower organizations
must be concentrated directly among the masses, and not as at present in countless inner meetings."*

The depression was not only a blow to the income position
of those who lost jobs and savings or whose pay was cut; it
brought wholesale reduction of deference (granted by self
and others) for those who had previously been somewhat successful. Participation in propaganda was a means of improv-
ing the deference position of persons who craved the immediate and excited response of an attentive crowd, or who
enjoyed sacrificial absorption in the stirring life of the mass
demonstration. The activity of parading, applauding, arguing,
planning, enhanced the emotional self-sufficiency of the unemployed. By paying deference to one another, forming, as it
were, a closed deference circuit, they were able to tide themselves over the blows of fate and to await the coming of recovery. Although Communist words were words of sacrilege
against the dominant ideology of American social life, the
words were the words of men who (for the most part) stayed
within the law.

When the older symbols became once more associated with
indulgences (as with relief), and protest symbols became
more frequently associated with failures, earlier loyalties re-
established themselves. So rapidly did the masses desert protest symbols of revolutionary radicalism that it is safe to assert
that the older sentiments were little modified by the divaga-
tion into protest. If there were early modifications of attitude
in the direction of accepting revolutionary radical symbols,
these attitudes were in turn revised when such symbols became differentially associated with negative aspects of the
context.

We must not dismiss, without careful discussion, the possibility that some readjustments which occurred during the
depression are to be attributed in some degree to Communist
propaganda. We have already cast doubt upon the statement
that large-scale relief came in response to Communist demands. If we assume, however, that Communist propaganda
did to some extent accelerate and augment the assumption of
the burden of relief by government agencies, and especially by
the federal government, we must recognize that the final
political consequences of this policy depend upon the methods
which will ultimately be used to meet the indebtedness of the
government. Meanwhile it may be noted that the increased
governmentalization of American society paralleled certain
salient features of the latest world revolutionary pattern. This
pattern included practices as well as symbols, and governmentalization was among the conspicuous practices.

Viewed in the perspective of world political development,
increased governmentalization of American society is an example of the partial incorporation of the most recent pattern
of world revolution. Since the assumption of relief by the
government immediately resulted in indulgences for the unemployed, and thereby in a diminution of their insecurity
level, the probability of revolutionary upheaval was reduced.
Hence we have here an instance of restriction of the world
revolutionary pattern by its partial incorporation outside of
its center.[2]

Centralization of government was a direct response to Communist propaganda in some instances, not in the sense of acquiescence in a Communist demand, but as a counter-measure
to Communist activity. A striking instance of this was the
creation of the central Public Relations Bureau of the Chicago
relief agencies in January 1933. A prominent relief administrator discussed the measure as follows:

[2] " Incorporation " does not necessarily mean " conscious " copying.
The term signifies only a parallelism between practices prevailing elsewhere and in the world revolutionary pattern.

"I have spoken at several [demonstrations] at the invitation of the unemployed council because I have felt that much of the following of the unemployed council was not communistic, or even extremely radical, but that these individuals were in a terrible situation, were bewildered and were willing to follow anyone who promised them something in the way of more relief and better conditions.

"For almost ten months the relief service attempted to work with the organized unemployed groups, receiving grievance committees at the relief offices, not only unemployed councils which were frankly communistic, but the Chicago Workers Committee [Socialist], the Workers League of America, and the Workers Ex-Service Men's League. The plan broke down because of the attitude expressed by some of the speakers at the meetings referred to. The unemployed groups were building up their membership by offering to get more relief for the individual. The individual had nothing to lose, and we found that our work was seriously hampered by having to talk with groups all day long who were presenting cases which in our opinion were being properly handled."

(Public statement; attitude corresponded to that expressed previously in conversation.)

Many of the measures adopted to restrict agitational activities were successful because they were strictly enforced and accompanied by indulgences granted to the relief population. Deprivations were inflicted on the "agitators"; indulgences were bestowed upon "unemployed American citizens."

When the Communists provoked greater centralization of administrative activities, they did not necessarily advance their own cause. If greater centralization increases the effectiveness with which the established élites in America are able to defend themselves against "subversive" influences, it weakens world revolutionary radical movements. The "completed shell of the socialized state" may be seized by very different élites from those which head up in Moscow.

Our survey of the facilitating and restricting factors with reference to the acceptance of Communist propaganda has emphasized the relative strength of restrictive processes. We have seen, however, that Communist propaganda in Chicago during the Great Depression did not fail for lack of skill in tactics. In both distinctiveness and adaptiveness it outshone the rival propagandas of world revolutionary radicalism.

We asked whether to attribute the relative failure of Communist propaganda to lack of skill in strategy. We summarized the canons of strategy in the principles of combination and precaution. The general object of strategy was said to be the predominance necessary to the goal pursued; this is sought by the proper combination of favorable groups, and by the exercise of precaution to prevent superior concentrations of opposing influences. Communist strategy was criticized for excessive attention to the unemployed (and also to unstable personalities). It was also criticized for flagrant violations of the principle of precaution. In so far as the Chicago Communists adhered to the line of the World Congress of 1928, offering a " United Front " to the rank and file of Socialist and liberal organizations and denouncing their leaders as " Social Fascists," they spread dissension among elements of the Left and the Center. Already there were indications, not only of bitter resentment against Communists by Socialists and liberals, but of the growth of extreme kinds of anti-Communist associations. These were characterized as the fumbling precursors of possible developments explicitly parallel to the national revolutionary radical propagandas which cut short the life of the German Republic and Italian parliamentarism.

Final judgment on the skillfulness of Communist strategy was deferred until we had more exhaustively considered factors facilitating and impeding acceptance of Communist propaganda in Chicago. Such factors were classified as belonging either to " environment " or to " predisposition." The data of the Chicago case confirm the proposition that the acceptance of revolutionary radical propaganda varies directly as magnitudes of deprivation. Communist propaganda spread at the onset of the depression when deprivations were largest, and dropped off when they were increasingly replaced by indulgences. Predispositions are pre-organized attitudes and levels of reactivity. One general hypothesis about predisposition is that the relative frequency of acceptance of revolutionary radical propaganda in response to deprivation varies directly as the extent to which persons are already favorably inclined toward such patterns and unfavorably oriented toward conflicting (especially established) patterns. Our Chicago data gave some confirmation of this hypothesis. The insecurity level was defined as varying directly with the frequency and intensity of anxiety among persons in a given context. Our general hypothesis is that the relative frequency of extreme responses within a certain group (such as the acceptance of world revolutionary radical propaganda) varies directly with the height of the insecurity level of the group. Data collected upon Communist-led and Socialist-led organizations of the unemployed gave some confirmation. In particular, attention was called to the role of the political " hyperreactives " (who may or may not be " radicals "); that is, of persons who take the initiative in political activism. Their social role is to intensify collective reactions through extreme statement and impetuous action. In general they belong to the " externalized (or partially internalized) rage type " of personality. In so far as the Communists relied upon dramatic methods of recruiting their members, they attracted a disproportionate number of persons of a type likely to play a disruptive role in organized political life.

Our survey of the restrictive factors in Chicago began with the consideration of American nationalism. The pattern of nationalism is a basic pattern of western European civilization; it is one of the most potent means by which the scope of a revolutionary élite which has seized power at a world center may be restricted by rival élites. So vigorous was American nationalism that there was a constant inducement for Chicago Communists to increase adaptiveness (by the incorporation of more elements of the American pattern) at the expense of distinctiveness. This process was restriction of world revolution by the modification of the "self" (rather than the "other"); some patterns of the non-revolutionary world are incorporated among the symbols and practices of those identified with the revolutionary center (at the expense of elements of the original world revolutionary pattern; in the usual sense of the word, such internal modification is "counter-revolutionary").

Since the officials of the Communist International continued to follow the line expressed in the World Congress of 1928, pressure was brought on local leaders to "purge" deviating elements from the party and to enforce strict compliance with the "general line." It was not until well after the triumph of National Socialism in Germany that the Communist International dropped its "third period" attitude toward Socialist and liberal elements and initiated the unprecedentedly conciliatory and co-operative strategy and tactic which was codified at the World Congress of 1935. Until this change in the central policy of the party, the local party in places like Chicago was condemned to chronic internal strife because of the concessions which it constantly tended to make to the strength of American nationalism.

We also examined the degree to which Communist propaganda was restricted by American individualism. The international leaders of Communism, thinking of themselves as the generals of an army of professional revolutionists, made membership in the party as much of a full-time occupation as possible. Such total absorption of the individual in the service of rather inclusive secondary symbols, while not unique, is exceptional in individualistic America. Recruits often found it disagreeable to sacrifice so much of their time and energy to the party, and withdrew, contributing to a turnover rate of party membership which was considered by the officials to be alarmingly high. Many persons who remained inside the party made certain adaptations (mostly unconscious) to protect themselves against party demands (evasiveness and indiscipline through seeming conformity).

By means of incessant pressure from the top (ultimately Moscow) the International sought to break up individualistic practices; but these efforts resulted in provoking and intensifying chronic crisis in such local areas as Chicago. As the party was unable to maintain a sufficiently permanent membership in its basic units, the "democratic" features of "democratic centralism" were practically nullified. The paid official staff of the party (and in the final analysis the staff of the Communist International in Moscow) exercised predominant and even conspicuous control. This gave rise to constant accusations of "bureaucratism" against the highly interlocking élites of the Third International and the Soviet Union.

The repeated accusations of the "bureaucracy" may be precursors of the next fundamental change in world political development. It was a turning-point in world politics when the revolution in France was "stigmatized" as the "bourgeois" revolution. This denied in a functional, as distinguished from a territorial, sense the claim of the revolutionary leaders and their followers to speak for all mankind.

The contemporary accusations of "bureaucracy" may represent the nuclei of the slowly emerging symbolism of the next world revolutionary wave. It is asserted that after the revolution in Russia, made in the name of the proletariat, the chief benefits of the new order accrued to the skill groups (the newer middle-class groups) like the party propagandists, party organizers, department officials, technologists, and officers.[3]

It may be that world revolutionary waves themselves are one of the permanent as well as basic features of the western European pattern of civilization. Before the Russian upheaval was the French upheaval; both of them were marked by the cataclysmic emergence at a circumscribed center of an élite which invoked new symbols to justify its control and new practices for the benefit of hitherto "underprivileged" class

[3] Something akin to this point of view has already found systematic and agitational expression in certain anarcho-syndicalist and "Trotskyist" circles.

formations. The élite in France spoke for the " rights of man " and predominantly benefited the bourgeoisie; the élite in Russia spoke for the " proletariat" and predominantly benefited the " skill groups," a part of the " lesser bourgeoisie," which in its turn is a layer of the "bourgeoisie."

If we decide to extrapolate the past into the future, we may add to our description of the world revolutionary waves as permanent features of western European civilization the following statement: the élite which seizes power at the eruptive center of a new revolutionary movement does not succeed in unifying the world. Another conspicuous feature of the western European pattern of civilization is the multiple state system, which is sustained by such symbolic formations as the demand for " sovereignty " and the expectation of violence. Most potent of all, the multiple state system is supported by nationalistic sentiment, whose significance in the American case has been vividly exhibited in the Chicago record. Thus it seems highly improbable that world unity will occur by the incorporation of all states within the U.S.S.R.

To predict that the scope of the élite which seizes power at a world center will fall short of the world does not imply that all elements of what was called before " the world revolutionary pattern " will fall short of (almost) universal diffusion. We must distinguish the *original* world revolutionary *pattern of the* revolutionary *center* from the world revolutionary *pattern of the epoch*. The first (the original center pattern) is no doubt destined to be restricted; the second (the epoch pattern) is moving toward universality among the major powers.

If we look back at the French case, we plainly see in the perspective of subsequent happenings that many of the innovations in symbol and practice which took place within the borders of France also appeared beyond France, without formal affiliation of the other states with the eruptive center. That is, practices concerning the relationship of governments to economic processes which favored the rise of the bourgeoisie at the expense of the aristocracy became more and more universal during the nineteenth century, although the world remained separated into independent states. The same may be said for a series of other practices (universal suffrage, supremacy of legislatures over executives, etc.) as well as for certain symbols ("rights of man"). In all of these cases the connection between them and the élite of the eruptive center of revolution in France was severed. It is evident, too, that the most extreme features of the original revolutionary pattern did not persist, even in France.

What are the features of the Russian center of world revolution which are also components of the world revolutionary pattern of our entire epoch? Perhaps one may attribute a preeminent place to the *moderation of income differences* by the abolition of private ownership of the instrumentalities of production (unaccompanied by reinstatement of differences of the same magnitude within governmentally controlled enterprises). Possibly another pattern is the increasing *governmentalization of organized social life.* Another is the *predominance of a party with privileged status.* (This is less likely to universalize than the two patterns mentioned before.) The Soviet Union is a *party bureaucratic state,* because the most influential élite is composed of specialists on party propaganda and party organization. Under certain conditions a *military bureaucratic state* (garrison state) may arise (in Japan, for example) in which the most influential élite is composed of specialists on violence. It is probable that in the present epoch transitions to both of these state-forms would be accompanied by moderation of income differences.[4]

In the perspective just established, the political developments in Russia are to be understood in relation to two interrelated,

---

[4] Certain other distinctions may be drawn: skill in bargaining distinguishes the élite of the *business state;* skill in " departmental " organization, the *official bureaucratic state.* See H. D. Lasswell: " Sino-Japanese Crisis; the Garrison State versus the Civilian State," *China Quarterly,* II (1937), 643–9.

though distinguishable, processes. In the early days of the revolution Russia was the scene where a world revolutionary pattern appeared; it was impeded from moving toward universality. Today only certain features of this original pattern survive (even in the Soviet Union). The present characteristics are the pattern of our epoch; they are appearing among all the major states of the world. Pattern I (of the center) aspired toward a unified proletarian world; pattern II (of the epoch) perpetuates a divided world, in which the skill groups (sections of the lesser bourgeoisie) are rising in influence at the expense of plutocracies and aristocracies.

Thus the original pattern of the Russian center has largely vanished, and in its place is the Russian form of the world revolutionary pattern of our epoch. Pattern I was restricted from without and within the Soviet Union; pattern II emerged in Russia — and elsewhere — as an outcome of complex processes of diffusion and restriction of pattern I. The continuity of symbols in the Soviet Union has veiled, to some extent, the fundamental transformations which have taken place.

This case study of Communist propaganda in Chicago during the Great Depression has demonstrated the strength of the restrictive factors which prevent the universalizing of the U.S.S.R. Despite some favorable circumstances, Communist propaganda was blocked by American nationalism and individualism and thus contributed more to the catharsis of insecurities than to the readjustment of American symbols and practices. It made only a modest contribution even to the appearance in America of the revolutionary pattern of the epoch.

The propaganda of the Communist International in Chicago in some cases achieved the opposite of what it aimed at. Organically affiliated with the élite of one of the great powers, the Third International was an easy butt of restrictive processes which mobilized nationalistic sentiments against " alien " influences. Rigid adherence by international officials to the conception of the party as an army of professional revolutionists led to chronic strife in the local party, because of the strength of individualistic practices in American life. The conspicuousness of the role played by the " alien bureaucracy " fostered restrictive processes in two directions, one proceeding by nationalistic self-assertiveness, and the other by strenuous denial of the claim of the Russian élite to speak for the world proletariat or even for the proletariat of Russia.

The chief role of Communist propaganda was to crystallize the conflicts between diffusion and restriction tendencies in relation to the Russian center of the latest wave of world revolution. Propaganda did not create many of the profound ideological and material differences which it did so much to bring before the collective focus of attention; propaganda accelerated the intensification of these conflicts. In this sense the chief function of the Third International in America has been to expedite the rejection of the Russian revolution (of the center). It was not sufficiently menacing, however, to stimulate greatly the appearance of an American version of the world revolutionary pattern of the epoch.

Chicago, a major metropolitan center of diversified industry, lying in the intermediate zone of proximity, bipolarity, and insecurity in reference to the Soviet Union, was a proving ground of Communist propaganda during the unparalleled crisis of the Great Depression. Communist propaganda contributed chiefly to the catharsis of the insecurities of the unemployed and to the strengthening of defensive tendencies against what was conceived as the threat of Russian control of American life and bureaucratic control of the destinies of the proletariat itself.

Appendix

WITHIN the United States itself, Chicago has more in common with Moscow and Petrograd than most urban centers. Like New York, Chicago has many workers in light industry, commerce, and transportation; in addition, Chicago is an important center of heavy industry. In 1919 the Chicago industries which hired the largest number of wage-earners (in order of importance) were:

> Slaughtering and meat-packing wholesale
> Clothing, men's, youths', and boys'
> Foundry and machine-shop products
> Printing and publishing, book and job
> Car and general construction and repair

Ten years later (1929) the picture had altered in several important respects:

> Electrical machinery, apparatus, etc.
> Iron and steel: steel workers and mills
> Foundry and machine-shop products
> Slaughtering and meat-packing wholesale
> Printing and publishing, book and job

The men's clothing industry had declined to eighth place; car and general construction had risen from sixth to first; iron and steel had been thirteenth in 1921, and was now second. The changes, expressed in percentages of the total wage-earning population for each of these industries, were:

	1919	1929
Electrical machinery	3.44	10.06
Iron and steel	1.73a	8.24
Foundry	6.53	6.37
Slaughtering	11.31	4.64
Printing	4.94	4.60
Clothing, men's	7.63	3.30
Car construction	2.64	2.01

a — 1921

It should be emphasized, however, that the industries of Chicago are by no means as important in the national economy of the United States as the factories of Moscow and Petrograd were in pre-revolutionary Russia. Russia was industrially undeveloped, with the exception of a few great centers, but the United States has an intricate network of industrial activity. The national position of the Chicago industries is shown by the proportion of national value output made in Chicago:

	1919	1929
Electrical machinery	7.85	18.36
Iron and steel	3.71a	15.01
Foundry	6.07	10.05
Slaughtering	25.50	19.06
Printing	17.45	16.92
Clothing, men's	16.77a	12.39
Car construction	3.25	4.90

a — 1923

The industrial pattern of Chicago differs in another important respect from Moscow and Petrograd, where the number of factory workers per enterprise was very high.[1] Also Chicago had fewer wage-earners employed per establishment. The figures for 1919 and 1929 are:

	1919	1929
Electrical machinery	99	252
Iron and steel	489a	1,261
Foundry	56	61
Slaughtering	993	449
Printing	21	24
Clothing, men's	66	62
Car construction	606	351

a — 1921

Chicago resembled Moscow and Petrograd in that Chicago had been a center of radical and revolutionary activities. The Haymarket riot and the resulting anarchist trials in 1886 gained world-

[1] Refer to Leon Trotsky: *History of the Russian Revolution*, I, 10.

wide notoriety. In the Pullman strike of 1894 federal troops were called in to suppress the strike, which had been called by Eugene Debs of the American Railway Union. As a gathering-place of casual laborers, Chicago was the national headquarters of the Industrial Workers of the World, and hence a stronghold of anarchist and syndicalist propaganda. In 1917 and 1918 Chicago and the state of Illinois stood next to New York in Socialist Party membership (between 8,000 and 9,000). In presidential elections the Socialist vote was usually ten times the paid party membership. The 61,000 votes cast in Illinois in 1916 were more than the Socialists mustered in any other state in the Union. Chicago had three Socialists in the City Council, and the party was occasionally represented on other local government boards. In 1919 Chicago was the scene of the convention which led to the organization of several Communist parties, which subsequently struggled with one another for the leadership of the movement in America.

The workers of Chicago were very hard hit by the Great Depression which followed the stock-market collapse in 1929. Of the ten largest cities in the United States, Chicago suffered among the most from the recession of economic activity. Over half of the employees of the electrical industries and a large proportion of those engaged in furniture, packing, clothing, printing, and transportation were discharged.

However, the Great Depression struck Chicago after a prolonged period of improvement in the money wage (and the real wage) of factory workers. This, we expect, would minimize the probability of recourse to revolutionary radicalism. We expect to find a higher frequency of revolutionary responses when deprivations continue to be inflicted upon people who have already been frustrated in the recent past, and who cherish a reminiscence (true or false) of happier days in the more remote past. This presumably was not the case with most of the south and southeastern European immigrants which constituted such an important quota of Chicago's proletariat.

The yearly average wage (in dollars) increased between 1919 and 1929 in the principal Chicago industries, save only slaughtering and packing:

		1919	1929
Electrical machinery	....	1,062	1,684
Iron and steel	....	1,511a	1,869
Foundry	....	1,357	1,697
Slaughtering	....	1,529	1,379
Printing	....	1,280	1,764
Clothing, men's	....	1,388	1,490
Car construction	....	1,350	1,659

a — 1923

However, the position of the wage-receiver was declining relative to the salary-receiver during these years. Wages rose relative to salary levels in electrical machinery and car construction, but declined in the other industries on the list (data missing for steel). Average wages depicted as a percentage of average salaries:

		1919	1929
Electrical machinery	....	56.69	75.72
Iron and steel	....	—	65.92
Foundry	....	57.53	53.75
Slaughtering	....	85.22	51.53
Printing	....	71.31	60.52
Clothing, men's	....	75.86	59.02
Car construction	....	53.96	60.27

It is probable that the "psychic" income of the workers was reduced in certain other respects during the post-war period. The degree of mechanization was increasing (defined as the amount of horsepower per wage-earner). It is to be presumed that the changes incident to industrial mechanization complicated the adjustment problems of the laboring groups (mechanization often means the obsolescence of the worker's skill, and the speeding up of his tempo of work). Increased mechanization is notable in slaughtering, foundry, and car construction:

		1919	1929
Electrical machinery	....	1.07	1.67
Iron and steel	....	—	23.82
Foundry	....	1.31	3.25
Slaughtering	....	1.47	4.27
Printing	....	1.06	1.45
Clothing, men's	....	0.19	0.33
Car construction	....	1.64	2.97

TABLE I

Quarterly Variations in Economic Conditions in Chicago,
1930–4, as Measured by Certain Indices
(expressed in % change over previous quarter)

Quarter	Employ-ment	Evictions	Case Count	Work Relief	Avg. Ex-penditure per case	Descrip-tions of Quarters [1]
1930						
1st			25.30			D
2nd	—3.95	16.88	— 5.65		— 4.31	D
3rd	—6.39	13.72	3.77		— 2.97	D
4th	—4.75	— 28.57	110.59		—23.69	I
1931						
1st	—3.28	28.44	81.73		10.27	A
2nd	—2.26	7.27	— 7.35		— 4.22	D
3rd	—5.40	50.65	9.78		7.52	D
4th	—6.11	— 52.89	86.32		13.65	I
1932						
1st	—3.76	181.82	35.57		2.73	D
2nd	—8.57	— 33.55	.23		— 5.78	D
3rd	—5.76	145.63	11.98		13.92	A
4th	1.22	— 43.38	15.71		2.62	I
1933						
1st	—7.57	— 29.49	15.40		9.46	A
2nd	3.57	72.28	— 2.41		—16.76	D
3rd	6.18	— 4.89	— 23.17	100.00	26.91	I
4th	.74	— 40.03	— 8.67	— 27.77	18.86	A
1934						
1st	— .59	13.85	— 20.40	— 47.75	— 8.28	D
2nd	6.51	27.88	25.58	154.68	12.10	I
3rd	.97	13.67	— 1.43	— 7.18	3.23	In
4th	.14	— 36.99	6.47	11.00(?)	11.03	I

[1] D: Deprivation; I: Indulgent; A: Active; In: Inactive.

TABLE II

Monthly Variations in Economic Conditions in Chicago

	Unemploy-ment	Evic-tions	Case Load	Work Relief	Work Relief Average Expenditures	Case Load Average Expenditures
1930						
Jan.						
Feb.	—1.25	— 25.84	— 1.27			— 1.50
Mar.	—1.25	24.24	— 4.18			9.89
Apr.	—1.26	30.49	.74			— 9.74
May	—1.39	— 21.50	— 4.67			2.56
June	—1.95	2.38	— .25			— 5.13
July	—3.75	40.70	4.53			— .84
Aug.	—1.93	— 24.79	1.91			— 2.23
Sept.	—1.16	13.19	— .63			6.07
Oct.	—2.34	— 9.71	14.12			2.66
Nov.	—1.92	— 41.94	81.44			—32.65
Dec.	—	44.44	49.37			— 3.70
1931						
Jan.	—2.32	8.97	14.65			9.13
Feb.	— .50	21.18	6.45			4.50
Mar.	— .13	— 1.94	9.60			25.57
Apr.	— .50	14.85	— 8.44			—21.22
May	—1.65	— 25.86	—10.40			5.44
June	—1.29	25.58	1.18			1.48
July	—2.61	39.81	2.89			1.34
Aug.	—1.20	1.32	8.74			— 1.57
Sept.	—1.16	6.54	11.38			11.54
Oct.	—2.63	— 41.10	38.57			—17.66
Nov.	—3.27	— 26.04	19.02			20.29
Dec.	.88	— 25.35	23.66			20.29
1932						
Jan.	—2.77	209.43	10.93			—15.18
Feb.	— .15	42.68	1.49			1.93
Mar.	—1.64	— 5.13	1.08			5.27

	Unemployment	Evictions	Case Load	Work Relief	Work Relief Average Expenditures	Case Load Average Expenditures
Apr.	−5.93	− 46.85	4.01			−12.52
May	−2.42	− 14.41	− 6.36			− .11
June	− .66	91.09	− 1.75			11.06
July	−5.67	6.22	6.83			4.64
Aug.	1.24	100.49	10.24			1.87
Sept.	1.05	− 3.65	4.48			.77
Oct.	1.21	− 31.82	3.04			−25.36
Nov.	− .34	− 35.56	4.49			48.13
Dec.	−2.23	− 25.86	7.93			−13.77
1933						
Jan.	−2.10		5.38			18.94
Feb.	1.25		2.70			− 4.83
Mar.	−1.41		2.58			3.87
Apr.	.72		− .09			− 7.84
May	2.31		− 3.82			−13.76
June	5.22		− 6.99			− 6.20
July	4.63		−10.85			5.52
Aug.	8.53		− 8.95	13.20	− 5.54	33.93
Sept.	2.77		− 7.60	33.50	− 1.98	15.90
Oct.	− .28		− 2.61	− 2.98	2.02	− 7.86
Nov.	−2.56		2.58	− 53.31	− 5.45	− 9.63
Dec.	− .87		1.51	14.43	− 11.31	33.02
1934						
Jan.	−2.50		17.75		8.58	−15.93
Feb.	2.56	− 26.92	−12.66	− 31.45	13.92	6.82
Mar.	2.35	59.65	11.91	− 26.30	149.19	13.62
Apr.	1.87	1.65	23.71	42.57	− 52.61	− 2.50
May	2.12	16.76	− .03	125.23	12.01	4.04
June	− .41	− 18.06	3.88	− 1.10	− 7.42	7.19
July	−1.38	14.12	.60	2.24	− 4.49	− 8.31
Aug.	.98	22.77	.25	− 11.89	35.00	12.50
Sept.	2.21	− 16.53	1.34	− 5.14	− 3.92	− 6.41
Oct.	− .14	− 14.98	3.73	24.09	− 26.63	8.09
Nov.	−2.71	− 22.16	1.59			
Dec.	.97	− 26.28	1.74			

TABLE III
Indices of Employment in Chicago

	1930	1931	1932	1933	1934
Jan.	97.0	79.9	66.8	55.9	66.3
Feb.	96.2	79.5	66.9	56.6	68.0
Mar. 9	95.0	79.4	65.8	55.8	69.6
Apr.	93.8	79.0	61.9	56.2	70.9
May	92.5	77.7	60.4	57.5	72.4
June	90.7	76.7	60.0	60.5	72.7
July	87.3	74.7	56.6	63.3	71.7
Aug.	86.4	73.8	57.3	68.7	72.4
Sept.	85.4	72.3	57.9	70.6	74.0
Oct.	83.4	70.4	58.6	70.4	73.9
Nov.	81.8	68.1	58.4	68.6	71.9
Dec.	81.8	68.7	57.1	68.0	72.6
Average for year	89.3	75.0	60.6	62.7	71.4

TABLE IV
Number of Evictions in Chicago
(1930–4)

	1930	1931	1932	1933	1934
Jan.	89	85	164	97	156
Feb.	66	103	234	123	114
Mar.	82	101	222	184	182
Apr.	107	116	118	202	185
May	84	86	101	248	216
June	86	108	193	246	177
July	121	151	205	229	202
Aug.	91	153	411	234	248
Sept.	103	163	396	199	207
Oct.	93	96	270	182	176
Nov.	54	71	174	119	137
Dec.	78	53	129	96	101
Total					
Writ in for Detainer	38,556	55,626	54,765		41,396

TABLE V

Total Active Case Count (Unduplicated Total) for the Five Major Family Welfare Agencies[1] *and C.P.W.*[2] *by Months, January 1930 to January 1935*

	1930	1931	1932	1933	1934
Jan.	13,726	46,695	127,485	188,589	111,093
Feb.	13,552	49,707	129,385	193,689	97,026
Mar.	12,985	54,477	130,784	198,677	108,586
Apr.	13,081	49,879	136,028	198,489	134,336
May	12,470	44,694	127,379	190,908	134,299
June	12,439	45,220	125,151	177,571	129,093
July	13,003	46,526	133,703	158,309	129,874
Aug.	13,252	50,593	147,395	144,136	130,205
Sept.	13,169	56,352	154,001	133,183	131,947
Oct.	15,028	78,085	158,683	129,712	136,865
Nov.	27,267	92,940	165,803	133,065	139,044
Dec.	40,728	114,926	178,958	135,071	141,463
Total	200,700	730,094	1,714,755	1,981,399	1,523,831
Average no. of cases monthly	16,725	60,841	142,896	165,117	126,986

[1] United Charities, Jewish Social Service Bureau, Central Charity Bureau, Salvation Army, American Red Cross (Chicago Chapter).

[2] Field Service Division and Aid to Veterans. Approximately 60% of the families cared for by the Cook County Bureau of Public Welfare also received aid from private agencies. Therefore 40 per cent of the " relief case load " and the " total active case load " of the County Bureau were added to the corresponding case counts of the private agencies in order to arrive at the number of different cases receiving relief and the number of different active cases. This applies through February 1932. After that date actual figures on amount of duplication were available.

TABLE VI

Total Relief Expenditures by Major Public and Private Agencies in Chicago
(1930–4)

	1930	1931	1932	1933	1934
Jan.	$ 274,827	$ 663,786	$ 2,372,678.88	$ 4,452,883.96	$ 2,672,872.53
Feb.	267,282	738,405	2,454,527.64	4,351,975.06	2,495,257.20
Mar.	280,436	1,016,269	2,612,211.05	4,636,707.04	3,170,462.59
Apr.	255,877	733,291	2,376,605.93	4,279,308.52	3,823,899.33
May	250,115	692,828	2,222,406.29 [1]	3,541,271.72	3,977,612.01
June	236,678	711,131	2,426,859.31	3,089,569.34	4,099,034.69
July	245,520	741,977	2,711,295.39	2,908,632.35	3,781,137.30
Aug.	244,544	793,913	3,044,386.47	3,544,503.15	4,264,467.58
Sept.	257,691	986,465	3,206,599.75	3,795,507.54	4,044,232.80
Oct.	301,884	1,125,342	2,466,308.54	3,987,934.55	4,534,390.60
Nov.	369,001	1,691,666	3,817,335.03	3,696,057.15	4,785,506.98
Dec.	530,620	2,524,904	4,331,173.89	3,866,103.31	4,968,292.59
Total	$3,591,424	$12,409,977	$34,042,388.17	$46,150,453.69	$46,617,156.20
Average monthly expenditures	$ 299,285	$ 1,034,165	$ 2,836,865.68	$ 3,845,871.14	$ 3,884,763.02

[1] Includes estimated figures for Catholic Charities.

TABLE VII

Average Expenditure per Case by Major Public and Private Agencies in Chicago (1930–4)

	1930	1931	1932	1933	1934
Jan.	$20.02	$14.22	$18.61	$23.61	$24.06
Feb.	19.72	14.86	18.97	22.47	25.70
Mar.	21.67	18.66	19.97	23.34	29.20
Apr.	19.56	14.70	17.47	21.51	28.47
May	20.06	15.50	17.45	18.55	29.62
June	19.03	15.73	19.38	17.40	31.75
July	18.87	15.94	20.28	18.36	29.11
Aug.	18.45	15.69	20.66	24.59	32.75
Sept.	19.57	17.50	20.82	28.50	30.65
Oct.	20.09	14.41	15.54	30.74	33.13
Nov.	13.53	18.24	23.02	27.78	34.42
Dec.	13.03	21.94	19.85	28.62	35.12
Average per case	$17.89	$17.00	$19.85	$23.29	$30.57

TABLE VIII

State Legislation for Financing Relief in Illinois

Citation	Date			Source of Funds	Amount	Purpose	Administration
	Approved	Effective	Expires				
H. B. 1 (1932 3d Ex.)[1]	Feb. 6, 1932	Feb. 6, 1932	Aug. 1, 1935	State: Emergency Relief Fund	$20,000,000	Relief: Funds or supplies or any other desirable means	Illinois Emer. Relief Comm.
H. B. 4, 5 (1932 3d Ex.)	Feb. 6, 1932	Feb. 6, 1932	Unspecified	State: Bonds[2]	$20,000,000	Emergency Relief Fund	Subj. to legislative app.
H. B. 2 (1932 3d Ex.)	Feb. 6, 1932	Feb. 6, 1932	Dec. 31, 1932	State: Property levy[3]	$25,000,000	Emergency Relief Fund	Subj. to legislative app.
H. B. 3 (1932 3d Ex.)	Feb. 6, 1932	Feb. 6, 1932	Unspecified	State: Tax anticipation notes[4]	$20,000,000	Emergency Relief Fund	Subj. to legislative app.

[1] As amended by H. B. 6 (1932 4th Ex.) approved Oct. 17, 1932, and S. B. 160 (1933) approved June 30, 1933.
[2] Approved by electorate Nov. 8, 1932, and financed from counties' allotment of motor-fuel tax.
[3] Provides funds appropriated by H. B. 1 (1932 3d Ex.); operative only in case of electorate's failure to approve bond issue authorized by H. B. 4 (1932 3d Ex.).
[4] Authorized sale of tax anticipation warrants, to be redeemed from either property levy or bond issue provided by H. B. 2 and/or H. B. 4 (1932 3d Ex.).

| Citation | Date | | | Source of Funds | Amount | Purpose | Administration |
	Approved	Effective	Expires				
S. B. 30 (1932 4th Ex.)	Oct. 17, 1932	Oct. 17, 1932	Dec. 31, 1933	County: Share of State Motor Fuel Tax[5]	Unspecified	Relief to unemployed and destitute residents	County & township boards
S. B. 31 (1932 4th Ex.)	Dec. 31, 1932	Dec. 31, 1932	Unspecified	Cook County: Bonds[6]	Unspecified	Payment of indebtedness heretofore incurred for relief of unemployed and destitute	County boards
S. B. 4 (1932 4th Ex.)	Nov. 29, 1932	Nov. 29, 1932	Dec. 31, 1933	County: Bonds[7]	Unspecified	Relief to unemployed and destitute residents	County & township boards
H. B. 51 (1932 4th Ex.)	Nov. 29, 1932	Nov. 29, 1932	Unspecified	Cook County: Bonds[8]	$17,000,000	Temporary Relief	County board

[5] Authorizes use of counties' share of motor-fuel taxes for relief, after payment of service of $20,000,000 relief bond issue provided by H. B. 4 (1932 3d Ex.).

[6] Authorizes for service of bonds a direct annual property tax, or any balance of county's motor-fuel tax allotment after payment of service of $20,000,000 relief bond issue provided by H. B. 4 (1932 3d Ex.).

[7] May be authorized by two-thirds vote of county board to amount not exceeding 6 times the county's share of motor-fuel tax. To be serviced by property tax or by counties' share of motor-fuel tax after payment of service on $20,000,000 relief bond issue (H. B. 4, 1932 3d Ex.).

[8] Subject to resolution of county board; to be serviced by property levy.

TABLE VIII (Continued)
State Legislation for Financing Relief in Illinois

Citation	Date Approved	Effective	Expires	Source of Funds	Amount	Purpose	Administration
H. B. 24 (1932 4th Ex.)	Dec. 5, 1932	Dec. 5, 1932	June 30, 1933	County: Sales Tax[9]	Unspecified	Relief to unemployed and destitute residents	County & township boards
S. B. 665, 738 (1933)	June 29, 1933	July 1, 1933	Dec. 31, 1933	State: Retailers' Occupation Tax	$25,000,000[10]	Relief to unemployed and destitute residents	IERC in co-operation with political subdivision
H. B. 1048 (1933)	July 12, 1933	July 12, 1933	Unspecified	State: Emergency Relief Fund	$750,000	Administration	Subject to legislative appropriation
S. B. 4, 5 (1933 1st Ex.)	Nov. 10, 1933	Nov. 10, 1933	Unspecified	State: Bonds[11]	$30,000,000	Emergency Relief Fund	Subject to legislative appropriation

[9] Effective upon two-thirds vote of county board; authority never invoked.

[10] Actual yield of tax, $17,300,000.

[11] Bond issue approved by electorate Nov. 4, 1934 and financed by motor-fuel tax. Counties and cities must divert their share of motor-fuel taxes in proportion to percentage of bond proceeds received. May sell anticipatory notes.

Citation	Date			Source of Funds	Amount	Purpose	Administration
	Approved	Effective	Expires				
S. B. 1 (1933 1st Ex.)	Nov. 10, 1933	Jan. 1, 1934	Dec. 31, 1934	State: Property Tax[12]	$38,000,000	Emergency Relief Fund	Subject to legislative appropriation
S. B. 2 (1933 1st Ex.)	Nov. 10, 1933	Nov. 10, 1933	Unspecified	State: Emergency Relief Fund	$30,000,000	Relief: Funds or supplies or any other desirable means	IERC
S. B. 3 (1933 1st Ex.)	Nov. 10, 1933	Nov. 10, 1933	Unspecified	State: Emergency Relief Fund[13]	$30,000,000	Retirement of & interest on tax anticipation notes	IERC
				State: General Fund	$9,000,000	Relief to unemployed and destitute residents	IERC
				State: 3% Sales Tax	33⅓% of yield	Emergency Relief Fund	IERC
				State: Emergency Relief Fund	$45,000,000[14]	Relief of residents in need	IERC

[12] Operative only in case of electorate's failure to approve bond issue authorized by S. B. 4, 5 (1933 1st Ex.), or in case motor-fuel tax service is inadequate.

[13] Notes issued in anticipation of sale of bonds or taxes to be collected under S. B. 1, 4, and 5 (1933 1st Ex.).

[14] To be expended at rate not to exceed $3,000,000 per month.

TABLE IX

Obligations Incurred for Relief and Administration, and Percentage from Federal, State, and Local Sources for the United States and Illinois, by Months, January 1933 through December 1934

Month	Percentage of total from each source United States				Percentage of total from each source Illinois			
	Obligations	Fed.	State	Local	Obligations	Fed.	State	Local
TOTAL 18 Mos.	$1,341,453,766	62.6	15.9	21.5	$120,230,605	66.5	28.9	4.6
Jan.	60,827,161	51.2	13.8	35.0	7,480,421	87.5	0.1	12.4
Feb.	67,375,423	59.2	7.6	33.2	6,947,846	87.3	0.3	12.4
Mar.	81,205,632	63.2	6.1	30.7	7,893,299	89.3	0.4	10.3
Apr.	73,010,800	62.1	10.9	27.0	7,284,616	92.1	0.4	7.5
May	70,806,338	68.9	6.8	24.3	6,545,185	90.5	0.4	9.1
June	66,339,207	64.1	11.9	24.0	6,201,486	93.5	2.1	4.4
July	60,155,874	62.3	11.8	25.9	5,811,176	94.4	2.2	3.4
Aug.	61,470,496	64.7	14.4	20.9	5,758,871	95.9	1.5	2.6
Sept.	59,346,338	61.1	18.4	20.5	5,982,051	50.6	46.8	2.6
Oct.	64,888,914	62.3	15.4	22.3	6,583,898	64.6	32.9	2.5
Nov.	70,810,514	56.2	25.5	18.3	6,307,236	33.0	64.7	2.3
Dec.	56,526,330	49.1	32.6	18.3	6,311,850	23.8	74.4	1.8

Meetings, Demonstrations, Parades, and Social Gatherings of Communist Affiliated Organizations in Chicago

Time period covered by data — 1919–34.
Area covered by data — Chicago, Cook County, and Chicago Region.

I. SOURCES. The following sources were used in the collection of these data:

A. *Official police records* (Industrial Squad of Chicago).
   1. File of permits for parades and outdoor meetings, 1931–4.
   2. File of reports of all meetings attended by the squad, 1931–4.
   3. Record of arrests of radicals in Chicago, 1931–4.
   4. File of leaflets, circulars, posters, and other advance notices of meetings, 1930–4.

B. *Newspaper sources.*
   1. *The New York Times,* 1919–34.
   2. *The Chicago Daily News* (from index in *Daily News* library), 1919–34.
   3. *The Chicago Tribune* (from index in *Chicago Tribune* library), 1919–29; (from page by page survey of the newspaper), 1930–2.
   4. *The Chicago Defender,* 1924–6, 1930–4.
   5. *The Daily Worker,* 1930–4.
   6. *The Hunger Fighter,* 1931–4.

II. FORM AND METHOD.

A. *Form.* The data on meetings, demonstrations, parades, and social gatherings in Chicago sponsored by Communist organizations were collected in the following form:

Type of gathering (e.g., meeting, demonstration, date, parade, or social gathering).

1. Place of meeting.
2. Reason or issue.
3. Name of organization or organizations sponsoring.
4. Number of persons present.
5. Account of violence, if any.
6. Number of persons arrested.
7. Number of persons injured. Number killed.
8. The names of the speakers.
9. Source of the above data.

B. *Method*. This information was recorded on 6 x 4 slips of paper, a separate slip being used for each meeting and for each source. The slips were stapled together in cases where more than one report was given about a single meeting (e.g., when the same meeting was reported by the police, by the *New York Times,* and by the *Daily Worker*). In such cases the police reports of meetings were placed on top, and the newspaper reports behind, with the more radical publications, like the *Daily Worker* and the *Hunger Fighter,* toward the bottom. In some cases of important meetings there are as many reports of the meetings as there are sources. In other cases there are only one or two reports.

The slips were filed in chronological order — according to the date on which the meeting was held. This file constitutes the " demonstration file " — which is one of the basic sets of data for this study.

III. ANALYSIS. The following types of analyses were made of the above data:

A. *Analysis of number and types of gatherings per month, 1930–4.*
Four categories were used in the classification of types of gathering:

1. Meetings — defined as indoor gatherings.
2. Demonstrations — defined as outdoor gatherings.
3. Parades — street marches.

4. Socials — including dances, parties, lectures, moving-picture showings, etc.

In some instances one occasion was classified in more than one way. The rules governing such double or triple entries of a single event are as follows:

1. Parades. In the case of parades, the gathering held at the beginning of the parade (i.e., the point at which the parade formed) was recorded as a demonstration.
2. Parades. In the case of parades, the gathering held at the end of the parade was recorded as a " meeting " or as a " demonstration," depending on whether it was held indoors or outdoors.
3. Parades. In some instances (notably hunger marches, May Day parades, and City Hall demonstrations) parades were started simultaneously in different parts of the city, merging downtown for a large parade through the Loop. In such instances each parade (including the parade through the Loop) was counted separately. Thus the case of the usual line of march (i.e., parades coming from the north, south, and west sides and parading through the Loop) would be recorded as four parades.
4. Socials. In some cases meetings were held in connection with socials. In such instances a double record was made.

B. *Place of meetings.* The place of meetings was coded as to census tract, census community area, relief district, and police district. This coding appears on each slip. The only record made from this information, however, is that of the number of gatherings occurring each month in each census tract in the city.

C. *Issues in the name of which gatherings were called.* An analysis was made of the number and types of issues raised each month at meetings, demonstrations, etc. The major classifications of the types of issues are as follows:

1. Issues protesting unemployment.
2. Issues protesting relief administration.
3. Issues protesting evictions.
4. Issues demanding freedom of action.

5. Issues in the name of major political symbols (War, Imperialism, Fascism, etc.).

6. Issues in the name of special days (May Day, Lenin Memorial, etc.).

7. Issues connected with party organization and activity (party conventions, conferences, etc.).

8. Issues making labor demands.

9. Issues in the name of institutions and groups (the church, the Jews, the Negroes, etc.).

10. Issues in the name of consumer's protection.

The number of issues falling under each classification were tallied by months for the years 1930–4. The following rules governed this procedure:

1. The issues recorded on all slips, regardless of source, were included in the analysis. Thus, for example, if the *New York Times* reported a parade " protesting against unemployment " and the same parade was reported by the Communist press as " protesting against evictions," both of these issues were recorded, the assumption being that since we have no criteria of selection and because of the scantiness of the data, it is most accurate to include all sources.

2. All issues reported by a single source were likewise included in the tabulation.

3. In order that a correlation could be validly run between the number of demonstrations per month and the degree of concentration of attention upon particular issues, a second tally was made. In this second instance the issues were tallied for as many times as the gathering had been tabulated (cf. above III, A, rules governing double or triple entries of a single event). Thus, for example, if a parade on " unemployment " had been recorded three times in the analysis of the number and types of gatherings — e.g., as a demonstration (gathering at starting-point), as a parade, and as a meeting (indoor meeting at termination of parade) — then the issue " unemployment " would likewise be recorded three times under the month in which it happened to fall.

In addition to this analysis of issues, the following analyses were made:

1. Record of the types of issues raised at meetings held in different census tracts.
2. Record of the types of issues raised at meetings, according to the organization sponsoring the meeting.

D. *Sponsoring organizations.* The following analyses were made with regard to sponsoring organizations:

1. Types of gatherings (meeting, demonstration, parade, or social gathering) held by each organization every month, 1930–4.
2. Types of issues (for classifications, cf. III, c, 1–10) presented by each organization every month, 1930–4.
3. Meeting-places of each organization according to census tract for the years 1930–4.

E. *Number present.* A table was drawn up showing all estimates as to number present, listed as to source. The following sources were included:

1. Estimates of police (official).
2. Estimates of the *Daily Worker* (Communist).
3. Estimates of the *Chicago Defender* (Negro).
4. Estimates of the *Chicago Tribune* (city press).
5. Estimates of the *Chicago Daily News* (city press).

F. *Speakers.* Record on each speaker appearing in the demonstration record — showing date on which he spoke, the place, and the organization under whose sponsorship the meeting occurred.

Strikes

Time period covered by data — 1919–34.
Area covered by data — Chicago, Cook County, and the Chicago region.

I. SOURCES. The following sources were used in the collection of these data:

A. *United States Department of Labor.*

1. *Monthly Labor Review,* Vols. 30–39.
2. List of Strikes in Chicago, submitted upon request by the Bureau of Labor Statistics.

B. *Illinois Department of Labor. — Annual Reports* (Nos. 2–13), 1919–29.

c. *Official police records* (Industrial Squad of Chicago).

1. Reports of industrial disturbances (strike meetings, etc.) attended by the squad, 1931–4.
2. Record of arrest of radicals in Chicago, 1931–4.
3. File of leaflets, bulletins, circulars, etc., distributed in connection with strikes.

D. *Newspapers.*

1. *The New York Times,* 1919–34.
2. *The Chicago Tribune,* 1930–2.
3. *The Chicago Defender,* 1924–6, 1930–4.
4. *The Daily Worker,* 1930–4.

II. FORM AND METHOD.

A. *Form.* The material on strikes in Chicago was collected in the following form:

Strike.   Date.

1. Place (name of plant and address).
2. Issue.

   3. Organization (union, local number, affiliation).
   4. Number out on strike.
   5. Account of violence.
   6. Number arrested.
   7. Number injured. Number killed.
   8. How long out on strike. Result of strike.
   9. Source of the above data.

B. *Method.* This information, as in the case of meetings and
   demonstrations, was recorded on 6 x 4 slips, a separate slip
   being used for each strike and for each source. The slips
   were stapled together in cases where more than one report on a single strike was given (e.g., the same strike was
   reported by the U.S. Bureau of Labor Statistics, by the
   New York Times, and by the *Daily Worker*). In such
   cases, the U.S. Bureau reports were given preference and
   were placed on top.

   The slips were filed in chronological order in accordance with the first date of the strike. The place where the
   strike took place (i.e., address of plant or factory) was
   coded according to census tract, census community area,
   and relief district.

III. ANALYSIS.

   A. Table showing the number of strikes called during each
      month, 1930-4.

   B. Table showing number of strikers out in those strikes called
      each month, 1930-4.

   C. Record of number of strikes each month occurring in each
      census tract of the city.

Group Complaints — through the Public Relations Bureau

Time period covered by data — 1933–4.
Area covered by data — Chicago and Cook County.

I. SOURCES. The following sources were used in the collection of these data:

A. Weekly and monthly reports of the Public Relations Bureau of the IERC, 1933–4.

B. The individual records of complaints filed with the Public Relations Bureau of the IERC, January 1933 to September 1934.

II. FORM AND METHOD.

A. *Weekly and monthly reports.* The records of these reports contain the following information for 1933:

1. Name (and local number) of organizations bringing complaints to the Bureau.

2. Number of complaints per week (or per month) per organization.

The records of these reports for 1934 contain the following information additional to that above:

3. Disposition of complaints. Disposition classified as follows: (a) referred to district office, (b) referred to district office after telephone conference, and (c) discussion and/or rejection with direct answer from PRB.

B. *Individual records of complaints.* From this source the following information was taken:

1. Date of complaint.

2. Name (and local number) of organization registering complaint.

3. Address of complainant.

The address of complainant was coded according to census tract, census community area, and relief district.

III. ANALYSIS.

A. *Weekly and monthly reports.*

1. Table showing the volume of complaints per month, 1933–4.
2. Table showing the number of complaints submitted each month by every organization, 1933–4.

B. *Individual records of complaints.*

1. Table showing the volume of complaints per month, January 1933 to September 1934.
2. Table showing the number of complaints submitted by each organization per month, January 1933 to September 1934.
3. Table showing the number of complaints made each month in each relief district, January 1933 to September 1934.
4. Record of the number of complaints each month coming from each census tract of the city.

Arrest of Radicals

Time period covered by data — 1931–4.
Area covered by data — Chicago.

I. SOURCE. Arrest books kept by the Industrial Squad of Chicago, 1931–4.

II. FORM AND METHOD.

A. *Form.* The following information was recorded for each individual arrested:

1. Date arrested.
2. Address of arrested individual.
3. Sex and Age.
4. Nativity.
5. Occupation.
6. Marital status.
7. Police district in which arrest took place. Address of complainant if any. Address of arrest.
8. Charges.
9. Disposition of the case. Date tried. Name of presiding judge.

B. *Method.* A separate slip bearing the above information was made for each individual arrested. This slip was coded twice — once for the address of the individual, and once for the address of arrest.

III. ANALYSIS.

A. The analyses were made as follows (in each case according to the following classifications: American, Negro, Foreign-Born, Nationality Not Given, and Total):

1. Table showing the number of arrests per month, 1931–4.
2. Table showing the sex distribution of the total number arrested each year, 1931–4.

3. Table showing the age distribution (by ten-year intervals), of the total number arrested each year, 1931–4.

4. Table showing the distribution by age (as in 3) and sex of the total number arrested each year, 1931–4.

5. Table showing the distribution according to marital status of the total number arrested each year.

B. Table showing country of nativity, indicating number arrested and percentage which this number represents of the total population (in Chicago) of that nationality.

C. The following tables were made regarding persons arrested individually:

1. Nationality — number and percentage.
2. Occupation.

D. The following tables were made regarding persons arrested in groups of from two to five persons:

1. Nationality — number and percentage.
2. Occupation.

E. The following tables were made regarding persons arrested in groups of over five persons:

1. Nationality — number and percentage.
2. Occupation.

F. Analysis of place of arrest.

1. According to police districts.
2. According to relief districts.
3. According to census tracts.

G. Analysis of home address of individual arrested.

1. According to police districts.
2. According to relief districts.
3. According to census tracts.

H. Analysis of disposition of cases. By years, 1931–4.

I. Analysis of presiding judges. By years, 1931–4.

Individual Complaints — Complaint Bureau of CPW Field Service

(Note: Record of complaints of individuals receiving relief from URS has been kept only since October 1934.)

Time period covered by data — August 1933 to December 1934.
Area covered by data — Cook County.

 I. Sources. These data on individual complaints were brought together from the files of the Bureau for individual complaints of CPW Field Service Division.

 II. Form and Method. The data consist of monthly reports carrying the following information by relief districts (August 1933 to December 1934):

 A. Nature of complaint: whether regarding clothing; water, gas, light; food; medical attention; relief discontinued; relief needed; rent; etc.

 B. Total number of new complainants.

 c. Total number of repeat complainants.

Personnel

Time period covered by data — 1919–34.
Area covered by data — Chicago.

I. SOURCES. The following sources were utilized in the collection of this material:

A. *Official police sources.* Personnel records of the Industrial Squad on radical leaders in Chicago, 1930–4.

B. *Public Relations Bureau of Illinois Emergency Relief Commission.* Correspondence and organization files.

C. *Demonstration record.*

D. *Newspapers and periodicals.*

1. *The New York Times,* 1919–34.
2. *The Chicago Daily News,* 1919–34.
3. *The Chicago Tribune,* 1919–34.
4. *The Chicago Defender,* 1924–6, 1930–4.
5. *The Daily Worker,* 1923–9 (in part), 1930–4 (complete).
6. *The Hunger Fighter,* 1931–4.

E. *Books.*

1. *American Labor Who's Who,* edited by Solon De Leon, (New York, 1925).
2. Elizabeth Dilling: *The Red Network* (Chicago, 1934).
3. Joseph J. Mereto: *The Red Conspiracy* (New York, 1920).
4. Lucia R. Maxwell: *The Red Juggernaut* (Washington, D.C., 1932).
5. R. M. Whitney: *Reds in America* (New York, 1924).

II. FORM AND METHOD.

A. *Official police sources.* The police personnel record contains the following type of information on individuals:

1. Name.
2. Address.

3. Date (year) when the individual first came to the attention of the police.
4. Chronological list of party activities, including:
   a. Speaking engagements.
   b. Membership in organizations.
   c. Positions of importance held in the party or in any party organization. Membership on committees, etc.
   d. Articles written for the *Daily Worker,* if any.
   e. Other activities.
5. Dates arrested. For leaders who have been arrested at any time the following information is also available:
   a. Nationality.
   b. Occupation.
   c. Age.
   d. Marital status.
6. Additional comments and information from various sources.

B. *Public Relations Bureau.* The information available on the personnel of the movement at this source consists primarily of enlightening excerpts from correspondence with leaders of protest organizations and also comments of social workers and interviewers on particular leaders of these organizations with whom they have come in contact.

C. *Demonstration record.* From the demonstration file we have compiled for every individual who has appeared at any time as a speaker at a radical meeting in Chicago, a chronological record of speaking engagements bearing the following information:

1. Date of meeting at which speaker performed.
2. Place where the meeting was held.
3. Organization under whose auspices the meeting was held.

From the newspapers, periodicals, and books listed above all possible information on any Chicago leaders has been carefully gleaned. As in the case of the other sources, the information is recorded on 6 x 4 slips with the source indicated and filed alphabetically under the name of the individual.

Evictions

Time period covered by data — January 1932 to August 1933.
Area covered by data — Chicago.

I. SOURCE. Records of the Bailiff's Office, City Hall.

II. FORM AND METHOD.

A. *Form*. The following information was collected in the case of each eviction:
  1. The date on which eviction occurred.
  2. Name of individual evicted.
  3. Address of eviction.

B. *Method*. The above information was recorded on slips — one slip for each eviction case. These were coded as to address of the eviction according to census tract, community area, and relief district.

III. ANALYSIS. A record was made according to the number of evictions occurring in each month. Record was also made of evictions occurring each month in the various census tracts of the city.

Foreclosures

Time period covered by data — 1928–34.
Area covered by data — Cook County.

  I. SOURCE. Chicago Title and Trust Co.

 II. FORM AND METHOD. The only record available was that of the
     then number of foreclosures made each month.

Self-criticism of Strategy: Over-emphasis on the Unemployed

In 1932 an organization report was summarized as follows in the *Communist* (February 1932):

" The results of the Party registration, which are now at hand from the districts in New York, Cleveland, Detroit, Chicago, Minneapolis, Dakota and Colorado, show plainly all the political and organizational weaknesses of our Party and mass work and bring to the fore the problem of cadres.

" Of the 6,500 registered members in the above-mentioned districts, 2,550 are unemployed. Yet in 187 unemployed committees in these districts, we have only 96 fractions, of which a large number are not even active.

" If we consider the trades of our members, we find that workers of the most important industries, and above all of the war industries, are very feebly represented in the Party. Out of the 6,500 registered members, only 65 members are railway workers; only 20 work in the chemical industries; in transport and on the docks we have only 76 members; in the textile industries only 61 members; 532 belong to the metal industries; and 147 to the mining industries. On the other hand, we have 618 clothing workers, 636 building trades workers, 161 office workers, 174 intellectuals, 118 petty shopkeepers and 486 housewives. . . .

" We have already seen that the most important industries are very feebly represented in the Party, and that as a result, we have practically no foothold at all in the large factories. Whereas in the factories having 100 workers or less, we have 515 Party members, and in the factories having from 100 to 500 workers, we have about 250 Party members, in the factories having over 5,000 workers, we have only 70 members, in the factories having 3,000 to 5,000 workers, we have only 37 members, in the factories having from 2,000 to 3,000 workers, we have only 47 members, and in the factories having 500 to 1,000 workers, 68 Party members.

" As to trade union membership, these figures show a similar picture. Out of the 6,500 registered Party members, only 2,300 are members of any trade union, and of these, 1,650 are members of the revolutionary trade unions, and about 650 are members of the reactionary trade unions. But these figures grow even worse if we take, for instance, the Chicago district. This most important district of heavy industry has, out of 1,700 registered members, only about 400 comrades who are members of any trade union, and of these 189 are in the revolutionary and 207 are in the reactionary trade unions."

In 1935 an organization report in the *Communist* (July 1935) gives the following picture:

" Out of a partial registration covering 27,000 members we record 700 steel workers, 1,250 metal workers, 1,073 miners, 550 auto workers, 365 textile workers, 406 marine workers, and 324 railroad workers. The 4,668 in this category, out of a membership of about 27,000, is approximately one-sixth. It is interesting to compare the recruiting in the last three months. The comparison shows recruiting results in the following categories: 123 steel workers, 208 metal workers, 179 miners, 100 auto workers, 254 marine workers, 65 textile workers, and 87 railroad workers — a total of 1,016, or one-fifth of the total recruitment, which is a slight improvement. As to the other workers in basic industries, we have 23 oil workers, 74 chemical workers, 162 transport workers (outside of marine and railroad), 281 teamsters, 222 lumber workers, 87 packinghouse workers, 23 agricultural workers, and 444 mechanics — *a total of 6,414 only.*

" In the lighter industries, the industrial workers total 7,173, a figure larger than in the basic industries, and divided as follows: 2,177 needle workers, 2,423 building workers (many of whom are engaged in trades that are considered basic and very important), 289 shoe workers, 1,373 food workers, 223 furniture workers, 206 laundry workers, 268 painters, and 114 sign-painters.

" Among the non-proletarian and white collar workers, we have a total of 5,195, out of which there are 1,061 office workers, 425 teachers, 233 artists, 450 sales clerks, 408 store-keepers, and 2,516 working-class housewives. Another category is 1,200 farmers. There are 5,000 still unclassified.

" On the basis of the figures that we have from Cleveland, Detroit, Chicago and other districts, we estimate, approximately, that there is an average of eight Party members in the shop nuclei throughout the country, i.e., 3,500 to 4,000 *Party members are organized in the basic units of the Party, the factory nuclei,* while the overwhelming majority, over 23,000 to 24,000 members, are still in street nuclei."

INDEX